Santore, Modern European History

Selected Reading Lists and Course
Outlines from American Colleges
and Universities

Modern European History: 1789 to the Present Vol. II: Topical and Thematic Courses

edited by John Santore
New York University

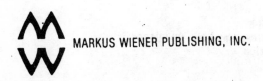

MARKUS WIENER PUBLISHING, INC.

© 1983 by Markus Wiener Publishing, Inc.

ISBN 0-910129-08-8
Library of Congress Card No. 83-061361
Printed in America

TABLE OF CONTENTS

Volume One:

Chronological and National Courses

1

2

Volume Two:
Topical and Thematic Courses

Military

Diplomatic

Economic and Social

Historical Methodology and Historiography

- -

*Institutional designations refer to the university or
college at which the course was taught, and not necessarily to
the school at which the author presently teaches. In all but a
few instances, the syllabi have been reproduced exactly as submitted, with little modification or change. All college courses,
of course, are subject to annual revision and updating, and the
reader is advised to check the syllabus for format and date. [Ed.]

Columbia University

Istvan Deak
1228 International Affairs Building
Tel.: 280-4627
Office hours: Tu. 11-5

History W 3969 y
Spring 1977
M 4:10-6:00

THE ARMY IN EUROPEAN POLITICS, 1815-1945

The purpose of this seminar is to investigate the political and social role officers played in modern European history. It is common knowledge that an enormous number of nations are governed today by generals and the notorious "colonels." Some of these officers abide by the constitution of their country: most, however, are dictators. Many are fascists, if not openly so, then in their style and methods; others appear peaceable and prefer to wear mufti. Some are outright reactionaries; others are liberals; again others see themselves (and can be regarded) as radicals and revolutionaries. But in each and every case these military rulers, and the armies they command, are modelled after the historic example of Europe: whether Asian, African, or Latin American, the military commanders and their armies wear European-style medals and uniforms; carry weapons invented or developed in Europe; bear titles and ranks that once had a meaning to Europeans only; and administer their system according to old Prussian, French or English models. Ironically, Europe itself is today free from military rule and the European armies can be said to abide by their country's constitution and to obey their civilian superiors.

Since military rule today seems to be the peculiarity of non-European states, and since military rule, where it existed in Europe in the twentieth century, seems to have been restricted to such less developed countries as Greece, Spain, Portugal, Romania, and Poland, or to such war-torn countries as Vichy France or Hungary in 1919, one question we must ask ourselves is whether military rule is simply an inevitable step in a country's socio-political development. There are also many other questions. For example, what exactly is the difference between military and civilian rule? Can we talk of military government when the head of state and the cabinet are soldiers but the administration is civilian? For a military rule to be real, must the officers have come to power illegally and by violence? Conversely, can we talk of civilian government when the civilians in power do their best to regiment and militarize society, as is the case of Soviet Russia or was the case in Nazi Germany? What exactly is militarism? Is it an expression of the political ambitions of officers or can militarism exist without the active assistance of officers? Is Alfred Vagts correct in distinguishing between militarism and what he calls "the military way"? Do officers tend to be conservative in a rapidly changing society, and progressive in a stagnant society? Does an officer's social background invariably determine his social-political outlook? What is the origin of the armies of modern Europe? What is more dangerous to freedom and orderly political process: a professional army or a people's army, an army of volunteers or an army of conscripts? And what is more dangerous to peace? Does the military traditionally prefer war to diplomacy? Do the generals always prepare for the last war, rather than the next war? Did all modern European wars come about because of the General Staffs' morbid fear of an enemy Blitzkrieg or what is called today "pre-emptive strike?" Why have the northern European and British, or British-founded, countries always succeeded in making their armies subservient to civilian leadership? And why have the Communist and Fascist countries? Was rule by the military, or decisive military influence, characteristic only of the Southern European and East Central European conservative states? Do the armies inevitably play a modernizing role even when the military themselves shun and abhor modernization? How old is the military-industrial complex and how real? How were the officers in Europe recruited, trained, paid, and employed? And how the NCO's and the enlisted men? How did the military live? How did they get along with the

6

civilians in garrison towns?
    I do not have any illusions about our ability to answer all the above
questions or the many others that will arise in our discussions. But we shall
try.
    Our seminar is organized chronologically, with the following rough divisions:
1815-1848, 1849-1914, 1914-1918, 1919-1939, and 1939-1945. For each period
there are short basic readings assigned, as well as some specific readings.
The latter you will divide among yourselves with each one of you assuming
responsibility for developments in a single European state. Of course, I realize
that several of you will chose England or France or Germany for your individual
specialization, whereas there might be no one willing to deal with such countries
as Spain, Russia, or Italy. But a wide distribution of individual specialties
would be useful to us all. All general readings and all special readings are
in English: you do not need to know any other language to successfully complete
this course. But if you wish to specialize on a small or rather exotic European
state, knowledge of a language other than English might become necessary.
    Our meetings will consist of two parts. In the first hour we shall discuss
general developments in a given period; during the second hour you will report on
developments in your chosen country for the same period.
    Naturally, you will have considerable freedom in selecting the country of
your specialty. There will also be a research paper: it should develop from
your "national" specialty. In order to facilitate the choice of the essay
topic, and the researching of the essay, I am distributing a list of suggested
topics, as well as a brief bibliography. Rough drafts of your research paper
will be submitted for classroom discussion during the semester. The end result
ought to be at least twenty pages long. On the other hand, there will be no
examination.
    All the readings indicated in the course outline are available in the
Columbia College Reading Room, including xerox copies of the articles. Most of
the books should also be available at the Columbia University Bookstore and at
Salter's. Unfortunately, few of the titles are paperbacks.
    The subject is fascinating and crucial. It is up to you, and to me, to
make the most of it.

COURSE OUTLINE

Jan. 24/Feb. 7.   Introduction. The origins of the European armies. Soldiers
of the French Revolution, the Napoleonic Wars, the Restoration period, the
first nationalist uprisings, and the revolutions of 1848. Levée en masse,
the first guerillas, middle class militias. The conflict between modern
ideologies and traditional dynastic loyalties.

General reading:
Alfred Vagts, A History of Militarism: Civilian and Military, Chapters 1-2, 4-6

Richard A. Preston and Sydney F. Wise, Men in Arms: A History of Warfare and Its
Interrelationship with Western Society, Chapters 1, 7-13

Some specialized readings:

Austria:
Gunther E. Rothenberg, "The Austrian Army in the Age of Metternich," Journal of
Modern History, 40: 155-165, June 1968.

Germany:
Gordon A. Craig, The Politics of the Prussian Army, 1640-1945, Chapters I-III

Frederick Engels, "Germany: Revolution and Counter-Revolution," in Engels,
The German Revolutions, Chapters VIII-XIX.

France:
Douglas Porch, Army and Revolution: France 1815-1848

J.M. Thompson, Louis Napoleon and the Second Empire, Chapters 2 and 4.

Feb. 14/28.   From the 1850's to World War I. Universal military service.
Aristocratic privilege versus the needs of modern war.

General reading:
Vagts, Chapters 7, 9-11

Preston and Wise, Chapters 14-15

Some specialized readings:

England:
Robert Blake, "Great Britain: The Crimean War to the First World War" in
Michael Howard, ed. Soldiers and Government: Nine Studies in Civil-Military
Relations, pp. 25-50

C.B. Otley, "Militarism and the Social Affiliation of the British Army Elite," in
Jacques Van Doorn, ed. Armed Forces and Society, pp. 84-108

E.S. Turner, Gallant Gentlemen, A Portrait of the British Officer 1600-1956,
Chapters XX and XXI

France:
Guy Chapman, "The French Army and Politics" in Michael Howard, ed. Soldiers
and Government , pp. 51-72

Paul-Marie de la Gorce, The French Army. A Military-Political History, Chapters 1-5

Germany:
Craig, Chapters IV-VII

Martin Kitchen, The German Officer Corps 1890-1914, Chapters II, III, and VI

Austria-Hungary:
Oscar Jaszi, The Dissolution of the Habsburg Monarchy, pp. 141-148.

Gunther E. Rothenberg, The Army of Francis Joseph

Russia:
O.R. Ray, "The Imperial Russian Army Officer," in Political Science Quarterly,
76: 576-592

G.H.N. Seton-Watson, "Army and Autocracy," in Michael Howard, ed. Soldiers and
Government, pp. 99-114

March 7/21.   World War I.   Annihilation of the professional officer corps.   War
of civilians in uniform.   Revolutionary and counterrevolutionary armies.

General reading:
Vagts, Chapter 8

Preston and Wise, Chapter 16

H.A. De Weerd, "Civilian and Military Elements in Modern War," in Jesse D. Clark-
son and Thomas G. Cochran, eds. War as a Social Institution: The Historian's
Perspective, pp. 95-112

Some specialized readings:

England:
A.J.P. Taylor, English History 1914-1945, Chapters 1-3 (Oxford University Press
paperback)

Turner, Chapter XXV

France:
de la Gorce, Chapters 6 and 7

Germany:
Erich Eyck, The History of the Weimar Republic, Vol. I, Chapter 1.

Russia:
Allen Wildman, "The February Revolution in the Russian Army," Soviet Studies,
22:3, July 1970.

March 28/April 4.   Between the World Wars.   The military and the totalitarian
parties.

General reading:
Vagts, Chapter 12

Some specialized readings:

England:
A.J.P. Taylor, pp. 227-232, 361-367, 409-413
Robin Higha m, Armed Forces in Peacetime Britain, 1918-1940: A Case Study,

9

Chapters 2, 3: pp. 68-70, 74-92

France:
de la Gorce, Chapters 8-12

Germany:
Craig, Chapters IX-XI

F.L. Carsten, The Reichswehr and Politics, Chapters VII and VIII.

Russia:
Raymond L. Garthoff, "The Military in Russia, 1861-1965," in Van Doorn, ed. Armed
Forces and Society, pp. 240-256

April 11-25.   World War II. The total war.

General reading:
Vagts, Chapter 13

Preston and Wise, Chapters 17 and 18

Some specialized readings:

England:
A.J.P. Taylor, pp. 477-500

Turner, Chapters 27-29

France:
de la Gorce, Chapters 13 and 14

Germany:
John W. Wheeler-Bennett, The Nemesis of Power: The German Army in Politics, 1918-
1945, Part III

Karl Dietrich Bracher, The German Dictatorship, Chapter VII: pp. 400-409, 431-460

Heinz Höhne, The Order of the Death's Head, Chapter 16

Craig, Chapter XII

May 2.   Conclusion.

    For general background reading, the following books are recommended:

E.J. Hobsbawm, The Age of Revolution 1789-1848

Norman Rich, The Age of Nationalism and Reform, 1850-1890

Felix Gilbert, The End of the European Era, 1890 to the Present

Gordon Wright, The Ordeal of Total War

All of these books are available in paperback.

HISTORY 442. WAR AND SOCIAL CHANGE:
EUROPE IN THE FIRST WORLD WAR

PREREQUISITES: There are no fixed prerequisites for this course, but
students who have not studied 19th-century European diplomacy or taken
one of the national surveys on modern France, Britain, or Germany will
find it very difficult. Two books recommended for background reading
are Laurence Lafore, The Long Fuse (1965) and J. Remak, The Origins of
World War I, 1871-1914 (1967). In addition, Cyril Falls, The Great War,
1914-1918 provides a fine account of the military conflict for those
unfamiliar with its course. Reading knowledge of French or German is not
required but would greatly enhance the range of research topics from which
you can choose.

REQUIREMENTS: Students may fulfill the requirements for this seminar in
either of two ways: (a) by writing a 15-20 pp. bibliographical essay on
a topic of controversy among historians and two 5-page book reports on
works drawn from the "recommended" list below, which would also be
delivered orally in class; or (b) by writing a research paper approximately
25 pages in length, based on both primary and secondary sources, and
delivering two oral book reports. History majors are urged to choose the
second option, which requires timely planning in order to guarantee that
your interests can be matched with the government documents, newspapers,
and other primary sources available in Sterling Library. All students
should consult me about paper topics within the first three weeks of the
semester and submit a brief description of their project by the end of
September.
     A written book review should include detailed analysis of the author's
thesis, premises, and use of evidence. Try to identify the author's view
of historical causality, i.e., what constitutes a satisfactory explanation
for a given phenomenon, and assess the quality of the empirical research
presented in support of that view. The purpose of an oral book report
is rather different. You should not simply read what you have written to
the class but should offer less formal remarks, 10-20 minutes in duration,
that seek above all to deepen your fellow students' understanding of the
topic covered that week. Include information on the author's background
and how your book elucidates or contradicts the major points made in the
general reading.

READINGS AND SYLLABUS: All required readings are on overnight reserve
(xeroxed articles on closed reserve) in CCL. Recommended readings are
not on reserve, so it is your responsibility to obtain them in good time.
The following required texts are also available in the Co-op:

     Harrison Wright (ed.), The "New Imperialism" (2nd edn., 1976).
     Immanuel Geiss (ed.), July 1914: The Outbreak of the First World
        War: Selected Documents (1967).
     Correlli Barnett, The Swordbearers: Supreme Command in the First
        World War (1963).
     Erich Maria Remarque, All Quiet on the Western Front.
     Arthur Marwick, The Deluge: British Society and the First World
        War (1965).

11

Gerd Hardach, The First World War, 1914-1918 (1980).
Harold Nicolson, Peacemaking 1919 (1965).
Robert Wohl, The Generation of 1914 (1979).
Charles Maier, Recasting Bourgeois Europe: Stabilization in France, Germany, and Italy in the Decade after World War I (1975).

September 8: Organizational meeting.

September 15: IMPERIALIST RIVALRIES IN PREWAR EUROPE.
    Required: Wright, The "New Imperialism" (articles by Hobson, Lenin, Schumpeter, Langer, Arendt, Robinson & Gallagher, Platt, & Fieldhouse); and Hans Ulrich Wehler, "Bismarck's Imperialism, 1862-1890," in James Sheehan (ed.), Imperial Germany.

September 22: GERMANY AND THE OUTBREAK OF WAR: AGGRESSION AS A FORM OF "PREVENTIVE COUNTER-REVOLUTION"?
    Required: Immanuel Geiss, July 1914, pp. 9-131;
    Wolfgang Mommsen, "Domestic Factors in German Foreign Policy before 1914," in James Sheehan (ed.), Imperial Germany;
    Herbert Butterfield, "Sir Edward Grey in July 1914," Historical Studies, vol. 5 (1965);
    I.V. Bestuzhev, "Russian Foreign Policy, February-June 1914," Journal of Contemporary History, vol. 1 #3.

September 29: THE OUTBREAK OF WAR (cont.):
    Required: Geiss, July 1914, pp. 132-375.

    Recommended: Fritz Fischer, War of Illusions (English edn., 1973);
    H.W. Koch (ed.), The Origins of the First World War (1972);
    Zara Steiner, Britain and the Origins of the First World War (1972).

October 6: THE UNCERTAINTY OF COMBAT.
    Required: Corelli Barnett, The Swordbearers, pp. xv-98, 193-361.

    Recommended: Aleksandr Solzhenitsyn, August 1914.
    Cyril Falls, The Great War 1914-18.
    Norman Stone, The Eastern Front 1914-17.

October 13: COMBAT AS EXPERIENCED BY THE COMMON SOLDIER.
    Required: Erich Maria Remarque, All Quiet on the Western Front.

    Recommended: Ernst Jünger, Copse 125.
    Stefan Zweig, Erziehung vor Verdun.
    John Ellis, Eye-Deep in Hell.
    William Faulkner, A Fable.

October 20: SOCIAL CHANGE ON THE HOME FRONT.
    Required: Arthur Marwick, The Deluge.

    Recommended: Marc Ferro, The Great War 1914-1918 (1973);
    J.C. King, Generals and Politicians: Conflict between France's High Command, Parliament and Government, 1914-18 (1951);
    Jürgen Kocka, Klassengesellschaft im Krieg (1973);
    Z.A.B. Zeman, The Break-up of the Habsburg Empire, 1914-18 (1961).

October 27: THE COLLAPSE OF GERMANY.

Required: Reinhard Rürup, "Problems of the German Revolution, 1918-19," Journal of Contemporary History, vol. 3 #4;
Gerald Feldman, "Economic and Social Problems of the German Demobilization, 1918-19," Journal of Modern History, March 1975;
Richard Comfort, Revolutionary Hamburg, pp. 1-130, 167-71.

Recommended: Francis L. Carsten, Revolution in Central Europe (1972);
Klaus Schwabe, Deutsche Revolution und Wilson-Frieden (1971, counts as two reports);
Robert Daniels, Red October: The Bolshevik Revolution of 1917 (1967);
V.I. Lenin, State and Revolution (September 1917).

November 3: THE COSTS OF THE WAR.
Required: Gerd Hardach, The First World War.

Recommended: D.H. Aldcroft & H.W. Richardson, The British Economy 1870-1939 (1969);
Tom Kemp, The French Economy: The History of a Decline, 1913-39 (1972);
John Nef, War and Human Progress (1950).

November 10: THE VERSAILLES CONFERENCE.
Required: Harold Nicolson, Peacemaking 1919 (1933) pp. 3-219, 326-71;
Arno Mayer, "The Problems of Peacemaking," in Hans Gatzke (ed.), European Diplomacy between two Wars, pp. 14-39.

Recommended: Arno Mayer, Politics and Diplomacy of Peacemaking (1967);
J.M. Keynes, The Economic Consequences of the Peace (1919) and E. Mantoux, The Carthaginian Peace, or the Economic Consequences of Mr. Keynes;
Arthur Link, Wilson: Campaigns for Progressivism and Peace.

November 17: THE TRAUMA OF THE WAR.
Required: Robert Wohl, The Generation of 1914 (1979).

Recommended: Paul Fussell, The Great War and Modern Memory (1975);
Sigmund Freud, "Thoughts for the Times on War and Death" (1915) and Beyond the Pleasure Principle (1919);
Beth Lewis, George Grosz: Art and Politics in the Weimar Republic 1971;
Michael Ledeen, The First Duce (1977), on Gabriele d'Annunzio.

December 1: A RETURN TO "NORMALCY"? LABOR'S BID FOR POWER.
Required: Charles Maier, Recasting Bourgeois Europe, pp. 3-231.

Recommended: Maurice Cowling, The Impact of Labour, 1920-24 (1971);
Robert Wohl, French Communism in the Making, 1914-24 (1966);
Paolo Spriano, The Occupation of the Factories: Italy 1920 (1975);
Werner Angress, Stillborn Revolution: Germany 1921-23 (1963).

December 8: A RETURN TO "NORMALCY"? PRECARIOUS STABILIZATION.
Required: Maier, pp. 272-420, 481-594.

Recommended: Henry Winkler (ed.), Twentieth-Century Britain (1976);
Ernst Nolte, Three Faces of Fascism (1965), Parts 1, 3-4;
David Abraham, The Collapse of the Weimar Republic (1981);
Alan Cassels, Fascist Italy (1968).

Columbia University

War and Revolution in Europe, 1914-1923: Comparative Studies

of Russia, Germany and Italy

For a brief moment at the end of the First World War, revolution was on the agenda of many European nations. Not since 1848 had Europe undergone such a period of turmoil and political crisis. This seminar will seek to examine the origins and forms of that unusual revolutionary outburst. We will begin with a treatment of the background to revolutionary upheaval in the period of the First World War and will then proceed with three case studies of revolutionary development ---Russia, Germany and Italy---each with a very different outcome. Course requirements in addition to the weekly required reading assignments will include: a brief oral presentation of one of the week's readings, a mid-term paper (5-7 pages), and a term paper (15-20 pages) which should offer a comparative analysis of one of the aspects of revolutionary situations discussed in the course.

Those readings which have been ordered in the bookstore and are available in paperback are marked with *. These and all others are on reserve in the College Library.

Week I: General Introduction

Week II: Defining the Context: Economic Impact of the First
World War
*Gerd Hardach, The First World War, 1914-1918

Week III: Defining the Context: Diplomacy and Peacemaking,
1917-1919
Arno Mayer, Politics and Peacemaking, 3-30
Arno Mayer, Political Origins of the New Diplomacy, 1917-
1918, 1-58
Charles Maier, Recasting Bourgeois Europe, 3-52

Week IV: Background to Revolution in Russia
Alexander Gerschenkorn, "Problems and Patterns of Russian
Economic Development," in Cherniavsky, ed., Structure of
Russian History, 282-308
Leopold Haimson, "The Problems of Social Stability in
Urban Russia, 1905-1917," in Cherniavsky, ed., Structure
of Russian History, 341-81

JLH Keep, The Russian Revolution. A Study of Mass Mobilization, 1-64

Victoria E. Bonnell, "Trade Unions, Parties and the State
in Tsarist Russia: A Study of Labor Politics in St. Petersburg and Moscow," Politics and Society, 9, 3, 1980,
299-322

G.R. Swain, "Bolsheviks and Metal Workers on the Eve of
the First World War," Journal of Contemporary History,
16, 1981, 273-91

Week V: Makers of the Revolution in Russia

William G. Rosenberg, "Russian Liberals and the Bolshevik
Coup," Journal of Modern History, 40, 1968, 328-47

Graeme J. Gill, "The Mainsprings of Peasant Action in 1917,"
Soviet Studies, XXX, no. 1, 1978, 63-78

Marc Ferro, "The Russian Soldier in 1917: Undisciplined,
Patriotic, and Revolutionary," Slavic Review, 30, 3,
1971, 484-512

Paul Avrich, "The Bolshevik Revolution and Workers' Control
in Russian Industry," Slavic Review, XXII, 1963, 47-63

Diane Koenker, "The Evolution of Party Consciousness in 1917:
The Case of the Moscow Workers," Soviet Studies, XXX, no.
1, 1978, 38-62

Week VI: Stabilizing the Russian Revolution

J.P. Nettl, The Soviet Achievement, 39-114

Richard Stites, "Zhenotdel: Bolshevism and Women, 1917-
1930," Russian History, v.4, 1977

Carol Eubank, "The Bolshevik Party and Work Among Women,"
Russian History, v.4, 1977

Alexandra Kollontai, Selected Writings, 151-200

Paul Avrich, Kronstadt 1921, 7-34

William Henry Chamberlain, The Russian Revolution, 1917-
1921, v. II, 430-63 ("The Crisis of War Communism..."
and "The Revolution in Retrospect")

Week VII: Background to Revolution in Germany

Gerald D. Feldman, "The Political and Social Foundations
of Germany's Economic Mobilization, 1914-1916," Armed
Forces and Society, 3, 1, 1976, 121-45

Jürgen Kocka, "The First World War and the Mittelstand,"
Journal of Contemporary History, VIII, 1973, 101-24

Robert G. Moeller, "Dimensions of Social Conflict in the
Great War: The View from the German Countryside," Central
European History, v. XIV, 2, 1981, 142-68

Jürgen Tampke, The Ruhr and Revolution, The Revolutionary
Movement in the Rhenish-Westphalian Industrial Region
1912-1919, 3-70

Dieter Groh, "The Unpatriotic Socialists and the State,"
Journal of Contemporary History, 1, 4, 1966, 151-77

Week VIII: In Search of the German Revolution
Reinhard Rürup, "Problems of the German Revolution 1918-19,"
Journal of Contemporary History," 4, 1968, 109-35
Robert F. Wheeler, "'Ex oriente lux?' The Soviet Example
and the German Revolution, 1917-1923," in Bertrand, ed.,
Revolutionary Situations in Europe, 1917-1922, 39-50
Gerhard P. Bassler, "The Communist Movement in the German
Revolution, 1918-1919: A Problem of Historical Typology?"
Central European History, v. VI, 1973, 233-77
Wolfgang J. Mommsen, "The German Revolution 1918-1920:
Political Revolution and Social Protest Movement," in
R. Bessel and E.J. Feuchtwanger, Social Change and Poli-
tical Development in Weimar Germany, 21-54
Barrington Moore, Jr., Injustice, 376-97

Week IX: A Failed Revolution in Germany?
Lothar Albertin, "German Liberalism and the Foundation of
the Weimar Republic: A Missed Opportunity," in A. Nicholls
and E. Matthias, German Democracy and the Triumph of Hit-
ler, 29-46
Gerald D. Feldman, "Social Policy and Social Conflict:
Labor as a 'Winner' in the German Inflation," (typescript)
Renate Bridenthal, "Beyond Kinder Küche, Kirche: Weimar
Women at Work," Central European History, v. VI, 1973,
148-66
Jeremy Noakes and Geoffrey Pridham, Documents on Nazism,
1919-1945, 31-63

Week X: Background to Revolution in Italy
Salvatore Saladino, "Parliamentary Politics in the Liberal
Era 1861 to 1914," in E. Tannenbaum and E. Noether, eds.,
Modern Italy. A Topical History Since 1861, 27-51
Alice Keikian, "From Liberalism to Corporatism: The Province
of Brescia during the First World War," in J.A. Davis,
Gramsci and Italy's Passive Revolution, 213-38
Frank Snowden, "From Sharecropper to Proletarian: The Back-
ground to Fascism in Rural Tuscany, 1880-1920," in Davis,
ed., Gramsci and Italy's Passive Revolution, 136-71
Gwyn A. Williams, Proletarian Order. Antonio Gramsci, Factory
Councils and the Origins of Italian Communism 1911-1921, 1-67

Week XI: Revolution and Counterrevolution in Italy
Martin Clark, The Failure of Revolution in Italy, 1919-1920
Adrian Lyttleton, "Revolution and Counter-revolution in Italy,
1918-1922," and Alan Cassels, "Rise of Fascism in Italy,
1918-1922: Revolution, Counter-revolution, or Re-arrange-
ment?" in Bertrand, ed., Revolutionary Situations, 63-82
A. Lyttleton, The Seizure of Power. Fascism in Italy, 1919-
1929, 42-93
Paul Corner, Fascism in Ferrara 1915-1925, Ch. 7, "The Rank
and File of Fascism," 137-69

Page 4

Week XII: A Contemporary Analysis of Revolution and Count-
    Revolution in Italy: The Writings of Antonio Gramsci
    *A. Gramsci, The Modern Prince and Other Writings, 28-51
    *A. Gramsci, Selections from Political Writings, 1910-
        1920, ed. Q. Hoare, selections # 17, 20, 21, 23-26, 28,
        48, 51-52, 56-57, 60-64, 66-68, 71-72
    *A. Gramsci, Selections from Political Writings, 1921-
        1926, ed. Q. Hoare, selections # 2, 3, 5, 8, 11, 13, 14,
        16, 19, 25, 27, 29, 36, 52, 53, 55-56, 61-63, 73

Week XIII: Presentation of Oral Reports on Papers

Week XIV: Comparative Persepctives on Causes, Consequences and
    Outcomes of Revolution in Europe
    James E. Cronin, "Labor Insurgency and Class Formation:
        Comparative Perspectives on the Crisis of 1917-1920 in
        Europe," Social Science History, 4, 1, 125-52
    Carmen Sirianni, "Workers' Control in the Era of World
        War I. A Comparative Analysis of the European Experience,"
        Theory and Society, 9, 1980, 29-88
    Charles Maier, "Political Crisis and Partial Modernization:
        The Outcomes in Germany, Austria, Hungary, and Italy after
        World War I," in Bertrand, ed., Revolutionary Situations,
        119-32
    Arno Mayer, "Internal Crisis and War since 1870," in Bertrand,
        ed., Revolutionary Situations, 201-38
    Barrington Moore, Jr., Injustice, 357-75

17

Fall Semester 1982-83　　　　　　　　Prof. Charles S. Maier
　　　　　　　　　　　　　　　　　Center for European Studies
　　　　　　　　　　　　　　　　　Harvard University
　　　　　　　　　　　　　　　　　456-4303; or Robinson 101
　　　　　　　　　　　　　　　　　495-2157

History 1338

TOPICS IN TWENTIETH-CENTURY HISTORY:

THE SECOND WORLD WAR

I. (September 20): Introduction to Course.

II. (September 27): Is there an Issue of Responsibility?

A. J. P. Taylor, The Origins of the Second World War (PB),
　　　　chaps. I-II, VI-XI.

Michael Howard, The Continental Commitment: The Dilemma of
　　　　British Defense Policy in the Era of Two World
　　　　Wars, chaps. 5-6.

Klaus Hildebrand, The Foreign Policy of the Third Reich
　　　　(U. Cal. PB), chaps. 4-7.

Recommended Reading:

　　Esmonde M. Robertson, Hitler's Prewar Policies and Military
　　　　Plans,1933-1939.

　　Esmonde M. Robertson, ed., The Origins of the Second World
　　　　War (includes Taylor-Trevor Roper and Taylor-Mason
　　　　debates).

　　Gerhard L. Weinberg, The Foreign Policy of Hitler's Germany:
　　　　vol. I, Diplomatic Revolution in Europe, 1933-1936 (1970)
　　　　vol. II, Starting World War II, 1937-1939 (1980).

　　Robert Young, In Command of France (a reassessment of French
　　　　policy).

Recommended for origins of East Asian war and American policy:

　　William L. Langer and S. E. Gleason, The Undeclared War, 1940-
　　　　1941, chaps. I-III, XXVI-XXVIII.

　　Herbert Feis, The Road to Pearl Harbor (PB).

　　Robert Dallek, Franklin Roosevelt and American Foreign Policy,
　　　　1932-1945 (PB).

　　Robert J. C. Butow, Tojo and the Coming of War.

III. (October 4): Strategic Options: The Case of the Second Front.

United States War Department, Office of Military History: The
U.S. Army in World War II:

　　Maurice Matloff and Edwin N. Snell, Strategic Planning for
　　　　Coalition Warfare, 1941-1932, pp. 174-194, 217-244,
　　　　279-293, 328, 347-349, 376-382.

Maurice Matloff, <u>Strategic Planning for Coalition Warfare,</u>
1943-1944, pp. 18-33, 37-42, 68-76, 120-138, 162-184,
280-306, 360-367, 376-382.

AND

History of the Second World War: U.K. Military Series:

J.M. A. Gwyer, <u>Grand Strategy</u>, vol. III, part I, pp. 1-33,
49-78.

J. R. M. Butler, <u>Grand Strategy</u>, vol. III, part II,
pp. 419-434, 563-582, 593-600, 617-650, 657-666.

John Ehrman, <u>Grand Strategy</u>, vol. V, pp. 47-57, 105-118, 225.

Recommended:

Forrest Pogue, <u>George C. Marshall</u>: vol. II, <u>Ordeal and Hope,</u>
1939-1942, and vol. III: <u>Organizer of Victory, 1943-</u>
<u>1945</u>.

Winston S. Churchill, <u>The Second World War</u> (6 vols. of memoirs).

Robert S. Sherwood, <u>Roosevelt and Hopkins</u>.

Albert Seaton, <u>The Russo-German War, 1941-1945</u>.

Andreas Hillgruber, <u>Hitler's Strategies: Politik und</u>
<u>Kriegsführung 1940-1941</u>.

IV. (October 18): Strategic Options: The Case of Strategic Bombing.

Sir Charles Webster and Noble Frankland, <u>The Strategic Air</u>
<u>Offensive Against Germany, 1939-1945</u>, vol. II, pp. 3-8,
32-52, 214-268;
vol. III, 103-119,
207-244, 283-311.

AND

Alan S. Milward, <u>War, Economy and Society, 1939-1945</u> (U.Cal. PB),
chap. 9.

Recommended:

Max Hastings, <u>Bomber Command</u>.

V. (October 25): Did Intelligence Make a Difference?

F. H. Hinsley, et al., <u>British Intelligence in the Second</u>
<u>World War</u>, vol. I, pp. 19-43, 52-85, 89-92, 115-125, 127-145,
159-190, 487-495, 528-548, 315-346.

Roberta A. Wohlstetter, <u>Warning and Decision: Pearl Harbor</u>.

VI. (November 1): Economic Mobilization: The Nazi Effort in
Comparative Perspective.

Alan Milward, <u>War, Economy and Society, 1939-1945</u>, chaps. 2-4.

Alan Milward, The German Economy at War, chaps. II-IV, VI.

R. J. Overy, "Hitler's War and the German Economy: A Reinterpretation," Economic History Review, 2nd Series, XXXV, No. 2 (May 1982): 272-291.

Recommended for further comparison of rearmament efforts:

R. A. C. Parker, "Economics, Rearmament and Foreign Policy: The United Kingdom before 1939 - A Preliminary Study," Journal of Contemporary History, vol. 10, no. 4 (Oct. 1975): 637-47.

Robert Frankenstein, "A propos des aspects financiers du réarmament français," Revue d'Histoire de la Deuxième Guerre Mondiale, Nr. 102 (April 1976): 1-20.

Fortunato Minniti, "Il problema degli armamenti nella preparazione militare italiana dal 1935 al 1943," Storia Contemporanea, IX, No. 1 (February 1978): 5-62.

Other recommended reading:

Albert Speer, Inside the Third Reich.

Burton Klein, Germany's Economic Preparations for War.

G. Jansens, Das Ministerium Speer. Deutschlands Rüstung im Krieg.

Gen. Georg Thomas, Geschichte der deutschen Wehr- und Rüstungswirtschaft (1918-1943/45).

W. K. Hancock and M. R. Gowing, British War Economy.

VII. (November 8): The War and Social Change: The Case of Britain.

Paul Addison, The Road to 1945.

Richard M. Titmuss, Problems of Social Policy (History of the Second World War: Civil Series), chaps. I, II, XX section iv, XXV section i.

Recommended:

Angus Calder, The People's War: Britain, 1939-1945.

Keith Middlemas, Politics in Industrial Society, chap. 10.

VIII. (November 15): Patterns of Occupation.

Robert O. Paxton, Vichy France: Old Guard and New Order, 1940-1944 (Norton PB), Prologue, Chaps. I, II, III, V.

Jan Tomasz Gross, Polish Society under German Occupation: The Generalgouvernement, 1939-1944, chaps. I-III, V, VII, IX-X.

Recommended:

Werner Warmbrunn, The Dutch under German Occupation, 1940-1945.

IX. (November 22): Occupation and the 'Final Solution'.

Lucy S. Dawidowicz, The War Against the Jews, 1933-1945 (Bantam PB), chaps. 1, 4, 6-8, 10-16.

Recommended:

Randolph Braham, The Politics of Genocide: The Holocaust in Hungary.

Gerald Reitlinger, The Final Solution.

Karl A. Schlernes, The Twisted Road to Auschwitz.

Hannah Arendt, Eichmann in Jerusalem (PB).

Isaiah Trunk, Judenrat: the Jewish Councils in Eastern Europe under Nazi Control.

Robert O. Paxton and Michael Marrus, Vichy and the Jews.

X. (November 29): How Important Was the Resistance?

M. R. D. Foot, Resistance (Paladin PB), chaps. 1-4, 6-8;
OR
Henri Michel, The Shadow War;
OR
Werner Rings, Life with the Enemy.

H. R. Kedward, Resistance in Vichy France: A Study of Ideas and Motivation in the Southern Zone, chaps. II-III, VII-X.

Recommended:

Walter Roberts, Tito, Mihailovic and the Allies, 1941-45.

André Kédros, La résistance grècque, 1940-1944.

Charles Delzell, Mussolini's Enemies.

Giorgio Bocca, Storia dell-Italia partigiana.

Peter Hoffmann, The German Resistance to Hitler.

XI. (December 6): Culture and Society: The Impact of the War on America.

John Morton Blum, "V" Was for Victory: Politics and American Culture during World War II.

Recommended:

Leila J. Rupp, Mobilizing Women for War: German and American Propaganda.

Thomas N. Havens, Valley of Darkness: The Japanese People and World War II.

XII.   (December 13): Aftermaths: Origins of the Cold War (PB).

   Vojtech Mastny, Russia's Road to the Cold War (PB).

   Charles S. Maier, ed., The Origins of the Cold War and
       Contemporary Europe, chaps. 1-2 (Maier & Schurmann pieces).

   Recommended:
       A. W. DePorte, Europe Between the Superpowers, chaps. 1-7 (PB).
       W. Averell Harriman and Elie Abel, Special Envoy to
           Churchill and Stalin, 1941-1946.

XIII. (to be scheduled): Explanation and/or Judgment: The
                           Decision to Use the Atomic Bombs.

   Martin Sherwin, A World Destroyed (PB).

   Michael Walzer, Just and Unjust Wars, chaps. 1-3, 8, 11, 16-19.

   Articles, distributed by Fussell, Sherwin, Walzer, Alsop, Joravsky.

NB: Gordon Wright, The Ordeal of Total War, 1939-1945 (Harper TB)
       should be consulted as a general reference throughout.

Written work: A 6-8 page paper on one of several assigned
questions if due in early November; a term paper (c. 20 pages)
on a topic selected by the student is due in reading period.

WAR

INTRODUCTION   Sept. 20

PART ONE: Why War?   Sept. 22 - Oct. 22

A. War and social thought   Sept. 22-24
B. The lessons of primitive war   Sept. 27
C. The search for causes   Sept. 29 - Oct. 22
     1. Biology: animal warfare and Darwinian mythology
     2. Psychology
         a. Individual psychology: human drives and war
         b. Social Psychology: national character
     3. Geography and demography
     4. Economics and the problem of imperialism
     5. Politics
         a. Domestic politics: regimes and ideologies
         b. International politics: nations in the state of nature

Hour examination   Oct. 25

PART TWO: War in history   Oct. 27 - Nov. 19

A. War and the international order   Oct. 27- Nov. 8
     1. War and international systems
         a. Types of wars
         b. Functions of wars
     2. War and foreign policy
         a. Ends and means
         b. Strategy
B. War and society   Nov. 10-Nov. 19
     1. War and the domestic order
         a. Societies in war
         b. Civil-military relations
     2. War and the individual

PART THREE: War in the nuclear age   Nov. 22 - Dec. 15

A. Violence since 1945   Nov. 22 - Dec. 10
     1. "Neither war nor peaee": the international system
         a. Rules of the nuclear game
         b. Iiｍited and revolutionary wars
     2. The control of force
         a. Taming the actors: International Law and Organization
         b. Taming the weapons: Disarmament and Arms Control
B. Society and the military   Dec. 13 - 15

CONCLUSION   Dec. 17

REQUIREMENTS

1. <u>Sections</u> - the course will be divided into sections. They will meet every other week for two hours, at times and in rooms to be announced.

2. <u>Readings</u> - (starred * items are in paperback)

Part One: Why War?

A. <u>War and social thought (Sept. 22 - 24)</u>

*Kenneth Waltz, MAN, THE STATE AND WAR, (New York: Columbia U. Press, 1959).

*Hobbes, LEVIATHAN Ch. 1-6, 13-19.

*S. Hoffmann, THE STATE OF WAR, (New York: Praeger) Ch. 3.

C.J. Friedrich, ed., THE PHILOSOPHY OF KANT, (Modern Library) "Idea for a Universal History," (pp. 116 ff.) and "Eternal Peace," pp. 430 ff.

D.J. Friedrich, ed., THE PHILOSOPHY OF HEGEL, (Modern Lsbrary) from the "Philosophy of Right," pp. 320-329.

*M.J. Forsyth (ed.), THE THEORY OF INTERNATIONAL RELATIONS (London Allen and Unwin) Ch. by Grotius. Rousseau and Treitschke.

B. <u>The lessons of primitive war (Sept. 27)</u>

*Leon Bramson and George Goethals (eds.), WAR (New York: Basic Books, 1970) pp. 269-274.

C. <u>The search for causes (Sept. 29 - Oct. 22)</u>

*Konrad Lorenz, ON AGGRESSION (New York: Bantam Books) Ch. 3-7, 13-14.

*Freud, CHARACTER AND CULTURE (Collier) IX and X.

*Bramson and Goethals (eds.), WAR, pp. 21-31, 329-345.

*Heath Series on Problems in Modern European Civilization: THE NEW IMPERIALISM, (Harrison Wright, ed.) Selections from Hobson, Lenin, Schumpeter, Langer, Robinson and Gallagher, Fieldhouse.

A. Gilbert, "Marx on Internationalism and War", PHILOSOPHY AND PUBLIC AFFAIRS, Summer 1978, pp. 346-69.

Part Two: War in History

A. <u>War and the international order (Oct. 27-Nov. 8)</u>

*Hedley Bull, THE ANARCHICAL SOCIETY (New York: Columbia U. Press, 1977) Chapters 1-5, 8.

*Michael Howard, WAR IN EUROPEAN HISTORY (New York: Oxford U. Press) entire.

*Arnold Wolfers, DISCORD AND COLLABORATION (Johns Hopkins) Ch. 5-6.

Clausewitz, ON WAR (Howard and Paret, eds., Princeton U. Press)
    Book I, Ch. 1-3, 7 and Book VIII.

*R.J. Art and K. Waltz, (eds.) THE USE OF FORCE (Boston: Little
    Brown) pp. 365-401.

*E.M. Earle (ed.), MAKERS OF MODERN STRATEGY (Atheneum) Ch. 7, 14.

Readings on specific wars: students will choose two of the four following wars:

The Peloponnesian War:

*Thucydides, PELOPONNESIAN WAR, Books, I and II, and Book V, Ch. XVIII.

The wars of the French Revolution and Napoleon:

Kyung-Won Kim, REVOLUTION AND INTERNATIONAL SYSTEM (New York:
    NYU Press(entire.

*Charles Breunig, THE AGE OF REVOLUTION AND REACTION (New York:
    Norton, second edition) chapters 1-3.

World War One:

Hajo Holborn, THE POLITICAL COLLAPSE OF EUROPE (New York: Knopf)
chapters 3-4.

Gerd Hardach, THE FIRST WORLD WAR (Berkeley U. of California Press),
Ch. 7-11.

*A.J.P. Taylor, THE FIRST WORLD WAR (New York: Capricorn) entire.

World War Two:

*Telford Taylor, MUNICH (New York: Vintage), Parts II-III, chapters.
24, 26, 29 -33.

Hajo Holborn, THE POLITICAL COLLAPSE OF EUROPE, Ch. 5-6.

*Gordon Wright, THE ORDEAL OF TOTAL WAR (Harper Torchbook) entire.

Alan Milward, WAR, ECONOMY AND SOCIETY (Berkeley U. of Calif. Press)
chapters 1, 2, 4, 9-10.

B. War and Society (Nov. 10-17)

*S.P. Huntington, THE SOLDIER AND THE STATE (Vintage Book) Part I
and Part III, Ch. 12.

*J. Glenn Gray, THE WARRIORS (Harper Torchbook) entire.
or
*John Keegan, THE FACE OF BATTLE (Vintage) entire.

25

Jean Giraudoux, TIGER AT THE GATES.
or
*Brecht, MOTHER COURAGE (New York: Grove Press).

André Malraux, MAN'S HOPE (New York: Grove Press).
or
*George Orwell, HOMAGE TO CATALONIA (Beacon Press).

Part Three: War in the nuclear age

A. Violence since 1945 (Nov. 22 - Dec. 10)

*Walter La Feber, AMERICA, RUSSIA AND THE COLD WAR, fourth edition
(New York: John Wiley) entire.

*Michael Mandelbaum, THE NUCLEAR REVOLUTION (Cambridge: Cambridge U.
Press), Ch. 1. 3-4, 6, 8.

*Ground Zero, NUCLEAR WAR (New York: Pocket, 1982), Part I and Ch. 16.

*Independent Commission on Disarmament and Security Issues, COMMON
SECURITY (New York: Simon and Schuster) Ch. 3-4.

*S. Hoffmann, THE STATE OF WAR, Ch. 4-5, 8, 9.

*Michael Mandelbaum in: David Gompert et al, NUCLEAR WEAPONS AND
WORLD POLITICS (New York: McGraw-Hill) pp 15-80.

Walter Laqueur, GUERRILLA (Boston: Little, Brown) Ch. 6-9.

*Walter Laqueur, TERRORISM (Boston: Little, Brown) Ch. 3, 5 and
conclusion.

*Frantz Fanon, THE WRETCHED OF THE EARTH (New York: Grove Press)
Ch. 1-3.

*John Hersey, HIROSHIMA (New York: Bantam) entire.

*S. Hoffmann, PRIMACY OR WORLD ORDER (New York: McGraw-Hill) Part Two.

*Hedley Bull, THE ANARCHICAL SOCIETY (New York: Columbia U. Press)
Part Three.

*Ava Myrdal, THE GAME OF DISARMAMENT (New York: Pantheon) Ch. III,
VIII-IX.

*Lewis Dunn, CONTROLLING THE BOMB (New Haven: Yale U. Press).

B. Society and the military (Dec. 13-15)

*Amos Perlmutter, THE MILITARY AND POLITICS IN MODERN TIMES (New Haven:
Yale U. Press) Ch. 4-9.

To be read throughout the term:

Tolstoy, WAR AND PEACE (Penguin or any unabridged edition.)

3. Other Requirements

   All undergraduates must

   1. Take an hour exam on Oct. 25. It will cover the lectures
      and readings of Part One.

   2. Write a paper of approximately 5,000 words, due Jan. 14,
      on a topic chosen in concultation with the instructor or
      with the section leaders. The paper can deal with any
      aspect of the course. Here are some suggestions which are
      indications and do not pretend to be exhaustive.

The treatment of war in literature, in art or in the movies (comparisons
can be made between countries, or, for a given country, between different
wars).

The attitudes of various social groups, leaders or political organizations,
toward war, in either World War I or World War II (especially the workers and
the intellectuals).

An examination of types of, or of a particular type of, pacifist or
bellicist arguments and attitudes (among soldiers or civilians).

An examination of the effects of war on the economy and social order or a
nation (for instance, on civil liberties or on the class structure).

The impact of the expectation of, and preparations for war on a nation
(the 1930's provide a wealth of examples).

The role of warfare in the creation and evolution of the modern state.

A study of an arms race (e.g. the British-German naval race before 1914).

The psychological and economic mobilization in a nation or in several nations
during World Wars I or II (here again comparisons could be made).

The role of ideology in war (e.g. the wars of the French Revolution).

The conflicts between national allegiance and other forms of loyalty
(from Antigone to collaborationism).

An examination of the role of the military in policy-making.

A discussion of strategic doctrines.

The effects of technology and technological innovations on war.

A critique of casual explanations and of philosophies of history dealing with
war.

A discussion of primitive war.

A study of a specific decision, such as the U.S. decision to enter WWI, the decision to use the A-bomb, France's declaration of war in 1792, Churchill's resort to mass air bombings, etc.

Why a particular conflict has been limited or has escalated.

A critique of suggestions and efforts made for controlling war and the arms race, such as just war theory, the international law of war, collective security and disarmament conferences.

A discussion of the relevance of earlier studies of war (say, Thucydides or Machiavelli) to the wars of the 20th century.

A study of peace-making after a war, and of the effects of the peace treaty.

A discussion of the origins of the cold war and of the conflicting interpretations presented in recent years.

A discussion of the relevance of earlier strategic doctrines or studies of war to the nuclear age.

A study of the comparative evolution of nuclear technology and of the strategic policies or doctrines of the superpowers.

A case study of a conflict involving the use of force or of a conflict that stopped short of the resort to force, since 1945.

A study of some of the methods or doctrines of revolutionary or unconventional warfare.

A study of the impact of nuclear weapons on the policy calculations of a state.

A critique of some of the efforts or suggestions for controlling or ending the arms race.

An examination of the role played by international or regional organizations in peace-keeping.

A study of the so-called "industrial-military complex" in the United States or elsewhere.

A comparison of the views of various writers on strategy.

A study of the attitudes toward and images of other nations, in the public of a contemporary nation.

A case study of the spread (or avoidance of the spread) of nuclear weapons.

A case study of decision-making leading to war or in a crisis.

A comparison of nuclear deterrence with previous strategies of deterrence or defense.

A study of the military policies of small states.

A study of the ways in which the superpowers "control" their clients or allies.

A study of some aspect of the dynamics of the arms race.

A study of army behavior during a crisis in post-World War II foreign policy.

A study of the implications of the internationalization of Civil Wars.

A discussion of the possible effects of disarmament.

An examination of the treatment of nuclear war in literature and in movies.

A discussion of the ethical problems raised by contemporary wars or strategies.

An examination of the uses of hostility for nation-building.

A study of different types of military service and military organizations at the present time.

A study of the development and effects of transnational terrorism.

A study of proposed and possible schemes for international or regional security.

3. Take the final examination on Jan. 21

All graduate students have a choice between

1. either writing a 5,000 word paper and taking the final examination, like undergraduates (but not the hour exam)

2. or writing a paper of seminar length (12,000 words), without taking either the hour or the final examination.

The graduate student papers are due Jan. 14.

Professor Stanley Hoffmann   Professor Michael Smith
Center for European Studies   Social Studies
5 Bryant Street   Hilles Library--Lower Level

Office hours will be announced.

HISTORY **201**

Graduate Seminar on

COMPARATIVE MILITARY SYSTEMS

Professor Peter Karsten
University of Pittsburgh

This is a reading seminar, designed to stimulate a research project of one's choice, on the nature of military systems throughout the world. Needless to say, while it should appeal to the sociologist and political scientist, it has a strong historical dimension. The literature we will be considering concerns: the social origins of military personnel; their recruitment, their training; the process of value inculcation; inter- and intra-service rivalries; mutinies; coups d'etat, civil-military relations; a˙ ˙˙ role of the military in "nation-building." We will also spend a week ˙n ˙ ˙la d topic, the laws of warfare and war-crimes. You will be asked to read a common reading and one other work each week.

The sorts of questions we will be asking in the next two months may be of interest to you now as you begin the readings. These questions include (but are by no means limited to) the following:

Stanislav Andreski (in _Military Organization and Society_) argues that the type of military organization or innovation a society adopts may cause sweeping changes in that society's political and social organizations. To what extent is this valid?

The readings reveal relationships between recruitment practices and the roles military systems play in society? What are they?

What consistent evidence exists of a "militarist" who tends to offer his services or to emerge from training?

Why do military coups occur? Of the several different causes which are associated with particular societies or conditions?

How does one evaluate the claim that "the military is a natural nation-builder"?

What values appear malleable in training? Does military training differ from culture to culture? If so, give examples and explain the differences.

What accounts for the emergence of any particular "law" or "rule" of warfare? What accounts for the fact that any particular "law" is not observed as scrupulously by some military personnel as its drafters had hoped?

You will each be asked to select a particular topic, formulate a question or hypothesis (not necessarily any one of those I've just jotted down, of course), and answer it either with an extensive analysis of the existing literature, or with original research.

30

WEEKLY TOPICS

Week	Subject	Common Reading (in addition to each individual's)
1.	Introduction: the Military & Society	S. Andreski, Military Organization & Society (skim read)
2.	Civil-Military Relations (in general)	S. Huntington, The Soldier & the State, pp. 1-97
3.	Recruitment & Social Background	P. Karsten, Soldiers & Society, pp. 1-20, 51-125
4.	Training & Value Inculcation	P. Karsten, Soldiers & Society, pp. 21-22, 126-144
5.	The "Military Mind" & Inter-Service Rivalries	A. Vagts, A History of Militarism, pp. 1-74
6.	The World of Combat	P. Karsten, Soldiers & Society, pp. 22-31, 145-231
7.	The Laws of Warfare & War Crimes	P. Karsten, Law, Soldiers & Combat, chpts. 1 & 2
8.	Mutinies	C. J. Lammers, "Strikes & Mutinies," Admin. Science Q (Dec. 1969)
9.	Coups d'Etat	Wm. Thompson, The Grievances of Military Coup-Makers
10.	"Nation-Building"	Lucien Pye, "Armies in the Process of Political Moderni-zation," in John Johnson, ed., The Role of the Military in Underdeveloped Countries
11.	Veterans	P. Karsten, Soldiers & Society, pp. 32ff, 232ff.
12.	Office Hours	
13.	Presentation of Papers	

Basic Comparative Military Systems Literature, Organized Topically

1. The Military and Society: General Intro. Readings

Stanislav Andreski, Military Organization and Society
F. Voget, "Warfare & the Integration of Crow Indian Culture," in W.H. Goodenough, eds., Explorations in Cultural Anthropology, pp. 483-509

Peter G. Foote & David M. Wilson, The Viking Achievement
Victor Alba, "Stages of Militarism in Latin Amer.," in John Johnson, ed.,
    The Role of the Military in Underdeveloped Countries
Thomas Barker, The Seige of Vienna
Ben Halpern, "Role of the Military in Israel," in Johnson, ed., Role of Military
Philip Kuhn, Rebellion & its Enemies in Late Imperial China: Militarization
    and Social Structure, 1796-1864.
Stanley Spector, Li Hung-Chang and the Huai Army: 19th Century Chinese
    Regionalism
P. J. Vatikiotis, Politics and the Military in Jordan
Ramsay MacMullen, Soldier and Civilian in the Late Roman Empire
M.D. Feld, "Middle-Class Society and the Rise of Military Professionalism:
    The Dutch Army, 1589-1609," Armed Forces & Society, I (1975), 419ff.
Bopegamage chapters in Jacques van Doorn. ed. Military Professions &
    Military Regimes and in Van Gils, ed., The Perceived Role of Military
Scott and Graczck chapters in On Military Ideology, eds. Morris
    Janowitz & J. van Doorn
Ayad Al-Qazzas, "Army & Society in Israel," Pacific Sociological Review,
    XVI (Apr. 1973), 143ff
S. Encel, "The Study of Militarism in Australia," in Jacques van Doorn, ed.,
    Armed Forces & Society, 126-147.
Leonard Humphreys, "The Japanese Military Tradition," in James Buck, ed.,
    The Modern Japanese Military System, 21-39.
J. Bayo Adekson, "Army in a Multi-Ethnic Society: Ghana," Armed Forces &
    Society, II (1976), 251ff. Chapter on Mamelukes in Ira Lapidus, Muslim
    Cities in the Late Middle Ages
Nikolai Galay, "The Relationship between the Structure of Society & the
    Armed Forces in the U.S.S.R.," Bulletin of the Institute for the Study
    of the U.S.S.R. (Nov. 1966).
Jeffrey Fadiman, Mountain Warriors: The Pre-Colonial Meru of Mt. Kenya
Andrew Vayda, "Maoris and Muskets in New Zealand," Political Science
    Quarterly, LXXXV (1970), 550-584
Thomas Forster, The East German Army
L.J.D. Collins, "The Military Organization & Tactics of the Crimean Tartars
    during the 16th and 17th centuries," in War, Technology & Society, ed.
    Vernon Parry & M.E. Yapp, 257-276
John Shy, "A New Look at Colonial Militia," William & Mary Quarterly (1963),
    175-183
Marcus Cunliffe, Soldiers & Civilians
Dennis Skiotis, "Mountain Warriors & the Greek Revolution," in War,
    Technology & Society in the Middle East, ed. Vernon Parry & M.E. Yapp,
    308-329
M.E. Yapp, "Middle Eastern Armies & Modernization," in Parry & Yapp, War,
    Technology & Society..., 343-366.
Joseph Smaldone, Warfare in the Sokolo Caliphate
Gwyn Harries-Jenkins, The Army in Victorian Society, chs. 1 & 2.
Jonathan Adelman, The Revolutionary Armies
Richard Divale, Warfare in Primitive Societies (introduction only)
Allan Millett, Guardians of the Dynasty
Halil Inalcik, :The socio-political effects of the diffusion of fire-arms in
    the Middle East," in War, Technology & Society, ed., Vernon Parry &
    M.E. Yapp, 195-217
Janes Guyot, "Ethnic Segmentation & the Function of the Military in Burma
    & Malaysia" I U.S. paper 1474.
Richard Hellie, Enserfment and Military Change in Muscovy
Tim Colton, "Impact of the Military on Soviet Society," in S. Bialer, ed.,
    Domestic Context of Soviet Foreign Policy. 119-38

2. Civil-Military Relations

I. Deak, "An Army Divided: Loyalty Crisis in Haps. Off. Corps, 1848,"
   Jahrbuch des I. für Deut. G., VIII ('79)

Claude Welch and Arthur Smith, Military Role and Rule
E. Joffe, Party and Army: Professionalism and Political Control in the
   Chinese Officer Corps
Louis Perez, Army Politics in Cuba, 1898-1958
A. Mazrui chapter in Jacques van Doorn, ed., Military Professions and
   Military Regimes
Nelson Kasfir, "Civilian Participation under Military Rule in Uganda and
   Sudan," Armed Forces and Society, I (1975), 344ff.
C. Moskos chapter [on U.N.] in Van Gils, ed., The Perceived Role of the Military
Charles Moskos, Peace Soldiers and Moskos essay in J.van Doorn and Morris
   Janowitz, eds., On Military Ideology
Gabriel Ben-Dor, "The Politics of Threat: Military Intervention...,"
   Journal of Political and Military Sociology, I (1973), 57ff
Gabriel Ben-Dor, "Civilianization of Military Regimes in the Arab World,"
   Armed Forces and Society, I (1975), 317ff.
Edwin Lieuwen, Mexican Militarism
Anton Bebler, The Military in African Politics
D. Herspring and I. Volgyes, "Political Reliability in Eastern Europe
   Warsaw Pack Armies," Armed Forces and Society, VI (1980), 270-296
Jorge Dominques, "The Civic Soldier: The Military as a Governing Institution
   in Cuba," 1973 IUS paper
Roman Kolkowicz, "Interest Groups in Soviet Politics: The Case of the
   Military," Comparative Politics (April 1970), 445-472.
Cynthia Enloe, Ethnic Soldiers

3. Recruitment

Richard Smethurst, A Social Basis for Prewar Japanese Militarism
Ithiel de Sola Pool, Satellite Generals
Summer Shapiro, "The Blue-Water Soviet Naval Officer" U.S. Naval
   Institute Proceedings (February 1971), 19-26
Christopher Duffy, The Army of Fredrick the Great 24-68
Shelby D vis, Reservoirs of Men: Black Troops of French West Africa
John Erickson, "Soviet Military Manpower Policies," Armed Forces and
   Society, I (Fall, 1974), 29ff.
H. Moyse-Bartlett, The King's African Rifles
Edward Lowell, The Hessians
Chapters by Dudley, Wiatr,Graczyk, and Cvrcek in Military Professions and
   Military Regimes, ed. Jacques van Doorn
D. Ayalon and S. Vryoni on recruitment, in War, Technology and Society in
   the Middle East, ed. Vernon Parry and M. E. Yapp, 44-68, 125-152
Coulombe chapter in On Military Ideology, eds., Morris Janowitz and J. van Doorn
Thomas Brendle, "Recruitment and Training in the SDF:," in James Buck ed.,
   The Modern Japanese Military System
G. T. Griffith, The Mercenaries of the Hellenistic World
H. W. Parke, Greek Mercenary Soldiers
Peter Karsten, The Naval Aristocracy, chapter 1 and religion (chapter 3)
Peter Karsten, Soldiers and Society, (section on "The Recruitment Process")
Moskos, Davis-Dolbeare, and Wamsley essays in Roger Little, ed., Selective
   Service and American Society
Sylvia Frey, "Common British soldier in late 18th century," Societas (1975
   (or '76)
Holger Herwig, "Feudalization of the Bourgeoisie: Role of Nobility in
   German Naval Officer Corps, 1890-1918," The Historian ('75-'76), 268ff.

Michel Martin, "Changing Social Morphology of French Mil. Est., 1945-75" (Mimeo)
Alan R. Skelley, The Victorian Army at Home
George Chessman, Auxilia of the Roman Imperial Army
Douglas Wheeler, "African Elements in Portugals' Armies in Africa," Armed Forces and Society, II (1976), 233ff.
John Schlight, Monarchs and Mercenaries
Michael Powicke, Military Obligation in Medieval England
Gianfranco Pasquino, "The Italian Army," Armed Forces and Society, II (1976), 205ff
JJ Sanders, Feudal Military Service in England
Fritz Redlich, The German Military Enterpriser and his work force (2 volumes)
F. Kazemnadeh, "The Origin and Early Development of the Persian Cossack Brigade," American Slavic and East European Review, XV, 351-63
D. Mantell, "Doves v. Hawks," Psychology Today, September 1974
G. Kourvetaris, "Greek Service Academies: Patterns of Recruitment and Organization Change," in G. Harries-Jenkins, ed., The Military and the Problems of Legitimacy, 113ff
E. H. Norman, Soldier and Peasant in Japan
E. Waldman, The Goose Step est Verboden
H. Desmond Martin, The Rise of Chingis Khan, 11-47
John Bassett, The Purchase System in the British Army, 1660-1871
Michael Lewis, A Social History of the Royal Navy, 1793-1815
F. Harrod, Manning The New Navy
Richard Gabriel, The New Red Legions, Volumes I and II
G. R. Andrews, "The Afro-Argentine Officers of B. A. Prov., 1800-1860," Journal of Negro History, 64 (1979), 85-100
Steven Cohen, "The Untouchable Soldier: Caste, Politics and the Indian Army," Journal of Asian Studies, XXVIII (May 1969)
Roger N. Buckley, Slaves in Red Coats: The Br. N.I. Regiments, 1795-1815
John Keegan, "Regimental Ideology," in War, Economy and the Military Mind, ed. G. Best, 3-18
Michael Lewis, The Navy in Trasition, 1814-1864
Michael Lewis, England's Sea-Officers
H. Hanham, "Religion and Nationality in Mid-Victorian Army," in Foot, ed., War and Society, 159ff
Norbert Elias, "Studies inthe Genesis of the Naval Profession," British Journal of Sociology, I (1950), 291-309
C. B. Otley essay in Armed Forces and Society, ed., Jacques Van Doorn
P. Razzell, "Social Origins of Officers in the Indian and British Home Army," British Journal of Sociology, XIV (1963), 248ff.
Peter Karsten, et al., "ROTC, Mylai and the Volunteer Army," Foreign Policy, 1 (1971), 135-60

4. Training and Value Inculation

Roghmann and Sodeur, "Impact of Military Service on Auth. Attitudes in W. G." American Journal of Soc. (September 72)
John Farris, "Recruits and Boot Camp," Armed Forces and Society, (Fall, 1975)
James Kelley, "The Education and Training of Porfirian Officers," Military Affairs (October 1975), 124-28
Peter Karsten, The Naval Aristocracy, chapters 2 and 5
W. Cockerham, "Selective Socialization: Airborne Trainees," Journal of Political and Military Sociology, 1 (1973), 215-29
Correlli Barnett, "The Education of Military Elites," in Rupert Wilkinson, ed., Governing Elites, 193-214

Charles Firth, Cromwell's Army
Peter Karsten, "Ritual and Rank: Religious Affiliation, Father's "Calling" and Successful Advancement in the U.S. Officers Corps of the 20th Century", Armed Forces and Society (Fall, 1981)

Law, Radine, The Taming of the Troops, Social Control in U.S. Army
Morris Janowitz, "Changing Patterns of Org. Auth." Admin. Science Quarterly
(1957)
William D. Henderson, Why The Vietcong Fought: Motivation and Control
Hassanein Rabie, "The Training of the Mamluk Faris," in War, Technology,
and Society in the Middle East, ed. Vernon Parry and M. E. Yapp, 153-163
Harold Wool, "The Armed Services as a Training Institution," in
Eli Ginsberg, The Nations Children, II, 158-185
Herbert Goldhammer, The Soviet Soldier
C. Lammers, "Midshipmen...," Sociologica Neerlandia, II (1965), 98-122
G. Wamsley, "Contrasting Institutions of AF Socialization," Amer. Journal of Soc.
(Sept.72)

5. "Militarism" and Military Ideologies

Hans Herzfeld, "Militarism in Modern History," in Germany History, ed.
Hans Kohn, 108-121
Alfred Vagts, A History of Militarism, 1-74
Peter Karsten, The Naval Aristocracy, chapters 3, 5 and 6
Hansen and Abrahamsson chapters in On Military Ideology, eds. Morris
Janowitz and J. van Doorn.
Martin Kitchen, The German Officer Corps, 1890-1914
Francis Carsten, "From Scharnhorst to Schleicher: The Prussian Officer
corps in Politics, 1806-1933, in Michael Howard, ed., Soldiers and
Governments, 73-98
Stanley Payne, Politics and the Military in Modern Spain
Bengt Abrahamson, "The Ideology of an Elite...the Swedish Military," in
Armed Forces and Society, ed. Jacques van Doorn, 71-83
Morris Janowitz, The Professional Soldier
Roman Kolkowicz, "Modern Technology and the Soviet Officer Corps," in
Jacques van Doorn, ed., Armed Forces and Society, 148-168
Richard Smethurst, A Social Basis for Prewar Japanese Militarism
chapter on Italy in Stephen ward, ed., The War Generation
Maurice Keen, "Brotherhood in Arms," History, XLVII (1962)
Marcus Cunliffe, Soldiers and Civilians (chapters on volunteers and on North-
South comparison)
Wallace Davies, Patriotism on Parade

6. Inter - and Intra - Service Rivalries

Louis Morton, "Army and Marines on the China Station," Pacific Historical
Review, X (1960), 51ff
Peter Karsten, The Naval Aristocracy, chapter 5, part 2
Fred Greene, "The Military View of American National Policy,"
American Historical Review (1961), 354ff
Perry Smith, The Air Force Plans for Peace
Vincent Davis, Postwar Defense Policy and the U.S. Navy, 1943-1946
Robert Gallucci, Neither Peace nor Honor
Lewis Dexter, "Congressmen and the Making of Military Policy," in
Nelson Polsby, ed., New Perspectives on the House of Representatives
Paul Hammond, Supercarriers and B-36s

7. The World of Combat

Peter Karsten, Soldiers and Society, pp. 22-31, 145-231
John Baynes, Morale
John Keegan, The Face of Battle
S. L. A. Marshall, Men Against Fire
Peter Bourne, Men, Stress, and Vietnam
Art Bareau, The Unknown Soldiers

J. E. Morris, The Welsh Wars of Edward I
M. Barton, Goodmen: Civil War Soldiers
R. Grinker and J. Spiegel, Men Under Stress
"Cincinatus," Self-Destruction
Pete Maslowski, "A Study of Morale in Civil War Soldiers," Military
    Affairs, (1970), 122-125
Cecil Woodham-Smith, The Charge of the Light Brigade
Albert Biderman, March to Calumny
Eugene Kinkead, In Every War But One
Ron Glasser, 365 Days
John Beeler, Warfare in Feudal Europe, 730-1200
J. Glenn Gray, The Warriors
John Mahon, The Second Seminole War
Peter Paret, The Vendée, 1792-1796
Eric Leed, No Man's Land: Combat and Identity in World War I
Dennis Winter, Death's Men
Shils and Janowitz, "Cohesion and Disintegration in Wehrmacht," in
    W. Schramm, ed., Process and Effects of Mass. Comm.

8. The Laws of War and War Crimes

Peter Karsten, Law, Soldiers and Combat
Maurice Keen, The Laws of War in the Late Middle Ages
Raymond Schmandt, "The Fourth Crusade and the Just War Theory,"
    Catholic Historical Review (1975), 191-221
Stan H ig, The Sand Creek Massacre
Seymour Hersh, Mylai 4
The Sand Creek Massacre, ed., John Carroll
Leon Friedman, ed., The Laws of War, Volumes I and II
John R. Lemis, comp., Uncertain Judgement: A Bibliography of War Crimes Trials
The Mylai Massacre and Its Coverup, ed., Burke Marshall, et al
W. H. Parks, "Crimes in Hostilities," Marine Corps Gazette (August 1976)

9. Mutinies

C. Lammers, "Strikes and Mutinies: A Comparative Study," Admin. Science
    Quarterly (December 1969)
J. A. B. Palmer, Mutiny Outbreak at Meerut (1857)
Christ. Hibbert, The Great Mutiny, India, 1857
Daniel Horn, The German Naval Mutiny of WWI
John Williams, Mutiny, 1917
50 Mutinies
Carl Van Doren, Mutiny in January
A. P. Ryan, Mutiny at the Curragh
Hayford, The Somers Mutiny Affair
Richard Watt, Dare Call It Treason
Ronald Spector, "The Royal Indian Navy Strike of 1946," Armed Forces and
    Society," VII (1981), 271-284
Peter Karsten, "Suborned or Subordinate? Irish Soldiers in the British
    Army, 1792-1922," AHA paper, 1981
AllanWildman, The End of the Russian Imperial Army....Soldier's Revolt
John Prebble, Mutiny: Highland Regiments in Revolt

10. Military Corps d'Etat

William Thompson, The Grievances of Military Coup-Makers
Richard Kohn, "The Inside History of the Newburgh Conspiracy,"
   William and Mary Quarterly (April, 1970), 1987-220
Harold Hyman, "Johnson, Stanton and Grant," American Historical Review,
   (October 1960), 85ff
Alfred Stepan, The Military in Politics...Brazil
John Ambler, Soldiers Against the State
Ph. Schmitter, "Liberation by Golpe...Portugal," Armed Forces and
   Society (Fall 1975), 5-33
Luigi Einandi, "U.S. Relations with the Peruvian Military," in Daniel
   Sharp, ed., U.S. Foreign Policy and Peru, 15-56
J. Rothschild, "The Military Background of Pilsudski's Coup d 'Etat,"
   Slavic Review, XXI (1962), 241-260
Egil Fossum, "Factors influencing....military Coups d 'etat in Latin
   America," Journal of Peace Res. (oslo), III (1967), 228-251
Douglas Porch, "Making an Army Revolutionary: France, 1815-1848," in
   Geof. Best, ed., War, Economy and the Military Mind
Morris Janowitz, Military Institutions and Coercion in Developing Nations,
   ch. 3
Fuad Khuri and G. Obermeyer, "The Social Bases for Military Intervention
   in the Middle East," in Catherine Kelleher, ed., Political-Military
   Systems, pp. 55ff

11. Nation - building

Donald Jackson, Custer's Gold
D. Lerner and R. D. Robinson, "Swords and Ploughshares: Turkish Army as
   Modernizing Force," World Politics, XIII (October 1960)
Henry Bienen, ed., The Military and Modernization [on L.A., Asia,
   Turkey, Soviet Union, Africa, and Huntington's caveat]
Willard Barber and C. N. Ronning, Internal Security and Military Power:
   Counterinsurgency and Civic Action in L.A.
Ellen K. Trimberger, Revolution from Above: Military Bureaucrats and
   Development in Japan, Turkey, Egypt and Peru
Theophilus O. Odetola, Military Politics in Nigeria: Economic Development
   and Political Stability
Stephen Cohen, The Indian Army: Its Contribution to the Development of a
   Nation
Charles Corbett, The L. A. Military Force as a Socio-Political Force:
   Bolivia and Argentina
R. L. Clinton, "The Modernizing Military: Peru," Inter-American Economic
   Affairs, 24:4 (1971) 43-66
Francis Prucha, Broadax and Bayonet
William Goetzmann, Army Exploration in the American West
Lucien Pye, "Armies in the Process of Political Modernization," in
   John Johnson, ed., The Role of the Military in Underdeveloped Countries
Jae Souk Sohn , "Political Dominance and Political Failure: The Role
   of the Military in the Republic of Korea," in Henry Bienen, ed.,
   The Military Intervenes 103-121
S. E. Finer, "The Man on Horseback-1974," Armed Forces and Society,
   I (Fall, 1974), 5ff
Hugh Hanning, The Peaceful Uses of Military Forces
Moshe Lissak, Military Roles in Modernization: Thailand and Burma
Robert Athearn, W. T. Sherman and the Settlement of the West

12. Veterans

H. Browning, et al., "Income and Veteran Status," American Sociological
   Review (1973), 74
Rodney Minott, Peerless Patriots
Steven Ross, "The Free Corps Movement in Post World War I Europe,"
   Rocky Mountain Social Science Journal (1968), 81-92
Forrest McDonald, "French Veterans..." Agricultural History (1951)
G. Wooton, The Politics of Influence: British Ex-Servicemen, Cabinet
   Decisions and Cultural Change, 1917-1957
Mary Dearing, Veterans in Politics: The Story of the G.A.R.
William Benton, "Pa. Reve. Officers and the Federal Constitution,"
   Pa. History (1964), 419-35
Peter Karsten, Soldiers and Society (section on veterans)
Al. Biderman and L. Sharp, "Convergence of Military and Civilian Careers,"
   American Journal of Sociology (1968).
N. Phillips, "Militarism and Grass-Roots...," Journal of Conflict
   Resolution (December 1973), 625-655
Stephen Ward, ed., The War Generation
Isser Woloch, The French Veteran From the Revolution to the Restoration

THE UNIVERSITY OF WISCONSIN
Department of History
First Semester,1963-64

HISTORY 531(162) (DIPLOMATIC HISTORY OF EUROPE, 1815-1914) -MR. HAMEROW

Textbook: R. Albrecht-Carrié, A Diplomatic History of Europe
List of Topics

I.   THE FALL OF THE OLD ORDER
      Textbook: pp. 3-9
            Readings:
            L. Gershoy. From Despotism to Revolution, Ch. 7
            C. Brinton. A Decade of Revolution, Chs. 3 and 7
            F. M. Anderson. Constitutions and other Select Documents,pp.383-416

II.   THE RECONSTRUCTION OF EUROPE
      Textbook: pp. 9-22
            Readings:
            R.W. Seton-Watson. Britain in Europe, Ch.1
            C.K. Webster. The Foreign Policy of Castlereagh,Vol.I, pp.379-412
            H. Temperley and L.M. Penson. Foundations of British Foreign Policy,
                              pp. 28-63

III. THE CONGRESS SYSTEM
      Textbook: pp. 23-31
            Readings:
            W.A. Phillips. The Confederation of Europe, pp. 151-218
            A.W. Ward and G.P. Gooch. The Cambridge History of British Foreign
                              Policy, Vol. II, pp. 51-83
            Memoirs of Prince Metternich, (N.Y. ed.), Vol. II, pp.322-337

IV.   LIBERALISM AND AUTOCRACY, 1822-1853
      Textbook: pp. 31-40, 55-83
            Readings:
            F.B. Artz. Reaction and Revolution, Ch. 9
            C. Webster. The Foreign Policy of Palmerston,Vol.I,pp.422-457
            E. Hertslet. The Map of Europe by Treaty,Vol.II,pp.979-998,
                              1061-1076, 1129-1138

V.   THE NEAR EASTERN QUESTION, 1812-1853
      Textbook: pp. 40-55
            Readings:
            J.A.R. Marriott. The Eastern Question, Ch.8
            F.S. Rodkey. The Turco-Egyptian Question, Ch. 6
            E. Hertslet. The Map of Europe by Treaty,Vol.II,pp.813-831,925-928

VI.   THE CRIMEAN WAR
            Textbook: pp. 84-94
            Readings:
            H. Temperley. England and the Near East: The Crimea, Ch. 14
            V.J. Puryear. International Economics and Diplomacy in the Near
                              East, Chs. 6-7
            E. Hertslet. The Map of Europe by Treaty, Vol.II,pp.1243-1283

VII. THE UNIFICATION OF ITALY
      Textbook: pp. 94-107
            Readings:
            R.C. Binkley. Realism and Nationalism, Ch. 10
            A.J.P. Taylor. The Struggle for Mastery in Europe, Ch. 6
            E. Hertslet. The Map of Europe by Treaty, Vol. II, pp. 1359-1375,
                              1380-1411
                                 39

VIII. THE UNIFICATION OF GERMANY
Textbook: pp. 112-141
Readings:
H. Friedjung. The Struggle for Supremacy in Germany, Chs. 3 and 5
H. Oncken. Napoleon III and the Rhine, pp. 38-69
O. Bismarck. The Man and the Statesman, Vol. II, Chs. 20 and 22

IX. THE DIPLOMACY OF IMPERIALISM
Textbook: pp. 186-194, 214-220, 223-226, 244-246
Readings:
P. T. Moon. Imperialism and World Politics, Ch. 3
W.L. Langer. The Diplomacy of Imperialism, Vol. II, Ch. 16
J.V.A. MacMurray. Treaties and Agreements with China, Vol.I,pp.278-308

X. THE NEAR EASTERN QUESTION, 1856-1913
Textbook: pp. 107-112, 167-177, 220-223, 280-286
Readings:
H.L. Hoskins. British Routes to India, Ch. 18
E.C. Helmreich. The Diplomacy of the Balkan Wars, Chs. 20-22
E. Hertslet. The Map of Europe by Treaty, Vol. IV, pp. 2759-2798

XI. THE EUROPEAN ALLIANCE SYSTEM, 1871-1890
Textbook: PP.145-167, 177-186, 194-206
Readings:
W. L. Langer. European Alliances and Alignments, Ch. 1
R. J. Sontag. European Diplomatic History, Ch. 2
A.F. Pribram. The Secret Treaties of Austria-Hungary,Vol. I,pp.18-73,
78-103

XII. THE EUROPEAN ALLIANCE SYSTEM, 1890-1907
Textbook: pp. 207-214, 226-243, 253-259
Readings:
E.L. Woodward. Great Britain and the German Navy, Chs. 2-3
G.P. Gooch. Before the War, Vol. I, pp. 287-331
E.T.S. Dugdale. German Diplomatic Documents, Vol. III, Chs. 28-29

XIII. THE CRUCIAL DECADE, 1904-1914
Textbook: pp. 246-253, 259-280, 286-295
Readings:
E.N. Anderson. The First Moroccan Crisis, Ch. 12
L. Albertini. The Origins of the War of 1914, Vol. I, pp. 190-225
G.P. Gooch and H. Temperley. British Documents on the Origins of the
War, Vol. VII, Ch. 55

XIV. THE COMING OF THE WAR
Textbook: pp. 299-332
Readings:
S.B. Fay. The Origins of the World War, Vol. II, Ch. 3
B.E.Schmitt. The Coming of the War, Vol. I, Ch. 6
M. Paléologue. An Ambassador's Memoirs, Vol. I, Chs. 1-2

HISTORY 532(163) (DIPLOMATIC HISTORY OF EUROPE, 1914-1945) - MR. HAMEROW

Textbook: R. Albrecht-Carrie. A Diplomatic History of Europe

List of Topics

I. THE FIRST WORLD WAR: THE YEARS OF STALEMATE
Textbook: Pp. 299-342
Readings:
A. Rosenberg   The Birth of the German Republic, Ch. 3
F. P. Chambers The War Behind the War, Chs. 13-14
R. H. Lutz, ed. Fall of the German Empire, Vol. I, Pp. 305-347

II. THE FIRST WORLD WAR: THE VICTORY OF THE ENTENTE
Textbook: Pp. 342-360
Readings:
J. W. Wheeler-Bennett The Forgotten Peace, Ch. 2
H. R. Rudin   Armistice 1918, Chs. 15-16
D. Lloyd George War Memoirs, Vol. V, Chs. 1 and 5

III. THE PEACEMAKERS AND THE PEACE
Textbook: Pp. 360-384
Readings:
H. Nicolson   Peacemaking 1919, Part I, Ch. 8
P. Birdsall   Versailles Twenty Years After, Chs. 7-8
E.M. House & C. Seymour, eds. What Really Happened at Paris, Ch. 6

IV. THE POSTWAR DIPLOMATIC SCENE IN THE WEST
Textbook: Pp. 385-400
Readings:
A. Wolfers   Britain and France Between the Wars,Chs.12-15
J.W. Wheeler-Bennett. Nemesis of Power, Pp. 102-142
A. Baltzly & A.W. Salomone. Readings in 20th Century European History,Pp.113-146.

V. THE POSTWAR DIPLOMATIC SCENE IN THE EAST
Textbook: Pp. 400-411
Readings:
L. Fischer   The Soviets in World Affairs,Vol. I, Ch. 6
H. Seton-Watson   Eastern Europe Between the Wars, Ch. 8
A. Baltzly & A.W. Salomone. Readings in 20th Century European History,p.146-172.

VI. THE ERA OF ILLUSION
Textbook: Pp. 411-447
Readings:
G.M. Gathorne-Hardy. Short History of International Affairs,Part II,Chs.9, 11-12
W.E. Rappard.   The Quest for Peace,Ch.IV, Pts.4-7.
J.W. Wheeler-Bennett,ed. Documents on International Affairs,1928,Pp. 1-14,
 33-50(Social Studies Reference, Rm. 320)

VII. THE BEGINNINGS OF THE WORLD CRISIS
Textbook: Pp. 448-477
Readings:
S. R. Smith. The Manchurian Crisis, Ch. 1

F. L. Neumann   Behemoth, Pt. I, Ch. 5
W.C. Langsam, ed. Documents and Readings in the History of Europe Since 1918,
   Pp. 146-177

VIII. THE COLLAPSE OF THE VERSAILLES SYSTEM
Textbook: Pp. 477-496
Readings:
M.H.H. Macartney & Paul Cremona.   Italy's Foreign and Colonial Policy,Ch.14
A.J. Toynbee,ed.   Survey of International Affairs,1937,Vol.II,
                                   Pp.138-177(Social Studies Reference,Room 320)
S. Heald & J.W. Wheeler-Bennett,eds. Documents on International Affairs,1936,
                                   Pp.35-82(Social Studies Reference,Room 320)

IX. THE RISE OF THE AXIS
Textbook: Pp. 497-513
Readings:
E. H. Carr.   International Relations Between the Two World Wars,Chs. 11,13
F. L. Schumann. Europe on the Eve, Ch. 8
G. Ciano.   Diplomatic Papers, Ch. 4

X. FROM APPEASEMENT TO WAR
Textbook: Pp. 513-540
Readings:
L. B. Namier   Diplomatic Prelude, Ch. 7
N. Henderson   Failure of a Mission, Pt. II, Chs. 4-5
M. Curtis, ed. Documents on International Affairs,1938,Vol. II, Pp. 292-321
                          (Social Studies Reference, Rm. 320).

XI. THE SECOND WORLD WAR: THE AXIS TRIUMPHANT
Textbook: Pp. 541-560
Readings:
W.S. Churchill. The Second World War,Vol. II(Their Finest Hour),Book I,Ch.10
M. Beloff.   The Foreign Policy of Soviet Russia, Vol. II, Ch. 14
E. L. Woodward & R. Butler, eds.   Documents on British Foreign Policy,
                Third Series, Vol. VII, Pp. 496-546.

XII. THE SECOND WORLD WAR: THE GREAT COALITION
Textbook: Pp. 560-597
Readings:
W. P. Hall   Iron out of Calvary, Chs. 11-12
R. E. Sherwood. Roosevelt and Hopkins, Chs. 32-33
J. Stalin.   The Great Patriotic War, Pp. 127-167

XIII. THE FOUNDATIONS OF THE PEACE
Textbook: Pp. 597-613
Readings:
G.F. Kennan.   American Diplomacy: Chs. 5-6
V.M. Dean.   The United States and Russia, Chs. 11-13
L.W. Holborn,ed. War and Peace Aims of the United Nations, Vol. II, Pp. 1-35

XIV. THE COMING OF THE COLD WAR
Textbook: Pp. 614-663
Readings:
B. Ward   The West at Bay, Chs. 1-2
H. Seton-Watson. The East European Revolution, Chs. 10-11
S. E. Harris.   The European Recovery Program, Ch. 2

NEW YORK UNIVERSITY
GRADUATE SCHOOL OF ARTS AND SCIENCE
DEPARTMENT OF HISTORY

History G57.1251   Diplomatic History of Europe 1789-1900   Professor Stehlin
                                                               Fall,1982

Readings:

For each lecture the student is expected to have read in advance the
pertinent sections of the following textbook: Rene Albrecht Carrie, A
Diplomatic History of Europe Since the Congress of Vienna. (Harper paperback) (revised ed.)

In addition, the student is expected to read the items under each weekly
topic. The bibliography contains further readings listed in order to
aid the student in delving more deeply into those topics discussed.

The required books are available in the Reserve Reading Room.

1. September 16   Introduction

2. September 23   1. Background of the period
                     2. The French Revolution
     C. Brinton, A Decade of Revolution, pp. 64-87, 90-104, 128-130, 164-
     189, 206-209, 221-245.

3. September 30   1. The Diplomacy of the Napoleonic Era
                     2. The Congress of Vienna
     G. Brunn, Europe and the French Imperium, pp. 29-32, 36-61, 83-108,
     109-139, 157-209
     H. Nicolson, The Congress of Vienna, chapters 8-15

4. October 7   1. Restoration Europe
                     2. The Eastern Question
     H. Kissinger, A World Restored, chps. X-XVII

5. October 14   1. The Revolution of 1848
                     2. The Crimean War
     L. Namier, The Revolt of the Intellectuals, entire book
     B. Jelavich, St. Petersburg and Moscow (Century of Russian Foreign
     Policy), pp. 71-113

6. October 21   1. The Second Napoleonic Era
     R. Binkley, Realism and Nationalism, pp. 27-31, 120-122, 124-139,
     157-193, 197-214, 227-230
     J. M. Thompson, Louis Napoleon and the Second Empire, chp. VII,
     chps, VIII-X (foreign affairs)

7. October 28   1. The Unification of Italy
     A. J. Whyte, The Evolution of Modern Italy, chps. I-XI

8. November 4   1.The Struggle for Supremacy in Germany
     E. Eyck, Bismarck and the German Empire, pp. 11-186

9. November 11   1. The New Europe
                      2. The League of Peace
   H. Kohn, Panslavism, Parts I & II

10. November 18   1. The Near Eastern Question
                      2. The Cracks in the Bismarckian System
    E. Eyck, Bismarck and the German Empire, pp. 187-323
    Gordon Craig, From Bismarck to Adenauer, chaps. I & II

11. December 2   1. The end of the Bismarckian System
                      2. The Diplomacy of Imperialism
    L. Lafore, The Long Fuse, pp. 13-127 (2nd ed.)

12. December 9   1. The Crises of Imperialism
    H. M. Wright, ed., The New Imperialism, 2nd ed. 1975 (entire book)

13. December 16   1. The Franco-Russian Alliance
                      2. The Weakening of the Triple Alliance and the
                         Formation of the Entente Cordiale
    H. Feis, Europe The World's Banker, pp. 26-32, 57-59, 78-80, 117,
       156-159, 187-188, 191-242, 258-360
    B.Jelavich, St. Petersburg & Moscow (Century of Russian Foreign
       Policy) pp. 213-256

14. December 23   1. The Rise of New Powers
                      2. Europe at the Turn of the Century
    B. Tuchman, The Proud Tower, chps. 2,4,5,8

History G57.1252   Diplomatic History of Europe 1900-1939 Prof. Stehlin

Readings:

For each lecture the student is expected to have read in advance the pertinent
sections of the following textbook: René Albrecht Carrié, A Diplomatic History of Europe
Since the Congress of Vienna. rev. ed. paperback.

In addition, the student is expected to read the items under each weekly topic. The
bibliography contains further readings listed in order to aid the student in delving more
deeply into those topics discussed.

The required books are available in the Reserve Reading Room.

Schedule of Lectures and Assignments:

1. February 4   1. Introduction
                       2. Europe at the Turn of the Century

2. February 11   1. The First Moroccan Crisis
                       2. The Formation of the Triple Entente
                          and the Annexation of Bosnia
                       ____   Oron Hale, The Great Illusion Chapters I,II, III, VII-XI

3. February 18   1. The Bosnia Crisis and its Consequences
                       2. The Second Moroccan Crisis and the War in Tripoli
                          Laurence Lafore, The Long Fuse 2nd edition

4. February 25   1. The Balkan Wars
                       2. The Great Powers on the Eve of the War
                          Dwight Lee, The Outbreak of the First World War 4th ed. 197.
                       ____ Jack Roth: World War I Chps. 1,2,3,6

5. March 3   1. The Outbreak of World War I
                       2. Diplomacy of World War I
                       ____ Hans Gatzke, Germany's Drive to the West, pp. 1-84,
                          126-195, 219-237, 271-294

6. March 10   1. The Making of the Peace
                       2. The Reorganization of Eastern Europe
                       ____ F. Czernin, Versailles 1919, Chps. I,II,VI,VII,IX,XI

7. March 17   1. The War after the War (1920-1922)
                       2. The Ruhr Problem
                       ____ A. Wolfers, Britain and France between Two Wars.
                          Chapters I-IX, XI-XVI, pp. 265, XVIII-XIX, Conclusion

8. March 31   1. The Search for Security
                       2. Disarmament
                       ____ Gordon Craig and F. Gilbert, The Diplomats, Chapters I,
                          2,5, Wolfers, Chapters X,XXI

9. April 7   1. Soviet Foreign Policy
                       2. The Turn of the Tide
                       ____ G. Kennan, Soviet Foreign Policy 1917-1941 just text
                       ____ Gordon Craig, Diplomats, Chapters 8,11 no documents

10. April 14   1. Appeasement in the Far East
                 2. The Beginnings of Nazi Foreign Policy
                 _____Gordon Craig, The Diplomats, Vol. II, Chapters 10,12-15

11. April 21   1. Fascist Foreign Policy and the Italo-Ethiopian War
                 2. The Two Camps: Democracies vs. Dictatorships Vol. II
                 _____Gordon Craig, The Diplomats, Vol. I, Chapters 7,9, Vol. 16-21

12. April 28   1. The Spanish Civil War
                 2. The Austrian Anschluss
                 _____Hugh Thomas, The Spanish Civil War, Book III, Chapters 40,48
                         54,58,60,64,65,69,70 conclusion and diplomatic sections.

13. May 5   1. The Betrayal of Czeckoslovakia
                 2. Munich and its consequences
                 _____A. Rowse, Appeasement

14. May 12   1. The Road to War
                 2. The Outbreak of World War II
                 _____L. Lafore, End of Glory Chapters 1,4-8

History 19: European Diplomacy, 1914-1939
Barnard College

Professor Santore   Fall 1980

I. The Diplomatic Background to the First World War (Sept. 4-Oct. 2)

Required:

Laurence Lafore, The Long Fuse (Lippincott).
Fritz Fischer, Germany's Aims in the First World War (Norton),
          pp. 1-92.
Fritz Fischer, World Power or Decline, pp. 3-45.
Fritz Stern, "Bethmann Hollweg and the War: The Limits of Respon-
          sibility", in Leonard Krieger and Fritz Stern (eds.),
          The Responsibility of Power, pp. 252-85.
Arno Mayer, "Domestic Causes of the First World War", in Krieger
          and Stern, The Responsibility of Power.
Joachim Remak, The Origins of the First World War (Holt, Rinehart,
          and Winston), pp. 60-96, 132-150.

Recommended:

James Joll, 1914: Unspoken Assumptions.
L.C.F. Turner, Origins of the First World War (Norton).
Gordon A. Craig, From Bismarck to Adenauer: Aspects of German
          Statecraft (Harper Torchbooks), chaps. 1-2.
H.M. Koch (ed.), The Origins of the First World War: Great Power
          Rivalry and German War Aims (Macmillian).
Imanuel Geiss, July 1914.
Wolfgang J. Mommsen, "Domestic Factors in German Foreign Policy
          before 1914", in James J. Sheehan (ed.), Imperial
          Germany (New York: 1976).
John A. Moses, The Politics of Illusion: The Fritz Fischer Contro-
          versy in German Historiography (New York: New York),
David Calleo, The German Problem Reconsidered: Germany and the
          World Order, 1870 to the present (1978), pp. 1-84.

II. The War and the Peace Settlement, 1914-1919 (Oct. 7-24)

Required:

A.J.P. Taylor, An Illustrated History of the First World War (Penguin)
Erich Maria Remarque, All Quiet on the Western Front (Fawcett).

Adam Ulam, Expansion and Coexistence: The History of Soviet Foreign
    Policy, 1917-1967, pp. 31-75.
Rene Albrecht-Carrie, The Meaning of the First World War (Spectum),
    pp. 90-172.

Recommended:

Cyril Falls, The Great War (Capricorn).
Harold Nicolson, Peacemaking 1919 (Grosset and Dumlap).
Arno J. Mayer, Wilson vs. Lenin: The Political Origins of the
    New Diplomacy (Meridan).
Arno J. Mayer, Politics and Diplomacy of Peacemaking (Knopf).
Leo J. Lederer (ed.), The Versailles Settlement: Was it Foredoomed
    to Failure? (D.C. Heath).

October 28: Midterm.

III. The Fragility and Collapse of the Postwar International Order,
    1919-1933 (Oct. 30-Nov. 18).

    Required:

    E.H. Carr, International Relations Between the Two World Wars, 1919-
        1939, pp. 1-152.
    Adam Ulam, Expansion and Coexistence: The History of Soviet Foreign
        Policy, 1917-1967, pp. 126-167, 183-208.
    Alan Cassels, "Fascist Diplomacy", in Alan Cassels, Fascist Italy,
        pp. 73-94.

    Recommended:

    Arnold Wolfers, Britain and France Between the Two World Wars.
    Pierre Renouvin, War and Aftermath, 1914-1929.
    Jon Jacobson, Locarno Diplomacy.
    Hans Gatzke (ed.), European Diplomacy Between the Two World Wars.
    Hugh Seton-Watson, Eastern Europe Between Two World Wars.

IV. The Nazi Triumph in Germany and the Outbreak of the Second World
    War, 1933-1939 (Nov. 20-Dec. 9).

    Required:

    Alan Bullock, Hitler: A Study in Tyranny (Penguin or Harpers).
    A.J.P. Taylor, The Origins of the Second World War (Penguin).
    William Roger Louis (ed.), The Origins of the Second World War:
        A.J.P. Taylor and His Critics (essays by Trevor-
        Hinsley, and Bullock), pp. 44-63, 69-81, 117-45).

48

Recommended:

Keith Eubank, The Origins of World War II.
T.W. Mason, "Some Origins of the Second World War", Past and Present, No. 29 (December 1964).
Laurence Lafore, The End of Glory: An Interpretation of the Origins of World War II.
Pierre Renouvin, World War II and Its Origins: International Relations, 1929-1939.
Christopher Thorne, The Approach of War, 1938-1939.
Gerhart Weinberg, The Foreign Policy of Hitler's Germany, 1933-1939.

Harvard University

HISTORICAL STUDY A-12

International Conflict in the Modern World

Spring Term, 1982

Professor Stanley Hoffmann
Associate Professor Michael E. Mandelbaum
Assistant Professors John S. Odell
and M. J. Peterson

Lectures will be given every Tuesday and some Thursdays at noon. Sections will meet once a week for two hours. Written requirements are a take-home midterm and regularly-scheduled three hour final examination.

All readings are on reserve at Lamont <u>and</u> Hilles. Books marked with an asterisk have been ordered at the Coop.

I.   The Origins of Twentieth Century Conflict

1.   4 Feb (Th.) The Enduring Logic of Conflict
     *Kenneth Waltz, <u>Man, the State, and War</u>, chs. 1, 2, 4, 6, and 8.

2.   9 Feb (T) The Peloponnesian War
     Discussion: Athens, Sparta, and their Allies
     *Thucydides, <u>The Peloponnesian War</u> (Penguin ed.) pp. 35-109
     and 400-9.

3.   16 Feb (T) International Systems and War
     18 Feb (Th) The Nineteenth Century Balance of Power
     Discussion: <u>Germany and the Balance of Power</u>
     A. J. P. Taylor, <u>The Struggle for the Mastery of Europe</u>,
     introduction.

     * Edward V. Gulick, <u>Europe's Classical Balance of Power</u>, chs 1-3.
     * Rene Albrecht-Carrie, <u>A Diplomatic History of Europe Since
     the Congress of Vienna</u>, pp. 3-31 and 121-86.
     * A. DePorte, <u>Europe and the Superpower Balance</u>, pp. 5-19.
     R. B. Mowat, <u>Europe, 1715-1815</u>, pp. 65-75 and 91-104.

4.   23 Feb (T) Imperialism
     Discussion: The Scramble for Africa

     * Benjamin Cohen, <u>The Question of Imperialism</u>, ch 2
     D. M. K. Fieldhouse, <u>Economics and Empire</u>, pp. 10-88, 260-311, and
     340-61.

II. The World Wars

5.   2 Mar (T) Origins of World War I
     4 Mar (Th) Versailles and Geneva
     Discussion: World War I

     * Barbara Tuchman, <u>The Guns of August</u>, pp. 1-157.
     Rene Albrecht-Carrie, <u>The Meaning of the First World War</u>,
     pp. 1-46.

6.   9 Mar (T) Origins of World War II
     11 Mar (Th) The World in 1945.
     Discussion: Munich and Appeasement

     Arnold Wolfers, <u>Discord and Collaboration</u>, ch. 16.
     Martin Gilbert, <u>The Roots of Appeasement</u>, pp. 138-88.
     *Klaus Hildebrand, <u>The Foreign Policy of the Third Reich</u>,
     chs. 4-7 and conclusion.

7.   16 Mar (T) Midterm Questions Distributed

III. Conflicts since 1945

8.   23 Mar (T) The Cold War Debate
     Discussion: Origins of the Cold War

     *DePorte, pp. 20-76.
     *Walter LaFeber, <u>America, Russia, and the Cold War</u>, pp. 1-65.
     George Kennan "The Sources of Soviet Conduct," in Kennan, ed.,
     <u>American Foreign Policy</u>.
     Arthur Schlesinger, Jr., "The Origins of the Cold War,"
     <u>Foreign Affairs</u>, October 1967.
     Thomas G. Patterson, ed., <u>The Origins of the Cold War</u>, pp. 225-60.

Week of March 28 Spring Break

9.   6 Apr (T) Nuclear Weapons
     8 Apr (Th) Superpower Relations Today
     Discussion: Deterrence and the Question of Soviet Intentions

     *Michael Mandelbaum, <u>The Nuclear Question</u>, pp. 1-157.
     David Holloway, "Military Power and Purpose in Soviet Policy,"
     <u>Daedelus</u>, Fall 1980.
     Richard Pipes, "Militarism and the Soviet State," <u>Daedelus</u>,
     Fall 1980.
     George Kennan, "Reflections: The Soviet Union," <u>The New Yorker</u>,
     2 November 1981.

10. 12 Apr (T) The Mideast Conflict
     14 Apr (Th) The Role of International Law and Organization
     Discussion: The Arab-Israeli Wars

     Nadav Safran, <u>From War to War</u>, ch. 1.
     John Stoessinger, <u>Why Nations go to War</u>, ch 6.
     Institute for Strategic Studies, <u>Strategic Survey, 1973</u>, pp. 13-55.
     Inis L. Claude, Jr., "Collective Legitimization as a Function of the
     United Nations," <u>International Organization</u>, summer 1966.
     L. Scheinman and D. Wilkinson eds., <u>International Law and
     Political Crisis</u>, pp. 91-126.
     Donald Neff, <u>Warriors at Suez</u>, chs. 13-17.

51

11.   20 Apr (T) The International and Domestic Politics of Oil
22 Apr (Th) International Inequality and Economic Conflict
Discussion: Struggles over Oil

*R. Keohane and J. Nye, Power and Interdependence, chs. 1 and 2.
*R. Vernon, ed., The Oil Crisis. Essays by Vernon, Girvan,
Stobaugh, Knorr, Smart, and Penrose.
Joesph Nye, "Energy Nightmares," Foreign Policy, fall 1980.
Robert Tucker, "Oil and American Power Five Years Later,"
Commentary, September 1979.

12.   27 Apr (T) Responses to Dependency
Discussion: North-South Conflict in the 1970's

Stephen Krasner, "North-South Economic Relations," in
K. Oye and others, eds., Eagle Entangled, pp. 153-203.
Mahbub ul Haq, The Poverty Curtain: Choices for the Third World,
pp. 153-203.
*Cohen, ch. 5.
*Joan Spero, The Politics of International Economic Relations
(2d ed.), pp. 182-245.

13.   4 May (T) Ethics in International Relations
6 May (Th) The Nation-State and the Future of International
Conflict
Discussion: The US in Southeast Asia

Arnold Wolfers, Discord and Collaboration, ch. 4.
Stoessinger, Why Nations go to War, ch. 4
Henry A. Kissinger, White House Years, pp. 457-521.
*William Shawcross, Sideshow, chs. 1, 4-9, 19, 23, and 24.
Irving Howe and Michael Walzer, "Were We Wrong about Vietnam?"
The New Republic, 18 August 1979.
Charles Horner, "America Five Years after Defeat,"
Commentary, April 1980.

Information

1.   Sections will hold their first meeting during the week of February
9th. For course purposes the week begins on Tuesday and ends on the
following Monday. Since February 15th, which would otherwise be the
day for the first meeting of Monday sections, is a holiday, special times
for those groups' first meetings will be announced.

2.   Lists of sections, indicating hour and place of meeting and section
leader, will be posted in the hallway outside the Government Tutorial
Office (which is in Room G-2 in the basement of Littauer) at noon
on Friday the 5th. You will have to consult the list yourself or send
a friend to check. The Tutorial Office staff do not have time to take
phone calls asking them to look on your behalf.

3.   This course does section early, so we realize that there are a
number of reasons for having to change section.

4.   Any student may change section through February 28th. No changes
will be allowed after that date. All changes must be done through the
head of sections.

5.   Professor Peterson is head of sections for the course. Her phone
number is 5-2616, and her office at Coolidge (1737 Cambridge Street,
next to Gund Hall) Room 411. She takes care of all administrative matters,
including the signing of study cards.

6.   Government concentrators may not take this course pass-fail. If
you think you will become a gov. concentrator, take the course for
a grade and avoid trouble later. (If you take the course pass-fail
and then decide to concentrate in Gov., you cannot count H.S. A-12
towards your concentration requirements. You would have to take Gov.
1720 or 1800 or Social Analysis 16 for a grade.) If you are taking the
course to fulfill Core/General Education requirements, the limits on
your ability to take courses pass-fail are set out on pages 12 and 14
of the Student Handbook. You will be responsible for keeping yourself
within the limits prescribed.

7.   Grades are determined using the following formula: 20% for section
participation, 30% for the midterm, and 50% for the final examination.

8.   The midterm will consist of two 5-page essays on topics to be
assigned. You will have a choice of questions. Questions will be
distributed in the lecture room at noon on March 16th, and completed
essays will be due the following Tuesday noon. Lectures and sections
are not held during this week, and you are not expected to read any
new material. You are expected to make effective use of what you have
heard and read up to that point.

9.   As a consequence of this suspension, lectures and sections are
held during the first week of reading period.

10. The final is a regularly-scheduled three-hour exam. Copies of
last year's exam are printed in the CUE Guide and will be available
at Lamont. It is now scheduled for Thursday, May 27th at an hour to
be set by the Registrar.

History 421A
Fall 1982

University of Pennsylvania MWF 11:00
Martin Wolfe

SOCIETY AND ECONOMY IN WESTERN EUROPE

Fall term: Industrial Capitalism and the Western Social Conscience, 1815-1914

(Spring term: Coping with Socioeconomic Crises during the First Postindustrial Era, 1914-1973)

The focus of this course is the enormous increases in wealth brought to western Europe by 19th century industrialization and the fundamental changes in social relations that resulted. A second aim is a better understanding of the British, French, Germans, and Italians through a study of how they made their living during the transformation of their societies from agrarian to industrial. We use the comparative approach--contrasting regions and groups as well as countries--rather than treating western Europe as a unit.

This is a history course and not one in economics or social science. It depends on description of concrete developments and relations rather than on theories or models. To "learn Europe from the ground up" we spend some time with historical geography. No previous work in European history is needed. Chronologies and maps plus parts of your instructor's presentations will help provide needed background. If you want to use History 421A to acquire a knowledge of general European history, you should buy a good text and read it not all at once but in tandem with our own weekly readings. A highly recommended general history is Gordon A. Craig, Europe since 1815, but there are many fine texts covering 19th and 20th century Europe.

The separate terms of History 421 are taught as independent units; it is not necessary to take both of them or to take them in chronological order.

Students are asked to wrote two short papers, the first an evaluation of some aspects of Zola's Germinal, the second a report on the industrial transformation of one region. Also required: three one-hour exams.

Topics and Assignments

Week

1. Sept. 8   The End of Agrarian Europe

The price of industrialization
"The world we have lost"

Hobsbawm, Intro. and chs. 1 and 2

2. Sept. 13   The Social Impact of Industrialization

The factory
Standards of living: Up or Down?
Speenhamland and All That

Cipolla, ch. 3; Stearns, ch.s 1 and 2

3. Sept. 20   New Socioeconomic Landscapes

Yorkshire and Lancashire
The Massif Central
The Ruhr

Cipolla, ch. 1; Hobsbawm, chs. 3 and 4

4. Sept. 27   Toward a Market Economy

Industrial capitalism formulates an ideology
Social control vs. liberalism on the Continent
"Backwash" in southern Italy

Cipolla, pp. 76-115, 278-296; Stearns,
ch. 3; Henderson, pp. 91-126

5. Oct. 4   The Bourgeois Triumph

"Palace of Industry": the Exhibition of 1851
Counter-industrial values and movements
(1st exam)

Stearns, pp. 116-143

6. Oct. 11   The Victorian Social Conscience

The new Poor Laws
The noble path: amelioration
Charles Dickens: cynical sentimentalist or welfare hero?

(1st paper due Oct. 15)

7. Oct. 18   High Tide of Industrial Capitalism

Louis Napoleon and "social caesarism"
Britain and France around 1900
Germany and Italy around 1900

Hobsbawm, ch. 6; Henderson, pp. 126-167

8. Oct. 25   Western Europe in the Age of "New Imperialism"

        The profits and perils of imperialism
        Beggaring neighbors
        A banker's world

              Cipolla, pp. 115-157

Nov. 1   Workers and Peasants under Industrial Capitalism

        A new social structure: labor unions
        Nobles and peasants: the agricultural scene around 1900
        The dilemma of reformist socialism

              Stearns, pp. 143-177

10. Nov. 8   "The Rise of the Masses"

        The quality of life under mature industrial capitalism
        New perceptions of social welfare
        (2nd exam)

11. Nov. 15   Edwardian Britain

        "Economic climacteric"
        The Fabians and "collectivism"
        Upstairs, Downstairs

              Hobsbawm, chs. 7, 8, and 9

12. Nov. 22   Wilhelmine Germany

        Class relations under paternal authoritarianism
        A paradigm of finance capitalism
        (Thanksgiving weekend)

              Henderson, pp. 44-74

13. Nov. 29   Belle Epoque France

        Backward-looking growth
        French economic nationalism
        Regional problems in prewar France

              Stearns, ch. 5; Henderson, pp. 167-201

14. Dec. 6   United (?) Italy

        Struggles over national economic policy
        The economic centaur
        Workers and peasants in pre-Fascist Italy

              Cipolla, pp. 297-325
              (Second paper due December 6)

TEXTS : Carlo Cipolla, The Emergence of Industrial Societies (Vol. 4,
        part 1 of "The Fontana Economic History of Europe")
      Peter N. Stearns, European Society in Upheaval, 2nd ed.
      E. J. Hobsbawm, Industry and Empire
      Emile Zola, Germinal

      (In Rosengarten: W. O. Henderson, Industrial Revolution in Europe)

Required texts

Carlo Cipolla, ed., The Fontana Economic History of Europe,
vol. 4 part 1: "The Emergence of Industrial Societies"
Raymond F. Betts, Europe in Retrospect

You might want to buy (but these are in Rosengarten)

E.J. Hobsbawm, Industry and Empire
Peter N. Stearns, European Society in Upheaval, 2nd ed.

Also required: a chapter or so each (in Rosengarten)

W.O. Henderson, The Industrial Revolution in Europe, 1815-1914
E.J. Hobsbawm, The Age of Revolution, 1789-1848
Jurgen Kuczynski, The Rise of the Working Class
E.C. Midwinter, Victorian Social Reform

Good (and easy) reading: recommended for reports

Duncan Bythell, The Handloom Weavers
Friedrich Engels, The Condition of the Working Class in England
Ross J.S. Hoffman, Great Britain and the German Trade Rivalry
J.L. and Barbara Hammond, The Town Labourer
David Landes, Bankers and Pashas
Donald McKay, The National Workshops
David Pinkney, Haussmann and the Rebuilding of Paris
Ralph Samuel, Village Life and Labour
Pierre-Jakez Helias, The Horse of Pride
Val Lorwin, Labor and Working Conditions in Modern Europe
Eugen Weber, Peasants into Frenchmen

57

SOCIETY AND ECONOMY IN WESTERN EUROPE

Second term: Coping with Socioeconomic Crises during the Post-
industrial Era, 1914-1973

(First term: Industrial Capitalism and the Western Social
Conscience, 1815-1914)

The focus of this course during the spring term is the successes and
failures of western European governments in dealing with the vital problems
of twentieth century war, depression, monetary crisis, and class conflict.
A second aim is a better understanding of the British, French, Germans, and
Italians through a study of what they wanted from their material and social
affairs with the help of their governments. One of the main aims of the course
is to understand the relative performance of west European governments and the
connections between that performance and the presumed national personality
characteristics of each nation.

This is a history course and not one in economics or social science.
It depends on description of concrete events and developments and only
incidentally on theory or models. Its approach is comparative ("transnational")
rather than international, and it tends to deal with national differences
rather than similarities within western Europe. No previous work in European history is needed. Chronologies and other materials will be provided
for background. Students who want at the same time to improve their general
knowledge of 20th century European history should acquire a good text and read
it along with our week assignments. One good short text is Michael Richards,
Europe 1900-1980: A Brief History. The separate terms of this course are
taught as independent units; it is not necessary to take both of them or to
take them in chronological order.

Students are asked to take three one-hour exams. One short paper (about
7 pp.) will be required; it will be on relations between collective mentali-
ties and socioeconomic achievements (or the lack of them), andshould be
based in part on two of the works in our reading list.

Class Topics and Week Assignments

WEEK ONE   Socioeconomic Policy and European History

Course aims and procedures
Course themes: some examples from the literature of economics
Some examples from the literature of sociology

> [For students who want background on the pre-1914 era:
> Hobsbawm, 9-33 and 172-193; Stearns, 59-90, 109-133, and
> 157-177]

WEEK TWO   Total War and Heightened Expectations

Involving the "home front"
Release of new economic energies
Long-run implications of economic warfare

> Stearns, 179-236; Marwick, 1-33 and 41-96; Aldcroft, Intro and
> chapter 1

WEEK THREE   Recasting Bourgeois Europe

Reconstruction: "homes for heroes"
The war debts and reparations fiasco
"Normalcy"?

> Stearns, 236-266; Aldcroft, ch. 2

WEEK FOUR   "Golden Twenties"?

Runaway inflation in Germany
Britain on the dole
Monetary stability and economic stagnation in France

> Hobsbawm, 207-225; Cipolla, 128-148; Stearns, 276-288;
> Wolfe, 73-104

WEEK FIVE   The Great Depression in Italy and Germany

The tragedy of the Weimar regime
Was there a Fascist economic system?
Fascism and modernization"

> Cipolla, 266-290 and 180-200; Tannenbaum, 89-112 and 119-143

WEEK SIX   The Great Depression in France and Britain

The French Popular Front
Stanley Baldwin's England
[first exam]

> Hobsbawm, 225-248; Aldcroft, ch. 3; Wolfe, 105-137 and 138-171

Class topics and week assignments, contd

WEEK SEVEN   The Nazi Socioeconomic Revolution

Nazi economic "miracles"
Class relations in Nazi Germany
Socioeconomic significance of the Nazi conquest of Europe

    Schoenbaum, Intro, pp. 1-42, 113-151, and 275-288

WEEK EIGHT   World War II

New forms of economic mobilization
Social change in wartime Britain
Social change in wartime France

    Marwick, pp. 98-123, 151-165, and 185-204

WEEK NINE   Laying the Groundwork for the Welfare State

The Liberation and Resistance mystique
The Keynesian Revolution
New social and economic structures

    Cipolla, 91-100; Cipolla, vol. 5, 366-399 (on Keynes)
    Stearns, 289-330; Aldcroft, ch. 4

WEEK TEN   Britain after 1950: A New Society?

"Dukes and Dustmen": establishing welfare state values
Nationalized companies: some mixed results
[second exam]

    Cipolla, 148-177; Hobsbawm, 249-293; Stearns, 33!-336; Shonfield,
    61-57 and 88-120

WEEK ELEVEN   France: New Values, New Structures

A long-delayed transformation
The Monnet Plan
"Embourgeoisement"

    Cipolla, 100-124; Shonfield, 71-87 and 121-150; Hoffmann,
    118-234; Aldcroft, ch. 5

WEEK TWELVE   The German Economic Miracle

The amazing 1948 currency reform
"Guided capitalism": Tucktigkeit and tycoons
"An economy in search of a nation"?

    Cipolla, 208-259; Shonfield, 239-297

WEEK THIRTEEN   The Italian Economic Centaur

An Italian economic miracle?
Southern Italian poverty: an uneradicable problem?
Economic failures and social turmoil

    Cipolla, 290-318; Shonfield, 176-198; Grindrod, 120, 38-46, and
    198-206

WEEK FOURTEEN   Conclusions

Prospects for better socioeconomic policy
1968: A turning point?

History 421B
Spring 1983

Texts

Derek H. Aldcroft, The European Economy, 1914-1980
Carlo Cipolla, ed., "Contemporary Economies," vol. 6, part 1 of the
      Fontana Economic History of Europe
E. J. Hobsbawm, Industry and Empire
David Schoenbaum, Hitler's Social Revolution
Peter N. Stearns, European Society in Upheaval

Required readings (in Rosengarten); a chapter or so in each

Carlo Cipolla, ed., "The Twentieth Century,", vol. 5, part 1 of the
      Fontana Economic History of Europe
Muriel Grindrod, The Rebuilding of Italy
Stanley Hoffmann, et el., In Search of France
Arthur Marwick, War and Social Change in the 20th Century
Andrew Shonfield, Modern Capitalism
Martin Wolfe, The French Franc between the Wars

For student papers

George Bailey, Germans
Luigi Barzini, The Italians
Ronald Blythe, Akenfield: Portrait of an English Village
Crane Brinton, The Americans and the French
Jacques Heliaz, A Horse of Pride [on Brittany]
Edwin Hartrich, The Fourth and Richest Reich: How the Germans Conquered
      the Postwar World
H. Stuart Hughes, The Americans and the Italians
Danilo Dolci, Sicilian Lives
Herbert Kubly, Stranger in Italy
Rudolf Leonhardt, This Germany: The Story since the Third Reich
Carlo Levi, Christ Stopped at Eboli
Edward Muir, Scottish Journey
Carlo Levi, Christ Stopped at Eboli
Peter Nichols, Italia, Italia
George Orwell, Down and Out in Paris and London
————————, The Road to Wigan Pier
————————, A Collection of Essays
Guido Piovene, In Searchof Europe
J. B. Priestley, English Journey
Laurence Wylie, Village in the Vauclause

History 126C
Fall, 1978

University of California
Berkeley

Mr. de Vries

EUROPEAN INDUSTRIALIZATION IN AN AGE OF IMPERIALISM

The following books have been ordered by the bookstore and are recommended for purchase:

Andrew and Lynn Lees, The Urbanization of European Society in the Nineteenth Century.
David Landes, Unbound Prometheus.
M.E. Rose, The Relief of Poverty, 1834-1914.
S.B. Saul, The Myth of the Great Depression, 1873-1896.
Harrison M. Wright, The New Imperialism

These books plus all other reading assignments are also available on 2-hour or 1-day reserve in Moffitt Library.

Evaluation is based on:

1. a mid-term exam
2. a short (7-8 page) paper, to be explained in class
3. a final examination

Reading Assignments:

26-28 September   Introduction
                   Simon Kuznets, "The Meaning and Measurement of Economic Growth,"
                   in Barry Supple, ed., The Experience of Economic Growth, pp.52-67.

3 - 5 October   The British Economy in the 19th Century
                   Students who have not taken History 126B will find it useful to
                   familiarize themselves with the material presented in T.S. Ashton,
                   "The Industrial Revolution in Great Britain," in Barry Supple, ed.
                   The Experience of Economic Growth, pp. 146-158 and David Landes,
                   Unbound Prometheus, Ch. 2, pp. 41-123.

                   Assignments: Eric Hobsbawm, Industry and Empire, Ch. 6, pp.
                   88-108; Phyllis Deane and W.A. Cole, British Economic Growth,
                   1688-1959, Ch. 4 and 5, pp. 136-181.

10-26 October   Development of the National Economies
                   David Landes, Unbound Prometheus, Chaps. 3-4, pp. 124-230.

                   France
                   Rondo E. Cameron, "Economic Growth and Stagnation in France,
                   1815-1914," in Supple, pp. 328-339.
                   David Landes, "French Entrepreneurship and Industrial Growth in
                   the Nineteenth Century," in Supple, pp. 340-353.
                   Dudley Kirk, "Population and Population Trends in Modern France,"
                   in Herbert Moller, Population Movements in Modern European History,
                   pp. 92-100.

Germany

Germany
Knut Borchart, "Germany, 1700-1914," in Carlo Cipolla, ed.,
Fontana Economic History of Europe, Vol. 4, The Emergence of
Industrial Societies, pp. 76-157;
Eric Maschke, "Outline of the History of German Cartels from 1873
to 1914," in F. Crouzet, W.H. Chaloner, and W.M. Stern, eds.,
Essays in European Economic History, 1789-1914, pp. 226-258.

Italy
Alan S. Milward and S.B. Saul, The Development of the Economies of
Continental Europe, 1850-1914, pp. 215-221, and 253-268.
Shepard B. Clough and Carlo Livi, "Economic Growth in Italy:
An Analysis of the Uneven Development of North and South," in
Supple, pp. 354-366.

Russia
Alexander Gerschenkron, "The Early Phases of Industrialization in
Russia and their Relationship to the Historical Study of Economic
Growth," in Supple, pp. 426-444.
William Blackwell, The Beginnings of Russian Industrialization, pp.22-
53.

General
Alexander Gerschenkron, "Economic Backwardness in Historical Perspective," available in Bobbs-Merrill Reprint, and in book of the same
name and author.

**31 October -
2 November**

Population, Migration and Urbanization
Alan S. Milward and S.B. Saul, The Economic Development of Continental
Europe, 1780-1870, Ch. 2, pp. 118-168.
Andrew and Lynn Lees, eds., The Urbanization of European Society
in the Nineteenth Century, articles by Weber, Sorlin, and Kollmann,
pp. 3-44.

7-9 November

Social Issues in Industrialization
M.E. Rose, The Relief of Poverty, 1834-1914.
Michael Anderson, "Family Structure in Nineteenth Century Lancashire,"
in Lees and Lees, pp. 180-192.
Peter Rassow, "Some Social and Cultural Consequences of the Surge
of Population in the 19th Century," in Herbert Moller, ed.,
Population Movements in Modern European History
T.S. Ashton, "The Treatment of Capitalism by Historians" and
"The Standard of Life of the Workers in England, 1790-1830," in
F.A. Hayek, ed., Capitalism and the Historians, pp. 31-61 and 123-155.
E.P. Thompson, The Making of the English Working Class, Chaps. 6, 9,
and 10, pp. 189-212, 269-349.
J.F. Bergier, "The Industrial Bourgeoisie and the Rise of the Working
Class 1700-1914," in Carlo Cipolla, ed., Fontana Economic History of
Europe, Vol. 3, Ch. 7, pp. 397-451.

14-21 November   Imperialism and the International Economy
                    Milward and Saul, The Development of the Economies of Continental
                        Europe, 1850-1914, Ch. 9, pp. 466-513.
                    Hobsbawm, Ch. 7, pp. 110-127
                    Harrison M. Wright, ed., The New Imperialism, articles by Hobson,
                        Lenin, and Schumpeter, pp. 4 - 38, 47 - 61.

28-30 November   The Climacteric
                    Landes, Unbound Prometheus, Ch. 5, pp. 231-358
                    Hobsbawm, Ch. 9, pp. 144-163.
                    S.B. Saul, The Myth of the Great Depression, 1873-1896.
                    Michael Tracy, "Agriculture in western Europe: The Great Depression
                        1880-1900," in Charles K. Warner, Ed., Agrarian Conditions in Modern
                        European History, pp. 98-111.
                    W.W. Rostow, The World Economy, History and Prospect, Ch. 14, pp.
                        163-202.

Fall Term, 1982-1983
Tuesday, Thursday, 11:00 am.
Sections; Thursday, 2 and 3 pm.,
        Friday, 2 pm.

Prof. Charles S. Maier
Center for European Studies,
5 Bryant St.; 495-4304/04
Harvard University

HISTORICAL STUDIES A 24

Historical Development of the International
Political Economy

How do we achieve high economic performance when economic
institutions no longer seem to function well on their own? Today's
debates over inflation, growth, the contributions of industry, the
appropriate rewards for labor, the incentives for investment, the
relief of poverty, draw upon a long tradition. This course examines
historically the successive policy alternatives that Europeans and
Americans have confronted since the framing of explicit economic-
policy agendas during the seventeenth and eighteenth centuries.

This is not a course in economic theory or in economic
history per se. It does, however, examine theories and institutions
in their historical context. It will seek to clarify the political
implications of economic systems and doctrines: their ideological
assumptions, the distributions of power they presuppose at home
and internationally, the class structures they tend to assume.
Some background in basic economics is helpful but not formally
required.

Lectures will concentrate on the evolving economic institutions,
their major crises, and the theoretical debates during the development of today's industrialized countries. Weekly discussions will
focus on the key issues raised by the reading, expecially by the
selections from the economic theorists. Written requirements
include a brief analytical paper at midterm; a course essay of
about 15 pages due in reading period (suggestions for topics will
be offered but students can propose their own); and a take-home
final examination.

Week I. September 21, 23: Introduction: the Concept of Political Economy.
                          The Crisis of "feudal" Europe and early modernization

Week II. September 28, 30: Discovery of the Economic Realm and the Idea of
                            National Wealth: Mercantilists, Whigs, Adam Smith.

        Discussion sessions (Sept. 30, Oct. 1): Wallerstein's scenario of
                                                 development.

    Required Reading:

        Immanuel Wallerstein, The Modern World System: Capitalist Agricul-
            ture and the Origins of the European World-Economy in the
            Sixteenth Century (Academic Press, 1967: PB), chaps. 1-2, 7.

        Jan De Vries, The Economy of Europe in an Age of Crisis, 1600-1750
            (Cambridge University Press, 1976: PB), chaps. 1-2, 4, 7-8.

    NB: Recommended Readings will be distributed in a separate bibliography.

Week III. October 5, 7: Commerce, Agriculture, and Industry: Smithian,
Physiocratic and Protectionist Strategies for
Development.

Discussions sessions (Oct. 7, 8): Smith's <u>Wealth of Nations</u>.

Required Reading:
Adam Smith, '<u>The Wealth of Nations</u>' (Pelican PB, Modern Library,
or other editions), Book I, chaps. 1-5, 7-8;
Book II, chap. 3;
Book III, chap. 4;
Book IV, chap. 2 (not included in the Pelican

Week IV. October 12, 14: Classical Political Economy and the Problems of
Distribution, Class Conflict, and Poverty.

Discussion sessions (Oct. 14, 15): Ricardo and Polanyi.

Required Reading:
David Ricardo, <u>The Principles of Political Economy and Taxation</u>,
chaps. 1-2, 5. Any edition. The standard is now that of Piero
Sraffa, ed., Works and Correspondence, vol. I. There is
also an "Everyman" PB issued by J.M. Dunt in London and E. P.
Dutton in New York.

Karl Polanyi, <u>The Great Transformation</u> (c. 1944; Beacon, 1957: PB),
chaps. 1, 3-10.

Week V. October 19, 21: Breaking with Economic Liberalism: Marx's Analysis.
Breaking with Liberalism: Tariffs, Cartels, and
the Sources of Imperialism.

Discussion sessions (Oct. 21, 22): Marx's <u>Capital</u>.

Required Reading:
Karl Marx, <u>Capital</u> (any edition), vol. I: chap. I, sections 1-2, 4;
chap. VII; chap. X;
chap. XXV, sections 2-4;
chap. XXVI.

Joseph Schumpeter, "The Sociology of Imperialisms" in <u>Imperialism
and Social Classes</u> (c. 1915; World Publishing Co. 1968).

Week VI. October 26, 28: Core and Periphery: Imperialism and the Issue of
Dependency.
The International Economy before World War I.

Discussion sessions (Oct. 28, 29): Theories of Imperialism.

Week VI, cont.

Required Readings:
Tony Smith, The Pattern of Imperialism (Cambridge UP, 1982: PB),
chaps. 1- 2.

Marcello De Cecco, Money and Empire: The International Gold Standard,
1890-1914 (Oxford, Basil Blackwell, 1974), chaps. 1-3.

V. I. Lenin, Imperialism: The Highest Stage of Capitalism (any
edition), chaps. 1, IV-VII, X.

Week VII. November 2, 4: The Political Economy of Twentieth-Century
Inflation (the German Hyperinflation).

Discussion sessions (Nov. 4, 5): Theories of Inflation.

Required Readings:
Costantino Bresciani-Turroni, The Economics of Inflation (Allen &
Unwin, 1937), chaps. 1, II, V, VIII-IX, XI.

Fred Hirsch & John Goldthorpe, eds., The Political Economy of
Inflation (Harvard UP, 1978: PB), chaps. 1, 2, 7, 8, conclusion.

Week VIII. November 9, 11: The Interwar Economy and the Sources of
the Great Depression.

Discussion sessions (Nov. 11, 12): What Caused the Depression?

Required Reading:
Charles P. Kindleberger, The World in Depression, 1929-1939
(University of California, 1976: PB), chaps. 3-8, 14.

Milton Friedman and Anna Schwartz, The Great Contraction (Princeton
University Press, 1965:PB), sections 2-5, 7. This is a separate
edition of their Monetary History of the United States, 1867-
1960 (Princeton PB), chap. VII.

Peter Temin, Did Monetary Forces Cause the Great Depression?
(Norton PB), chaps. I, IV.

Week IX. November 16, 18: The Impact of the Depression. Mass Unemployment
and Comparative Policy Responses.

Discussion sessions (Nov. 18, 19): Keynes's General Theory.

Required Readings:
John Garraty, Unemployment in History (Harper & Row, 1978: PB), chaps. 7-

John Maynard Keynes, The General Theory of Employment, Interest and
Money (c. 1936, Macmillan PB), chaps. 1-3, 5, 11-13, 18, 24.

Week X. November 22 only: The Keynesian Legacy.

Week XI. November 30, December 2: Alternatives to the Market: Soviet
Collectivization and Nazi Economic Policies.

Discussion sessions (Dec. 2, 3): Stalin's Political Economy.

Required Readings:
Alex Nove and James Millar debate: "Was Stalin Really Necessary?" in
Problems of Communism (July-August, 1976).

Alexander Ehrlich, The Soviet Industrialization Debate (Harvard UP,
1967), chaps. I-V, IX;
OR
Stephen F. Cohen, Bukharin and the Bolshevik Revolution (Vintage
1973: PB), chaps. V-IX.

Week XII. December 7,9: The Rise and Fall of Dollar Leadership: Bretton
Woods (1944) to the Present.

Discussion sessions (Dec. 9, 10): America's Role in the World Economy.

Required Readings:
Peter J. Katzenstein, ed., Between Power and Plenty: Foreign Economic
Policies of Advanced Industrial States (University of Wisconsin,
1978: PB): Introduction, essays by Maier, Krasner, Blank.

David P. Calleo, The Imperious Economy (Harvard UP, 1982),
chaps. 1-7, conclusion.

Week XIII. December 14, 16: The Age of Stagflation: Domestic and International
Distributive Conflicts since the late 1960's.
(Labor Militancy, OPEC, the Claims of the Public
Sector)

Discussion sessions (Dec. 16, 17): Are we in a Crisis of Capitalism?

Required Readings:
Leon Lindberg and C. S. Maier, eds., "The Politics of Inflation and
Economic Stagnation." Xeroxed essays will be on reserve.

Joseph Schumpeter, Capitalism, Socialism and Democracy (c. 1943), part II

Fred Hirsch, Social Limits of Growth (Harvard UP, 1978: PB),
Introduction, chaps. I, III, IV.

Mr. Moeller
History 299
Spring 1981

Colloquium in Modern European Social History

The purpose of this seminar is to provide students with a general
introduction to the recent literature in European social history. We will
begin with a discussion of the nature of social history and then proceed
to a consideration of individual topics. The readings are intended very
much as a "state of the art" survey of the variety of approaches currently
being employed and the sorts of topics being studied by social historians.
Since this is a new and in some senses still undefined field in which there
are still few "classic" works, we will attempt a broad survey primarily
of journal literature, rather than concentrating on a limited number of
monographs. Each student will be expected to prepare a presentation on
one or more of the week's readings, and in addition, to write a twenty
page paper, reviewing the literature on one of these topics. This paper
should include a review of the appropriate monographic literature and
other relevant articles as well. In order to facilitate an information
exchange in the seminar, each student will also prepare and distribute an
annotated bibliography on his or her topic.

I.01 General Introduction -- What is Social History?

  Hobsbawm, E. J., "From Social History to the History of Society,"
      in: Felix Gilbert and Stephen R. Graubard, Historical Studies
      Today, 1-26.

  F. Braudel, "History and the Social Sciences," in P. Burke, ed.
      Economy and Society in Early Modern Europe, 11-42.

  Ann D. Gordon, Mari Jo Buhle, Nancy Schrom Dye, "The Problem of
      Women's History," in: Vernice, A. Carroll, Liberating Women's
      History, Urbana, 1976, 75-92.

  Elizabeth Fox-Genovese and Eugene Genovese, "The Political Crisis of
      Social History," JSH, X, 1976.

  Tony Judt, "A Clown in Regal Purple: Social History and the
      Historians," HWJ, VII, Spring, 1979, 66-94.

II. Rural Society and Economy Before the Industrial Revolution

  Jack Goody, Joan Thirsk, E. P. Thompson, eds., Family and Inheritance.
      Rural Society in Western Europe, Cambridge, 1976, articles by
      Goody, Sabean, Berkner.

  William N. Parker and Eric L. Jones, European Peasants and their
      Markets. Essays in Agrarian Economic History, Princeton, 1975,
      essays by Cohen and Weitzman, deVries, and Grantham.

III. Proto-Industrialization

Rudolf Braun, "The Impact of Cottage Industry on an Agricultural Population," in D. Landes, ed., The Rise of Capitalism, New York, 1964, 53-64.

Hermann Kellenbenz, "Rural Industries in the West from the end of the Middle Ages to the Eighteenth Century," in: Essays in European Economic History 1500-1800, ed. by Peter Earle, Oxford, 1974, 45-88.

Jan de Vries, Economy in Europe in an Age of Crisis, 1600-1750, Cambridge, 1976, 84-112.

Franklin F. Mendels, "Proto-industrialization: The First Phase of the Industrialization Process," JEH, XXXII, 1, 1972, 241-261.

Olwen Hufton, "Women and the Family Economy in Eighteenth Century France," French Historical Studies, 9, 1975, 1-22.

Hans Medick, "The Proto-industrial Family Economy: The Structural Function of Household and Family during the Transition from Peasant Society to Industrial Capitalism," Social History, 1, 3, 1976.

IV. Changing Patterns of Work

E. P. Thompson, "Time, Work-Discipline and Industrial Capitalism," Past and Present, 38, 1967.

E. P. Thompson, The Making of the English Working Class, New York, 1963, 189-313.

Joan Scott and Louise Tilly, "Women's Work and the Family in Nineteenth Century Europe," CSSH, 17, 1975, 36-64.

Ivy Pinchbeck, Women Workers and the Industrial Revolution, 1750-1850, London, 1969 (selections)

Raphael Samuel, ed., Village Life and Labour, London, Boston, 1975, editor's introduction.

Michelle Perrot, "Workers and Machines in France during the First Half of the 19th Century," (with comment). Proceedings of the Annual Meeting of the Western Society for French History, 1977, Santa Barbara, 1978, 198-217.

V. Fertility and Birth Control

Charles Tilly, ed. Historical Study of Changing Fertility, Princeton, 1975, 3-55.

Pierre Goubert, "Legitimate Fecundity and Infant Mortality in France during the Eighteenth Century: A Comparison," Dacdalus, Spring 1968, 593-603.

70

E. A. Wrigley, "Family Limitation in Pre-Industrial England,"
    EcHR, 2nd series, 19, April 1966, 89-109.

Louise Tilly, Joan Scott and Miriam Cohen, "Women's Work and European
    Fertility Patterns," *JIH*, VI, 1976, 447-476.

Knodel, John, "Infant Mortality and Fertility in Three Bavarian
    Villages: An Analysis of Family Histories from the Nineteenth
    Century," *Population Studies*, 22, 1968, 293-318.

McLauren, Angus, "Abortion in France: Women and the Regulation of
    Family Size, 1800-1914," *French Historical Studies*, 10, 1978,
    461-85.

Neuman, R. P., "Working Class Birth Control in Wilhelmine Germany,"
    CSSH, 20, July 1978, 408-428.

VI. Family Structure

Peter Laslett, ed., *Household and Family in Past Time*, Cambridge,
    1972, editor's introduction, 1-90.

Lawrence Stone, "The Rise of the Nuclear Family in Early Modern
    England: The Patriarchal Stage," in: C. Rosenberg, ed.,
    The Family in History, Phila., 1975, 13-57.

John Knodel and Mary Jo Maynes, "Urban and Rural Marriage
    Patterns in Imperial Germany," *Journal of Family History*, 1,
    Winter, 1976.

Roderich Phillips, "Women and Family Breakdown in Eighteenth
    Century France: Rouen 1780-1800," *Social History*, 2, May
    1976, 197-218.

Humphries, Jane, "The Working Class Family, Women's Liberation
    and Class Struggle: The Case of Nineteenth Century British
    History," *Review of Radical Political Economy*, 9, 1977, 25-41.

Peter Czap, Jr., "Marriage and the Peasant Joint Family in the Era
    of Serfdom," in: David L. Ransel, ed., *The Family in Imperial
    Russia. New Lines of Historical Research*, Urbana, Chicago,
    London, 1978, 103-123.

VII. Cities and Urbanization

E. A. Wrigley, "A Simple Model of London's Importance in Changing
    English Society and Economy 1650-1750," in P. Abrams, E. A.
    Wrigley, eds., *Towns in Societies*, Cambridge, London, New York,
    Melbourne, 1978, 215-243.

Asa Briggs, *Victorian Cities*, London, 1963, 55-82.

David Cannadine, "Victorian Cities; how different?" *Social History*,
    No. 4, Jan. 1977, 457-482.

J. J. Lee, "Aspects of Urbanization and Economic Development in
    Germany, 1815-1914," in: Abrams and Wrigley, eds., 279-293.

John Foster, "Nineteenth-Century Towns: A Class Dimension," in Flinn and Smout, eds., Essays in Social
History, Oxford, 1974, 178-196.

Ronald Aminzade, "Breaking the Chains of Dependency:
From Patronage to Class Politics, Toulouse,
France, 1830-1872," Journal of Urban History,
3, no. 4, 1977, 485-506.

VIII. Forms of "Pre-industrial" Social Protest?

Michelle Perrot, "Delinquency and the Penitentiary
System in Nineteenth-Century France," in:
Robert Forster and Orest Ranum, ed., Deviants
and the Abandoned in French Society, Baltimore
and London, 1978, 213-245.

D. Hay, P. Linebaugh, J. Rule, E.P. Thompson, C.
Winslow, Albion's Fatal Tree. Crime and
Society in Eighteenth-Century England, New
York, 1975 (selections).

Colin Jones, "Prostitution and the Ruling Class in
18th Century Montpelier," HWJ, Issue 6, Autumn.
1978, 7-29.

John K. Walton, "Lunacy in the Industrial Revolution:
A Study of Asylum Admissions in Lancashire,
1848-50," JSH, 13, 1979, 1-22.

Neil B. Weissman, "Rural Crime in Tsarist Russia:
The Question of Hooliganism, 1905-1914,"
Slavic Review, 37, 1978, 228-240.

H. Zehr, "The Modernization of Crime in Germany and
France, 1830-1914," JSH, VIII, Summer 1975,
117-141.

IX. "Pre-Industrial" Forms of Collective Action

E.P. Thompson, "The Moral Economy of the English
Crowd in the 18th Century," P&P, 1971.

Louise Tilly, "The Food Riot as a Form of Political
Conflict in France," JIH, 2, Summer 1971,
24-57.

Charles Tilly, "Changing Nature of Collective Vio-
lence," in: Melvin Richter, ed., Essays in
Theory and History: An Approach to the Social
Sciences, Cambridge, MA, 1970, 139-164.

Charles A. Tamason, "From Mortuary to Cemetery:
Funeral Riots in Lille, 1779-1870," SSH,
4, 1, February 1980, 15-31.

Robert J. Bezucha, "The 'Preindustrial' Worker
Movement: The Canuts of Lyon," in Bezucha, ed.,
Modern European Social History, Lexington,
Toronto, London, 1972, 93-123.

Lüdtke, Alf, "The Role of State Violence in the
Period of Transition to Industrial Capitalism:
The Example of Prussia from 1815 to 1848,"
Social History, 4, 1979, 175-221.

Ted Margadant, "Modernisation and Insurgency in
December 1851: A Case Study of the Drome,"
in: Roger Price, ed., Revolution and Reaction.
1848 and the Second French Republic, London,
New York, 1975, 254-279.

X. Politics in the Countryside

Ian Farr, "Populism in the Countryside: The Peasant
Leagues in Bavaria in the 1890s," in: Richard
Evans, Society and Politics in Wilhelmine
Germany, New York, London, 1978, 136-159.

Teodor Shanin, The Awkward Class. Political Sociology
of the Peasantry in a Developing Society: Russia
1910-1925, Oxford, 1972 (selections).

Mark Harrison, "Resource Allocation and Agrarian
Class Formation: The Problem of Social Mobility
among Russian Peasant Households, 1880-1930,"
JPS, 4, 1977, 127-161.

Edward E. Malefakis, "Peasants, Politics, and Civil
War in Spain, 1931-1939," in: Bezucha, ed.,
Modern European Social History, 192-227.

Gavin Lewis, "The Peasantry, Rural Change and Conservative Agrarianism: Lower Austria at the
Turn of the Century," P&P, Nr. 81, 1978.

Tony Judt, "The Origins of Rural Socialism in Europe:
Economic Change and the Provencal Peasantry,
1870-1914," Social History, 1, January 1976,
45-65.

J. Harvey Smith, "Agricultural Workers and the French
Wine-Growers' Revolt of 1907," P&P, 1978, 101-125.

XI. Changing Nature of Work in Industrial Societies

    Rose L. Glickman, "The Russian Factory Woman, 1880-1914," in: D. Atkinson, et al., Women in Russia, Stanford, 1977, 63-84.

    Peter N. Stearns, "The Unskilled and Industrialization. A Transformation of Consciousness," Archiv für Sozialgeschichte, v. 16, 1976, 249-282.

    Raphael Samuel, "The Workshop of the World: Steam Power and Hand Technology in mid-Victorian Britain," HWJ, 3, Spring 1977, 6-72.

    Laura Owen, "The Welfare of Women in Labouring Families: England, 1860-1914," in: Hartmann and Banner, Clio's Consciousness Raised. New Perspectives on the History of Women, New York, Evanston, San Francisco, London, 1974.

    Theresa McBride, The Domestic Revolution: The Modernization of Household Service in England and France 1820-1920, London, 1976 (selections).

XII. Models for Understanding Labor Protest

    E.J. Hobsbawm, "Economic Fluctuations and Some Social Movements," in: Labouring Men, Garden City, 1967.

    Peter Stearns, "Measuring the Evolution of Strike Movements," IRSH, 9, 1974, 1-27.

    James E. Cronin, Industrial Conflict in Modern Britain, Totowa, 1979 (selections).

    Charles Tilly and Edward Shorter, Strikes in France, 1830-1968, Cambridge, 1968 (selections).

XIII. Community, Labor Organization, and Changing Forms of Labor Protest

    Stephen Hickey, "The Shaping of the German Labour Movement: Miners in the Ruhr," in Evans, ed., Society and Politics in Wilhelmine Germany.

    Joan Scott, "The Glassworkers of Carmaux, 1850-1900," in: Sennett and Thernstrom, eds., Nineteenth-Century Cities, Yale, 1969, 3-42.

David Crew, <u>Town in the Ruhr. A Social History of
Bochum, 1860-1914</u>, New York, 1979 (selections).

Lawrence Schofer, "Patterns of Labor Protest: Upper
Silesia 1865-1914," <u>JSH</u>, 5, 1972.

Michael P. Hanagan, "The Logic of Solidarity.   Social
Structure in Le Chambon - Feugerolles," <u>Journal
of Urban History</u>, 3, 4, 1977, 409-426.

William H. Sewell, Jr., "Social Change and the Rise of
Working-Class Politics in Nineteenth-Century
Marseille," <u>P&P</u>, 65, 1974, 75-109.

XIV.   <u>Workers' Lives and Workers' Culture</u>

Gareth Stedman Jones, "Working-Class Culture and
Working Class Politics in London, 1870-1900:
Notes on the Remaking of a Working Class,"
<u>JSH</u>, 7, 1974, 460-507.

Gerhard A. Ritter, "Workers' Culture in Imperial
Germany: Problems and Points of Departure for
Research," <u>JCH</u>, 13, 1978.

Klaus Tenfelde, "Mining Festivals in the Nineteenth
Century," <u>JCH</u>, 13, 1978, 377-412.

Reginald E. Zelnik, "Russian Bebels: An Introduction
to the Memoirs of Semen Kanatchikov and Matrei
Fisher," <u>Russian Review</u>, v. 35, 1976, 249-289,
417-447.

Guenther Roth, <u>The Social Democrats in Imperial
Germany: A Study in Working Class Isolation and
Negative Integration</u>, Totowa, 1963 (selections)

History 5710 - Course Syllabus   Mary Jo Maynes
Fall, 1982   523 Social Science Tower
University of Minnesota   373-4430

History 5710 - <u>Introductory Proseminar in 18th and 19th-Century Europe:</u>
                        <u>Social History</u>

The aim of this course is to introduce students to the literature of modern
European social history, with an emphasis on France, Germany and England in the
18th and 19th centuries. Class time will be devoted largely to discussions
of this literature and discussion will be organized around a different theme
each week. Students will also be required to write a series of evaluations
of the works they read.

Course Requirements

The first requirement is to prepare for each class discussion by careful reading
of the week's <u>Required Readings</u> and of <u>at least one</u> selection from the <u>Supplementary</u>
<u>Reading</u> list. All of the required readings for each week have been placed on
reserve at Wilson, as have been those supplementary readings marked with an
asterisk. A 1 - 2 page evaluation of the supplementary reading should be turned
in at the beginning of the class session.
In addition, each student must do intensive reading around the theme of one
week's discussion, and be prepared to participate in the preparation of the
class discussion for that week. During the course of the discussion, a summary
of the main problems, sources and methods of the selected readings should be
presented to the class.

Finally, each student will be required to write a bibliographic essay of around
15 - 20 pages on a topic chosen in consultation with the instructor.

List of Abbreviations Used in the Reading List

AHR - American Historical Review
CSSH - Comparative Studies in Society and History
JCH - Journal of Contemporary History
JFH - Journal of Family History
JIH - Journal of Interdisciplinary History
JSH - Journal of Social History
P&P - Past and Present
SH - Social History

I. Introduction (9/30)

II. <u>Social</u> <u>History</u> - Theory and Method   (10/7)

Required:

＊F. Braudel, "History and the Social Sciences: The Longue Durée," in
F. Braudel, <u>On History</u> (Chicago, 1980)

＊E.J. Hobsbawm, "From Social History to the History of Society,"
<u>Daedalus</u> (1971), 20-45.

Supplementary:

P. Anderson, <u>Arguments Within English Marxism</u> (London, 1980).

E.F. & E.D. Genovese, "The Political Crisis of Social History,"
<u>Journal of Social History</u>, 10 (1976), 205-220.

P. Goubert, "Historical Demography and the Reinterpretation of Early
Modern French History," <u>Journal of Interdisciplinary History</u>, 1 (1970)
37-48.

＊K. Hausen, "Family and Role Division: The Polarization of Sexual Stere-
otypes in the Nineteenth Century - An Aspect of the Dissociation of
Work and Family Life," in R.Evans and W.R. Lee, eds. <u>The German Family</u>
(London, 1981).

G. Stedman Jones, "From Historical Sociology to Theoretical History,"
<u>British Journal of Scoiology</u> 27 (1976), 295-305.

T. Judt, "A Clown in Regal Purple," <u>History Workshop</u>, 7 (1979), 66-94.

G. McLennan, <u>Marxism and the Methodologies of History</u> (London, 1981).

B. Moore, <u>Social Origins of Dictatorship and Democracy</u>, (Boston, 1967).

M. Richter, ed. <u>Essays in Theory and History</u> (Cambridge, 1970).

R. Samuels, "History and Theory," in R. Samuels, ed., <u>People's History</u>
<u>and Socialist Theory</u> (London, 1981).

T. Skocpol, <u>States and Social Revolutions</u> (Cambridge, 1979).

T. Stoianovitch, <u>French Historical Method: The Annales Paradigm</u>

E.P. Thompson, <u>The Poverty of Theory and Other Essays</u> (London, 1978).

D. Thorner,ed. , <u>The Theory of the Peasant Economy</u> (Homewood, Ill., 1966).

C. Tilly <u>As Sociology Meets History</u> (New York, 1981).

✳ C. Tilly, "Did the Cake of Custom Break?" in J. Merriman, ed., Consciousness and Class Experience in Nineteenth-Century Europe (New York, 1979).

L.Tilly and M. Cohen, "Does the Family Have a History? A Review of Theory and Practice in Family History," Social Science History, 6 (1982), 131-180.

III. Agrarian Social Structure and the Peasant Family Economy (10/14) Required:
✳ L. Berkner, "The Stem Family and the Developmental Cycle of the Peasant Household," American Historical Review, 77 (1972), 398-418.

✳ G. Lefebvre, "The Place of the Revolution in the Agrarian History of France, " in R.Forster and O. Ranum, eds., Rural Society in France (Baltimore, 1977).

✳ D. Sabean,"Small Peasant Agriculture in Germany," Peasant Studies 7 (1978), 218-224.

Supplementary:

L.K.Berkner and J. Shaffer, "The Joint Family in the Nivernais," Journal of Family History 3(1978), 150-162.

P. Goubert, "The French Peasantry of the Seventeenth Century," Past and Present, 10(1956), 55-77.

J.Lehning, The Peasants of Marlhes (Chapel Hill, 1980).

E. Leroy Ladurie, The Peasants of Languedoc (Urbana, 1976).

R.R.Palmer, "Georges Lefebvre," Journal of Modern History, 31 (1959), 329-342.

A. Plakans, "Peasant Farmsteads in the Baltic Littoral, 1797," Comparative Studies in Society and History, 17(1975), 2-55.

A. Soboul, "The French Rural Community in the Eighteenth and Nineteenth Centuries," P&P, 10 (1956), 78-95.

✳ ---------, "The Persistance of 'Feudalism' in the Rural Society of Nineteenth-Century France," in R. Forster and O.Ranum, eds., Rural Society in France (Baltimore, 1977).

E. Weber, Peasants into Frenchmen (Stanford, 1976).

E van de Walle, "Household Dynamics in a Belgian Village, 1847-1866," JFH, 1(1976), 80-94.

IV. Protoindustry and Proletarianization (10/21)

Required:

✶ C.H.Johnson, "Patterns of Proletarianization: The Parisian Tailors and Lodeve Woolen Workers," in J. Merriman, ed., Consciousness and Class Experience in Nineteenth-Century Europe (New York, 1979).

✶ H.Schomerus, "The Family Life Cycle: A Study of Factory Workers in Nineteenth- Century Württemberg," in R. Evans and W.R.Lee, eds., The German Family (London, 1981).

✶ E.P. Thompson, "The Weavers," Chapter IX of The Making of the English Working Class

Supplementary:

R.Braun, "Early Industrialization and Demographic Change in the Canton of Zurich," in C.Tilly, ed., Historical Studies in Changing Fertility (Princeton, 1978).

L. Chevalier, Laboring Classes, Dangerous Classes

O. Hufton, The Poor of Eighteenth-Century France (Oxford, 1974).

D. Levine, Family Formation in an Age of Nascent Capitalism (New York, 1979).

---------, "Proletar ization, Economic Opportunity and Population Growth in W. Conze, ed., Sozialgeschichte der Familie in der Neuzeit Europas (Stuttgart, 1976).

H. Medick, "The Proto-Industrial Family Economy: The Structural Function of Household and Family During the Transition from Peasant Society to Industrial Capitalism," Social History, 3(1976), 291-315.

F. Mendels, "Agriculture and Peasant Industry in Eighteenth-Century Flanders," in E.L.Jones and N,Parker, eds., European Peasants and Their Markets (Princeton, 1976).

----------, "Proto-industrialization: the First Phase of the Process of Industrialization," Journal of Economic History, 32 (1972), 241-261.

C. Tilly, "Proletarianization: Theory and Research," In C.Tilly, As Sociology Meets History (New York, 1981).

V. Urban Social Structure (10/28)

Required:

✶ G. Lefebvre, "Urban Society in the Orleannais in the Late Eighteenth Century," P&P, 19 (1961), 46-65.

✶ L.A. Tilly, "The Family Wage Economy in a French Textile City," JFH, 4 (1979), 381-394.

*James Jackson, Jr., "Overcrowding and Family Life: Working-Class Fami-
lies and the Housing Crisis in Late Nineteenth-Century Duisberg,"
in R. Evans and W.R. Lee, eds., The German Family (London, 1981).

Supplementary:

M. Anderson, "Family and Household in the Industrial Revolution,"
in P. Laslett, ed., Household and Family in Past Time (Cambridge, 1972).

-----------, Family Structure in Nineteenth Century Lancashire(Cambridge, 19

L. Berlanstien, "Illegitimacy, Concubinage and Proletarianization in
a French Rural Town, 1760-1914," JFH 5 (1980), 360-374.

D. Crew, "Definitions of Modernity: Social Mobility in a German Town,
1880-1901," in P. Stearns and D. Walkowitz, eds., Workers and the
Industrial Revolution (New Brunswick, N.J., 1974).

R. Dasey, "Women's Work and the Family: Women Garment Workers in
Berlin and Hamburg before the First World War," in R. Evans and W.R.
Lee, eds., Ther German Family (London, 1981).

F. Ford, Strasbourg in Transition (New York, 1966[2])

O. Hufton, Bayeux in the Late Eighteenth Century

G. Stedman Jones, Outcast London (Oxford, 1971).

W. Köllmann, "The Process of Urbanization in Germay..." Journal of
Contemporary History, 4 (1969), 59-76.

* L.H.Lees, "Getting and Spending: The Family Budgets of the English
Industrial Workforce," in J. Merriman, ed., Consciousness and Class
Experience in Nineteenth-Century Europe (New York, 1979).

H. Liang, "Lower-class Migration in Wilhelmine Berlin," Central European
History, 3 (1970), 94-111).

T. McBride, The Domestic Revolution (New York, 1976).

R.P. Neumann, "Industrialization and Sexual Behavior: Some Aspects of
Working-Class Life in Imperial Germany," in R, Bezucha, ed., Modern
European Social History

J. Scott, The Glassworkers of Carmaux (Cambridge, Mass., 1974).

W. Sewell, Jr., "Social Mobility in a Nineteenth-Century European City,"
JIH, 7 (1976), 217-233.

T.F. Sheppard, Lourmarin in the Eighteenth Century (Baltimore, 1971).

N. Smelser, Social Change in the Industrial Revolution (Chicago, 1959).

P. Smith, Ladies of the Leisure Class: The Bourgeoises of Northern France in the Nineteenth Century (Princeton, 1981).

L.Tilly, "Individual Lives and Family Strategies in the French Proletariat," JFH, 3 (1979), 137-152.

L. Tilly and J. Scott, "Women's Work and the Family in Nineteenth-Century Europe," CSSH, 17 (L975), 36-64.

✱L. Trenard, "The Social Crisis in Lyons on the Eve of the French Revolution," in J. Kaplow, ed., New Perspectives on the French Revolution (New York, 1965).

M. Walker, German Home Towns (Ithaca, 1971).

VI. Social Structure and Education (11/4)

Required:
✱R. Colls,"'Oh Happy English Children': Coal, Class and Education in the North -east," P&P, 73 (1979), 75-99.

✱T.W. Margadant, "Primary Schools and Youth Groups in Pre-War Paris: Les Petites A's," JCH, 13 (1978), 323-336.

✱M.J.Maynes, "Work or School? Youth and the Family Economy in the Midi in the Nineteenth Century," In D. Baker and P.J. Harrigan, eds., The Making of Frenchmen (Waterloo, 1980).

Supplementary:

P. Burke, The Popular Culture of Early MOdern Europe (New York, 1978).

H. Chisick, The Limits of Reform in the Enlightenment: Attitudes toward the Education of the Lower Classes in Eighteenth-Century France (Princeton, 1981).

R. Darnton, "The High Enlightenment and the Low Life in Literature in Pre-Revolutionary France," P&P, 51 (1971), 81-115.

✱R. Gildea, "Education and the Classes Moyennes in the Nineteenth Century," in D. Baker and P.J.Harrigan, eds., The MAking of Frenchmen (Waterloo, 1981).

P.J. Harrigan, "Secondary Education and the Professions in France during the Second Empire," CSSH, 17 (1974), 349-371.

R. Johnson, "Educational Policy and Social Control in Early Victorian Britain," P&P, 49 (1970), 96-119.

G. Stedman Jones, "Working-Class Culture..." JSH, 7 (1974), 460-508.

T. Laqueur, "Literacy and Social Mobility in the Industrial Revolution," P&P, 64 (1974), 96-107.

T Laqueur, Religion and Respectability (New Haven, 1976).

D. Levine, "Education and Family Life in Early Industrial England," JFH, 4 (1979), 368-380.

M. Sanderson, "Literacy and Social Mobility in the Industrial Revolution in England," P&P, 56 (1972), 75-104.

------------, "Social Change and Elementary Education in Industrial Lancashire," Northern History, 3 (1968), 131-154.

J. Shaffer, "Family. Class, and Young Women's Occupational Expectations," JFH, 3 (1978), 62-77.

L. Stone, "Literacy and Education in England," P&P, 42 (1969), 69-139.

R. Thabault, Education and Change in a Village Community

C. Tilly, "Population and Pedagogy in France," History of Education Quarterly, 13 (1973), 113-129.

C. Truant, "Solidarity and Symbolism Among Journeymen Artisans: The Case of the Compagnonnage," CSSH, 21 (1979), 214-226.

VII. The Dominant Classes and Changing Styles of Domination (11/11).

Required:

D. Hay, "Property, Authority and the Criminal Law," in D. Hay, ed., Albion's Fatal Tree (New York, 1975).

M. Foucault, Discipline and Punish (New York, 1975) Chapter 1. "The Body of the Condemned."

Supplementary:

R. Braun, "Taxation, Socio-political Structure and Statebuilding in Great Britian and Brandenburg-Prussia," in C. Tilly, The Formation of National States in Western Europe (Princeton, 1975).

R. Cobb, The POlice and the People (Oxford, 1970).

A. Goodwin, ed., The European Nobility in the Eighteenth Century

F. Ford, Robe and Sword (Cambridge, Mass., 1953).

R. Forster, The Nobility of Toulouse in the Eighteenth Century (N.Y., 1967)

C.H. Friedrichs, "Capitalism, Mobility and Class Formation in the Early Modern German City," P&P, 69 (1975), 24-49.

A. Ludtke, "The Role of State Violence in the Period of Transition to INdustrial Capitalism." SH, (1979), 175-221.

L. O'Boyle, "The Middle Classes in Western Europe," <u>AHR</u>, 71 1966), 826-845.

H. Rosenberg, <u>Bureaucracy, Aristocracy and Autocracy</u> (Cambridge, Mass. 1958).

E.P.Thompson, "Time, Work-Discipline and Industrial Capitalism," <u>P&P</u>, (1967), 56-96.

C. Tilly, "Food Supply and Public Order in Modern Europe," in C. Tilly ed., <u>The Formation of National States in Western Europe</u> (Princeton, 1975).

✱ M. Vovelle and D. Roche, "Bourgeois, Rentiers and Property-owners," in J. Kaplow, ed., <u>New Perspectives on the French Revolution</u> (New York, 1965).

VIII. Changing Forms of Popular Protest (11/18)

Required:

✱ L. Tilly, "The Food Riot as a Form of Political Protest," <u>JIH</u>, 2 (1971), 23-59.

✱ J. Merriman, "The Demoiselles of the Ariege, 1829-1831," in J. Merriman, ed. <u>1830 in France</u>. (New Tork, 1975).

✱ T. Judt, "The Origins of Rural Socialism in Europe," <u>SH</u>, 1 (1976), 45-65.

Supplementary:

R. Aminzade, <u>Class, Politics and Early Industrial Capitalism</u> (Albany, 1981).

J. Foster, <u>Class Struggle and the Industrial Revolution</u> (London, 1974).

✱ D. Hay, "Poaching and the Game Laws in Cannock Chase," in <u>Albion's Fatal Tree</u> (New York, 1975).

E.J. Hobsbawm, <u>Primitive Rebels</u> (Manchester, 1959).

-------------- and G. Rude, <u>Captain Swing</u> (New York, 1968).

✱ E. Neumann, "What the Crowd Wanted in the French Revolution of 1830," in J. Merriman, ed., <u>1830 in France</u> (New York, 1975).

W. Reddy, "The Textile Trade and the Language of the Crowd at Rouen, 1752-1871," <u>P&P</u>, 74 (1977), 62-89.

G. Rudé, <u>The Crowd in History, 1730-1848</u> (New York, 1964).

W. Sewell, "Social Change and Working-Class Politics in 19th-Century Marseilles," <u>P&P</u>, 65 (1974), 75-109.

E.P. Thompson, "The Moral Economy of the English Crowd in the Eighteenth Century," P&P, 50 (1971), 76-113.

C. Tilly, The Changing Place of Collective Violence," in M. Richter, ed., Essays in Theory and History (Cambridge, Mass., 1970).

IX. The Social History of Revolution   (12/2)

Required:

✳ C. Johnson," The Revolution of 1830 in French Economic History," in J. Merriman, ed., 1830 in France (New York, 1975).

✳ G. Lefebvre, "Revolutionary Crowds..." in J. Kaplow, ed. New Perspectives on the French Revolution (New York, 1965).

✳ C. Lucas, "Nobles, Bourgeois and the Origins of the French Revolutions," P&P, 60 (1973), 84-126.

Supplementary:

R. Bezucha, The Lyon Uprising of 1834 (Cambridge, Mass. 1974).

T. Hamerow, Restoration,Revolution and Reaction (Princeton, 1966).

L. Hunt,Revolution and Urban Politics in Provincial France (Stanford, 1978).

    J. Kaplow, ed., New Perspectives on the French Revolution (New York, 1965).

G. Lefebvre, The Great Fear of 1789 (New York, 1973).

J. Merriman, The Agony of the Republic (New Haven, 1978).

P.H. Noyes, Organization and Revolution (Princeton, 1966).

G. Rude, The Crowd in the French Revolution (Oxford, 1959).

W. Sewell, Work and Revolution in France (Cambridge, 1980).

A. Soboul, "Classes and Class Struggle During the French Revolution," in Science and Society.

C. Tilly, The Vendée, (New York, 1964).

C.,L. and R. Tilly, The Rebellious Century (Cambridge, Mass., 1975).

Yale University

HISTORY 429b

Comparative American and Western European Social

History, 1770-1870

John Merriman
Paul Johnson

AGENDA

DATE	GENERAL TOPIC	READING
January 17	Introduction	
January 24	An Overview	Barrington Moore, Social Origins of Democracy and Dictatorship
January 31	Rural Society	Eugene Genovese, Roll Jordon, Roll E.J. Hobsbawm-George Rudé, Captain Swing
February 7	The State and Centralization	Charles Tilly, "Food Supply and Public Order in Modern Europe;" Charles Tilly, The Vendée; John Merriman, "The 'Demoiselles' of the Ariège, 1829-31"
February 14	Revolution, I: 1776, 1789	Robert Gross, Minutemen and Their World; Georges Lefebvre, The Coming of the French Revolution
February 21	Revolution, II: 1830 and 1848	Charles Tilly, "How Protest Modernized, 1845-55;" Tilly and Lynn Lees, "The People of June, 1848;" George Rudé, "Why was there no Revolution in England in 1830 or 1848?" and Karl Marx, The Eighteenth Brumaire of Louis Napoleon Bonaparte (Recommended: John Merriman, Agony of the Republic)
February 28	Urbanization	Lynn Lees and John Modell, "The Irish Countrymen Urbanized: A Comparative Perspective on the Famine Migration;" Charles Tilly, "The Chaos of the Living City;" S.B. Warner, The Private City
March 7	The Bourgeoisie	Philippe Aries, Centuries of Childhood, conclusion; Peter Gay, "On the Bourgeoisie: Towards a Psychological Interpretation" (Recommended: Paul Johnson, A Shopkeeper's Millennium)

85

DATE	GENERAL TOPIC	READING
March 28	Artisans	Joan W. Scott, "The Glassworkers of Carmaux;" Mack Walker, "Work and Community;" E.P. Thompson, Making of the English Working Class, Part I; Paul Faler, "Cultural Aspects of the Industrial Revolution: Lynn, Massachusetts Shoemakers and the Industrial Morality, 1826-1860"
April 4	Proletarianization	E. P. Thompson, Part 2; H. Gutman, "Work, Culture, and Society;" E.P. Thompson, "Time, Work Discipline and Industrial Capitalism;" Christopher Johnson, "Patterns of Proletarianization: Parisian Tailors & Lodève Woolens Workers;" Charles Tilly, "Did the Cake of Custom Break?"
April 11	Socialism	William Sewell, Jr., "Social Change and the Rise of Working-Class Politics in 19th Century Marseille;" Christopher Johnson, "Communism and the Working-Class before Marx: The Icarian Experience;" Alan Dawley, Class and Community, conclusion
April 18	Popular Religion	David Montgomery, "The Shuttle and the Cross;" Bruce Laurie, "Nothing on Compulsion: Life Styles of Philadelphia Artisans, 1820-1860;" Brian Harrison, "Religion and Recreation in Nineteenth Century England"
April 25	Women, Work, and the Family	Louise Tilly and Joan Scott, Women, Work, and Family; Thomas Dublin, "Women, Work, and the Family: Female Operatives in the Lowell Mills, 1830-1860;" Nancy Cott, The Bonds of Womanhood: 'Woman's Sphere in New England, 1780-1830,' chapter I.

Mr. Moeller   **Columbia University**
Winter/Spring 1982
History W3990y

Workers' Lives, Workers' Culture, the Working Class Movement:
Topics in European Labor History, 1780-1914

          This seminar will present a general introduction to central
issues in modern European labor history. We will be examining
not only the historical development of the European working class,
but in addition, the variety of methodological approaches to the
study of this vast subject. Students will be expected to have
a general knowledge of European history in the period covered by
the seminar, and this background will be essential. Readings
will offer a comparative European perspective, drawing in particular
on examples from England, France and Germany, and will include
investigations of such important topics as the impact of the
industrial revolution on workers' lives and the working class
family, the problems of stratification within the working class,
the emergence of trade union organizations and political parties
representing labor's interests, the changing nature and function
of working class collective action and strike activity, and the
emergence of a uniquely working class culture. Requirements for
the course will include a short paper, due at midterm, one or two
brief oral presentations, and a term paper concentrating on one
of the topics covered in the seminar. All readings for the course
are on reserve in the College library, and in addition, I have
ordered one general text, John Gillis, The Development of European
Society which is available in the college bookstore. This text
provides a background to many of the topics which we will be
covering, and in addition, serves as an excellent introduction to
the study of social history in this period. You should complete
it by Week VI.

          Please note that the reading for the first assignment should
be completed before the first class meeting.

Week I -- Why Study Labor History?

E.J. Hobsbawm, "From Social History and the History of Society,"
    in: Felix Gilbert and Stephen R. Graubard, Historical Studies
    Today, 1-26.

E.J. Hobsbawm, "Labor History and Ideology," Journal of Social
    History, Vol. 7, #4, 1974

Elizabeth Fox-Genovese and Eugene Genovese, "The Political Crisis
    of Social History," Journal of Social History, X, 1976.

Geoff Eley and Keith Nield, Social History, 1980 (currently at
    bindery, will be available by 1/15/82)

Week II -- The Changing Nature of Work in Industrial Society

E.P. Thompson, "Time, Work Discipline and Industrial Capitalism,"
Past and Present, 38, 1967

E.J. Hobsbawm, "Custom, Wages and Workload," in Labouring Men

Michelle Perrot, "Workers and Machines in France during the First
Half of the Nineteenth Century," (with comment), Proceedings
of the Western Society for French History, 1977, Santa Barbara,
1978, 198-217

Ivy Pinchbeck, Women Workers and the Industrial Revolution, 1750-
1850, London, 1969 (selections)

WeekIII -- The Debate over the Standard of Living

Friedrich Engels,"The Conditions of the working class in England,"
selections in James J. Sheehan, ed., Industrialization and
industrial Labor in Nineteenth Century Europe, 13-32

E.J. Hobsbawm, "The British Standard of Living, 1790-1850,"
Economic History Review, August 1957 (also, Labouring Men, 64-
104)

R.M Hartwell, "The Rising Standard of Living in England, 1800-
1850," in: The Industrial Revolution and Economic Growth

E.J. Hobsbawm, "The Standard of Living during the Industrial
Revolution: A Discussion," Economic History Review, 2nd ser.,
vol. 16, 1963

R.M. Hartwell, "The Standard of Living: An Answer to the
Pessimists," in: The Industrial Revolution and Economic Growth

Week IV -- "Preindustrial" Forms fo Labor Protest

E.P. Thompson, "The Moral Economy of the English Crowd in the
18th Century," Past and Present, 1971

Alf Ludtke, "The Role of State Violence in the Period of Transition
to Industrial Capitalism,....," Social History, 4, 1, 1980, 15-31

Robert J. Bezucha, "The 'Preindustrial' Worker Movement: The Canuts
of Lyon," in Bezucha, ed., Modern European Social History, 93-123

George Rudé, The Crowd in History, Chapter Ten, "Captain Swing"
and "Rebecca's Daughters," pp. 149-163

Week V -- The Development of "Class Consciousness"

Christopher H. Johnson, "Patterns of Proleterianization: Parisian
Tailors and Lodève Woolen Workers," in John Merriman, ed.,
Consciousness and Class Experience in Nineteenth-Century Europe,
65-84

Frederick D. Marquardt, "A Working Class in Berlin in the 1840s?" in: H.-U. Wehler, ed., Sozialgeschichte Heute, 191-210

Laura S. Strumingher, Women and the Making of the Working Class: 1830-1870, selections

William H. Sewell, Jr., "Social Change and the Rise of Working-Class Politics in Nineteenth-Century Marseille," Past and Present, 65, 1974, 75-109

Week VI -- Work in "Advanced" Industrial Societies

Raphael Samuel, "The Workshop of the World: Steam Power and Hand Technology in mid-Victorian Britain," History Workshop, 3, spring 1977, 6-72

Peter N. Stearns, "The Unskilled and Industrialization. A Trans-formation of Consciousness," Archiv fur Sozialgeschichte, v. 16, 1976, 249-282

E.J. Hobsbawm, "The Labour Aristocracy in Nineteenth Century Britain," in Labouring Men

G. Stedman Jones, "Class Struggle and the Industrial Revolution," New Left Review, 90, 1975

Week VII -- Women in the Labor Force

Sally Alexander, "Women's Work in 19th Century London," in J. Mitchell and A. Oakley, The Rights and Wrongs of Women, 59-111

Joan W. Scott and Louise A. Tilly, "Women's Work and the Family in Nineteenth Century Europe," Comparative Studies in Society and History, 17, 1975, 36-64

Peter N. Stearns, "Working Class Women in Britain, 1890-1914," in Vicinus, ed., Suffer and be Still

Rose L. Glickman, "The Russian Factory Woman, 1880-1914," in D. Atkinson, et al., Women in Russia, 63-84

Laura Oren, "The Welfare of Women in Laboring Families: England, 1860-1950," Hartmann and Banner, ed., Clio's Consciousness Raised

Week VIII -- Trade Unions and Political Socialism, I -- An Overview

Peter N. Stearns and Harvey Mitchell, The European Labor Movement, the Working Classes and the Origins of Social Democracy 1890-1914

Marily J. Boxer and Jean H. Quataert, Socialist Women, 1-18

Week IX -- Trade Unions and Political Socialism, II -- Case Studies

Stephen Hickey, "The Shaping of the German Labour Movement: Miners in the Ruhr," in Richard Evans, ed., Society and Politics in Germany

Michael P. Hanagan, "The Logic of Solidarity, Social Structure in Le Chambon-Feugerolles," _Journal of Urban History_, 3, 4, 1977, 409-426

Donald H. Bell, "Worker Culture and Worker Politics: The Experience of an Italian Town, 1880-1915," _Social History_, 3, 1, 1978, 1-21

Victoria E. Bonnell, "Trade Unions, Parties, and the State in Tsarist Russia: A Study of Labor Politics in St. Petersburg and Moscow," _Politics and Society_, 9, 3, 1980, 299-322

Dorothy Thompson, "Women and Radical Politics: A Lost Dimension," in Mitchell and Oakley, _The Rights and Wrongs of Women_, 112-138

Week X -- Models for Understanding Labor Protest

Charles Tilly and Edward Shorter, "The Shape of Strikes in France," _Comparative Studies in Society and History_, 13, 1970, 60-86

E.J. Hobsbawm, "Economic Fluctuations and Some Social Movements," in _Labouring Men_, 126-157

James E. Cronin, "Theories of Strikes: Why Can't They Explain the British Experience?" _Journal of Social History_, Vol. 12, #2, 194-220

Dieter Groh, "Intensification of Work and Industrial Conflict in Germany, 1896-1914," _Politics and Society_, v. 8, nos. 3-4, 1978, 349-387

Week XI -- Presentations of Rough Drafts of Papers -- to be scheduled

Week XII -- Workers' Lives

John Burnett, ed., _The Annals of Labour_ (selections)

John Burnett, ed., _Useful Toil_ (selections)

Maud Pember-Reeves, ed., _Round About a Pound a Week_

Reginald E. Zelnik, "Russian Rebels: An Introduction to the Memoirs of Semen Kanatchikov and Matrei Fisher," _Russian Review_, 35, 1976, 249-289, 417-447

Peter N. Stearns, ed., _The Impact of the Industrial Revolution_ (selections)

Week XIII -- Workers' Culture

Gareth Stedman Jones, "Working-Class Culture and Working-Class Politics in London, 1870-1900: Notes on the Remaking of a Working-Class," _Journal of Social History_, 7, 1974, 460-507

Gerhard A. Ritter, "Workers' Culture in Imperial Germany: Problems and Points of Departure," _Journal of Contemporary History_, 13, 1978, 377-412

Klaus Tenfelde, "Mining Festivals in the Nineteenth Century," _Journal of Contemporary History_, 13, 1978, 377-412

Peter N. Stearns, "The Effort of continuity in Working-Class Culture," _Journal of Modern History_, 52, Dec. 1980, 626-55

Workers and Social Change in Twentieth Century Europe

New York University
History
Fall 1981
Nolan

   This course will examine the social, cultural and political
history of workers in Western Europe from the 1890s to the present.
It will investigate the composition of the working class, the
nature of work, types of working-class culture, forms of working-
class protest and the theory and practice of workers' movements.
We will look at the lives of both those workers usually studied--
skilled, organized males--and those generally neglected--women,
the unskilled, the unorganized and migrants. Readings and
lectures will explore how workers and workers movements were
shaped by and helped shape such major developments as war,
the rise of the welfare state, the Russian Revolution and fascism.
Throughout the course we will compare and contrast developments
in Britain, France, Germany and Italy.
   Readings for the course include a textbook, historical
monographs and articles, a novel, and letters and memoirs from
the period.
   There will be a mid-term, a paper on a topic of your choice
(but you should discuss that choice with me) and a final. The
readings will be discussed in class, so you should do them for
the weeks assigned. A few class sessions will be devoted entirely
to discussion and these are indicated on the syllabus.
   All reading assignments are on reserve in Bobst. All articles
can be purchased in a packet of xeroxes (details to be announced).
   The following books are available at the book store.

Abendroth, Wolfgang. A Short History of the European Working Class

Tressell, Robert. The Ragged Trousered Philanthropists (Monthly Review)

Davies, Margaret L. (ed.) Maternity (Norton)

Orwell, George. The Road to Wigan Pier (Harcourt Brace)

Kramer, Jane. Unsettling Europe (Vintage)

Tourraine, Alain. The May Movement (Random)

Boggs, Carl and Plotke, David. The Politics of Eurocommunism (South End)

Procacci, G. The Italian Working Class from Risorgimento to Fascism

Part I: The 1890s to 1914

I. T. Sept. 22   Introduction
   Th. Sept. 24   Patterns of Industrialization and Working-class
                  Formation

Abendroth, W. Short History of European Working Class, Chap. 1-3.

T. Sept. 29 Holiday
Th. Oct. 1   Community, Culture and Consciousness Among British
             Workers

Tressell, Robert. <u>The Ragged Trousered Philanthropists</u>. first half

III. T. Oct. 6   Socialism and Syndicalism in France
     Th. Oct. 8   Holiday

Tressell. Finish the book

IV. T. Oct. 13 Women, Work and Family
    Th. Oct. 15 Discussion of Tressell and Davies

Davies, M. L., ed. <u>Maternity</u>, entire

V. T. Oct. 20 A Social History of German Workers
   Th. Oct. 22 German Social Democracy

Nettl, J. P. "German Social Democracy As A Political Model"
     in <u>Past and Present</u>, 1965.

Hickey, Stephen. "The Shaping of the German Labour Movement:
     Miners in the Ruhr," in Evans, Richard. <u>Society and
     Politics in Wilhelmine Germany</u>.

VI. T. Oct. 27 Economic Backwardness and the Working Class in Italy
    Th. Oct. 29 Internationalism and Nationalism

Procacci, G. <u>The Italian Working Class from Risorgimento to
     Fascism</u>. entire

VII. T. Nov. 3 Holiday
     Th. Nov. 5 mid-term exam

Part II: 1914 to 1945

VIII. T. Nov. 10 Workers and World War I
      Th. Nov. 12 Revolution and Counterrevolution, 1917-1920

Abendroth. Chapter 4
Cronin, James. "Labor Insurgency and Class Formation: Comparative
     Perspectives on the Crisis of 1917-20" <u>Social Science
     History</u>, Vol. 4, 1980.

Sirianni, Carmen. "Workers' Control in the Era of the First
     World War" <u>Theory and Society</u>, vol. 9, 1980.

IX. T. Nov. 17 Economy, Culture and the Working Class in the 1920s
    Th. Nov. 19 The Changing Face of Social Democracy

Gramsci, Antonio, "Americanism and Fordism," in Gramsci,
     <u>Prison Notebooks</u>, pp. 277-320.

Maier, Charles, "Between Taylorism and Technocracy," <u>Journal of
     Contemporary History</u>, Vol. 5, 1970.

Nolan, M. "The Infatuation with Fordism: Social Democracy and
     Rationalization in Weimar Germany,"

X. T. Nov. 24 Communist Parties and the Communist International
   Th. Nov. 26 Holiday

Abendroth. Chapters 5-6.

XI. T. Dec. 1 Workers and Fascism in Germany and Italy
   Th. Dec. 3 Popular Front in France

Bridenthal, Renata. ".Something Old; Something New: Working
   Women Between the Wars," Becoming Visible.
Mason, Tim. "National Socialism and the Working Class," New
   German Critique, 1977.
De.Grazia, Victoria. The Culture of Consent. Preface, Introduction,
   Chapters 3 and 8.

XII. T. Dec. 8 Britain in the Depression. Part lecture and part
   discussion of Orwell, Mason and De Grazia.
   Th. Dec. 10 War, Resistance and Collaboration

Orwell, George. Road to Wigan Pier. Part I

Part III: 1945 to the Present

XIII. T. -Dec. 15 Working Class and Post World War II Settlements:
   Italy and France
   Th. Dec. 17 Working Class and Post World War II Settlements:
   Britain and Germany

Abendroth. Chapter 7 and Postscript.

Block, Fred. "Eurocommunism and the Stalemate of European
   Communism," in Boggs and Plotke, The Politics of Euro-
   Communism, pp. 255-70.

XIV. T. Dec. 22 The Welfare State and Corporatism in Britain and Germany
   Th. Dec. 24 Holiday

Kramer, Jane. Unsettling Europe, Read Chapters on "The San
   Vincenzo Cell," "The Invandrare," and "The Uganda Asians"

XV. T. Jan. 5 Migrant Workers. Part lecture and part discussion of
   Kramer
   Th. Jan. 7 The Resurgence of Class Conflict in France

Touraine, Alain. The May Movement, Cahpters I, IV-V, conclusion.

XVI. T. Jan. 12 Eurocommunism
   Th. Jan. 14 Prospects for the 1980s--discussion of Eurocommunism
   readings.

Boggs, Carl and Plotke, David. Politics of Eurocommunism. Introduction, articles by G. Ross, J. Barkan, and A. Buttafuoco.
   Finish the article by F. Block.

Harvard University
Graduate Course

Prof. Donald H. Bell
Robinson L-24
Spring, 1981

HISTORY 1335

THE EUROPEAN WORKING CLASS IN COMPARATIVE PERSPECTIVE

This conference course will focus on reading and
discussion.(It is therefore vital that you keep up with
the assignments and come prepared to discuss them). You
will be required to submit a mid-term paper of 10-12 pages
and a final paper of 18-20 pages. In addition, class participation
and attendance will count in your final grade.

Books marked with an asterisk are for student purchase.
Unless otherwise noted, all books and articles are on
Reserve at Lamont and Hilles libraries.

My office is in Robinson Hall L-24; My office
phone is 495-5146. My office hours are to be announced.

The course deals with the formation and development of
the European working class, principally in the period 1750-1914
(and also makes comparative reference to U.S. examples). It
will examine the social and economic conditions created by
industrialization, the changing character of work and life,
and working class response in the form of organization and
protest. Special attention will be paid to the role and
significance of worker culture and to important historiographical debates and methodological issues involved in the
study of the working class.

INTRODUCTION

1). Edward Shorter, "The History of Work in the West:
an Overview"

2). Jurgen Kuczynski, The Rise of the Working Class*, pp. 7-37.

PART I: BRITAIN AND THE INDUSTRIAL REVOLUTION

A. The Economic Background:

1). E.J. Hobsbawm, Industry and Empire*, Ch. 1-5.

2). David S. Landes, The Unbound Prometheus*, Introduction,Ch.2.

B. Living Standards and the Quality of Life: Optimist vs. Pessimist:

1). C. Stuart Doty, The Industrial Revolution, pp. 53-130,
(Reserve).

2). Friedrich Engels, The Condition of the Working Class, Ch. 3.

C. The Factory System and the Changing Nature of Work:

1). E.P. Thompson, "Time, Work Discipline, and Industrial Capitalism," in Past and Present, 38, December 1967 (Reserve

2). Karl Marx, Capital, Vol. I, Ch. IO, sections 1-4,6; Ch. XIV, sections 4-5; Ch. XIV, sections 3c,4,8.

Stephen Marglin, "What Do Bosses Do? The Origins and Functions of Hierarchy in Capitalist Production," Review of Radical Political Economies, VI, 2, 1974 (Reserve)

4). W.H. Hutt, "The Factory System in the Early 19th Century", in F.A. Hayek, Capitalism and the Historians

D. Class Formation and Class Conflict I:

1). E.P. Thompson, The Making of the English Working Class*, Part II, pp. 198-447.

Optional, but suggested:
Thompson, Part I, pp. 9-198.
Jurgen Kuczynski, The Rise of the Working Class, Ch. 2.

E. Class Formation and Class Conflict II:

1). E.P. Thompson, The Making of the English Working Class, Part III.

2). John Foster, Class Struggle and the Industrial Revolution, Ch. 1,2,4,5,7,8 (pp. 251-254).

F. Women and Work:

1). Louise Tilly and Joan Scott, Women, Work, and Family, Introduction, Parts I and II (Part III, optional).

2). Heidi Hartmann, "Capitalism, Patriarchy, and Job Segregation by Sex," in M. Blaxall, Barbara Reagan (eds.), Women and the Workplace, pp. 137-170.

3). Rosalyn Baxandall, et al, eds., America's Working Women, pp. xiii-xxii, 13-22, 38-68, 82-125.

Optional:
1). Ivy Pinchbeck, Women Workers in the Industrial Revolution, (pages to be announced).
2). Donald H. Bell, "The Male Role in Historical Perspective: From Pre-Industrial to Post-Industrial Society"

95

PART II: THE EUROPEAN CONTINENT AND THE UNITED STATES

A. The Industrial Revolution on the Continent and the Changing Character of Work

    1). D.S. Landes, The Unbound Prometheus, Ch. 3-5

    2). E.J. Hobsbawm, Industry and Empire, Ch. 6,8.

    3). E.J. Hobsbawm, "Custom, Wages, and Work Load,"in Hobsbawm, ed., Labouring Men, pp. 344-370.

    4). Peter Stearns, ed., The Impact of the Industrial Revolution, pp. 139-154.

B. France: Organization, Culture, Protest:

    1). Joan Scott, The Glassworkers of Carmaux* (entire).

    2). William H. Sewell, Jr."Social Change and the Rise of Working-Class Politics in 19th Century Marseille," in Past and Present, 65, 1974 (Reserve)

    3). Robert J. Bezucha,"The 'Pre-Industrial' Worker Movement: The Canuts of Lyon," in Robert Bezucha (ed).,Modern European Social History, 93-123 (Reserve)

    4). Edward Shorter and Charles Tilly, "The Shapes of Strikes in France," in Comparative Studies in Society and History, 13, no. 1, Jan. 1971 (Reserve)

    Optional, but suggested:
    Bernard Moss, "Towards a Sociology of Labor Movements: The Socialism of the Skilled Workers").

C. Germany: Organization, Culture, Protest:

    1). Barrington Moore,jr, Injustice: The Social Bases of Obedience and Revolt *, Part II, Ch. 4-7.

    2). Carl Schorske, The German Social Democratic Party, 1905-1917, Pts. I-IV

    3). Lawrence Shofer, "Patterns of Labor Protest: Upper Silesia, 1865-1914," Journal of Social History, vol. 5, no.4, 1972 (Reserve)

    4). Peter Stearns, "Adaptation to Industrialization: German Workers as a Test Case," Central European History, III, 1970 (Reserve)

5). Peter Stearns, The Impact of the Industrial Revolution, pp. 154-177 (Reserve ⎯ ⏜   ⏜)

6). David Crew,"Definition of Modernity: Social Mobility in a German Town, 1880-1901, " Journal of Social History,7,1973 (Reserve)   ⏜⏜⏜⏜.

Optional:
J.P. Nettl, "The German Social Democratic Party,1890-1914 as a Political Model," Past and Present, 30, 1965 (Reserve ⏜⏜
⏜⏜⏜⏜

D. Italy: Organization, Culture, Protest:

1). Louise Tilly, "I Fatti di Maggio: The Working Calss ⎯of Milan and the Rebellion of 1898," in Bezucha (ed)., Modern European Social History, 124-158 and   ⏜ .

2).Louise Tilly, "Skilled Workers and Collective Action, Milan, 1870-1898, ⏜.

3). Donald H. Bell , "Worker Culture and Worker Politics: The Experience of an Italian Town,1880-1915," Social History, Vol. 3, No. 1, Jan 1978, pp. 1-21.

4). Nunzio Pernicone, "The Italian Labor Movement," in Edward Tannenbaum and Emiliana Noether,(eds.), Modern Italy, A Topical History Since 1861, pp. 197-227.

Optional:

1). Luciano Cafagna, "Italy, 1830-1914" in Carlo Cipolla, ed., The Fontana Economic History of Europe, The Emergence of Industrial Societies, Part I, pp. 279-325 (Reserve)   ⏜ ⏜⏜ ,

2). John Cammett, Antonio Gramsci and the Origins of Italian Communism, Ch.1-6 .

3). Antonio Gramsci, Prison Notebooks

4). Antonio Fiore, Antonio Gramsci: Life of a Revolutionary

5). Paolo Spriano, The Occupation of the Factories : Italy 1920

E. The United States: Organization, Culture, Protest:

1). Herbert Gutman, Work, Culture, and Society in Industrializing America, pp. 3-79

2).Alan Dawley, Class and Community*, (entire)

5). Jeremy Brecher, Strike!, pp. 15-132, 283-320.

6). Katherine Stone, " The Origins of Job Structures in the Steel Industry," in Radical America, VII, 6, 1973 (Reserve) and

7). Jack Russell, The Coming of the Line" Radical America, Vol 12, no 3,1978, pp. 28-45 and   .

Optional:

Paul Faler and Alan Dawley, "Working Class Culture and Politics in the Industrial Revolution: Sources of Loyalism and Rebellion," Journal of Social History, 9,4, June, 1976

Leon Litwack, The American Labor Movement, pp. 1-17,28-51.

Jerold S. Auerbach, American Labor: The 20th Century, pp. 19-49, 60-99.

John H.M. Laslett and S.M. Lipset, Failure of A Dream?: Essays in the History of American Socialism, pp. 3-24., 300-340.

Stephen Thernstrom, "Urbanization, Migration, and Social Mobility in 19th Century America"

PART III: THE PRE-WAR YEARS: NEW FORMS OF WORK AND PROTEST

1). Gareth Stedman Jones "Working Class Culture and Working Class Politics in London, 1870-1900: Notes on the Re-making of a Working Class."

2).Peter N. Stearns, "The European Labor Movement and the Working Classes, 1890-1914, in Harvey Mitchell and Peter N. Stearns, eds., Workers and Protest

3). Edward Shorter, Work and Community in the West pp 80-138

4). George Orwell, The Road to Wigan Pier, Part I

Optional:

Gareth Stedman Jones, Outcast London
Harry Braverman, Labor and Monopoly Capital, Parts I-III

KAPLAN
U:45 30Y

School of International
Affairs
Columbia University
Spring 1979

WOMEN IN SOCIETY:
EUROPEAN WOMEN IN THE   19th AND   20th CENTURIES

This course presents an overview of women in European society
using three core books and a great variety of reprints. The
course design suggests the general themes of the survey, but
I would like to add that several objectives are implied in
every section:

1) Students will attempt to analyze the complex interplay
of work and family in women's experience, that is, women's
relationship to the overlapping spheres of reproduction and
production.

2) We will try to contrast the general condition of women
with the lives of specific groups of women, to juxtapose
"women's" experience of work and family with the experiences
of women of a particular class, ethnicity, religion, culture
or nation and in a particular life stage and family pattern.

3) We have to be aware, at all times, of the overriding
themes in European social, economic and political history.
For example, for the 20th century we look at the impact
of two world wars and the economic crises associated with
inflation, rationalization and depression in Europe.

4) Within any given time frame, we call attention to
gender-specific changes, because the periods commonly regarded
as "turning points" by historians are not necessarily the same
for women as for men. When we look at the industrial revolution, for example, we try to examine how new jobs, economic
mobility and urbanization may have been experienced differently
by men and women. There were often time lags in the way men
and women adapted to transitional periods resulting from the
limitations imposed upon women as well as internalized values
and self images.

5) Students are asked to bring in family memoirs, diaries,
photos, as well as novels and poetry collections pertinent
to the period.

I. INTRODUCTION: THEORETICAL AND CRITICAL APPROACHES TO
WOMEN'S HISTORY

   Juliette Mitchell, "Four Structures in a Complex Unity"
      in Liberating Women's History, by Berenice Carroll

   Joan Kelly, "History and the Social Relations of the
      Sexes."

   Sheila Rowbotham, Hidden from History: Rediscovering
      Women in History from the 17th Century to the Present
      (introduction)

II. REBELLIOUS WOMEN: EARLY FEMINISM IN THE REVOLUTIONARY
ERA

   Ruth Graham, "Women in the French Revolution," in Becoming
      Visible, by Renate Bridenthal and Claudia Koonz (Hereafter
      referred to as BV)

John Stuart Mill and Harriet Taylor, On the Subjection of Women

or

Mary Wollstonecraft, A Vindication of the Rights of Women

(Supplementary Reading:)(for individual class presentations)
George Rudé, The Crowd in the French Revolution (chaps. 5,12,13)
Olwen Hufton, "Women in Revolution, 1786-96," in Past and Present, Nov. 1971
Scott Lytle, "The Second Sex, 1793," in Journal of Modern History, #27 (1955)

III. DEMOGRAPHY, SEXUALITY, MARRIAGE AND THE FAMILY

Elaine and English Showalter, "Victorian Women and Menstruation," in Suffer and be Still: Women in the Victorian Age, by Martha Vicinus

Edward Shorter, "Female Emancipation, Birth Control and Fertility in European History," American Historical Review, #78 (June 1973)

M. Llewellyn-Davies, Maternity. Letters from Working Women

(Supplementary Reading:)
J.A. and Olive Banks, Feminism and Family Planning

Laura Oren, "The Welfare of Women in Laboring Families: England, 1860-1950," in Clio's Consciousness Raised, by Mary Hartman and Lois Banner

Anna Davin, "Imperialism and Motherhood," History Workshop #5 (Spring 1978)

(Supplementary Reading:)
Nancy Tomes, "A 'Torrent of Abuse': Crimes of Violence between Working -Class Men and Women in London, 1840-1875," Journal of Social History (Spring 1978)

IV. WOMEN'S WORK

A. Women in Pre-Industrial Capitalism

Richard Vann, "Toward a New Lifestyle: Women in Pre-Industrial Capitalism," in BV

B. Middle Class Women

Barbara Pope, "Angels in the Devil's Workshop: Leisured and Charitable Women in Nineteenth Century England and France," in BV

M. Jeanne Peterson, "The Victorian Governess: Status Incongruence in Family and Society," in Suffer and be Still

Patricia Branca, "The Myth of the Idle Victorian Woman," in Clio's Consciousness

Eleanor Riemer and John Fout (eds.), European Women:
A Documentary History, parts III and IV

Catherine Bodard Silver, "Salon, Foyer, Bureau: Women
and the Professions in France," in Clio's Consciousness

(Supplementary)
Edward Bristow, Vice and Vigilance: Purity Movements
in Britain since 1700

Bonnie Smith, Ladies of the Leisure Class

C. Working Class Women

(1) The Industrial Revolution
Mary Lynn McDougall, "Working-Class Women during
the Industrial Revolution," in BV

European Women, parts I and II

Theresa McBride, "The Long Road Home: Women's
Work and Industrialization," in BV

(Supplementary)
Ivy Pinchbeck, Women Workers and the Industrial
Revolution
Ann Oakley, Woman's Work

(film)
"The Song of the Shirt" (the"sweated"clothes industry)

(2) Prostitution
Judith and Daniel Walkowitz, "We are not Beasts of the
Field:Prostitution and the Poor in Plymouth and
Southhampton under the Contagious Diseases Act," in
Clio's Consciousness

Richard Evans, "Prostitution and the State in Imperial
Germany," Past and Present, #70 (1976)

E.M.Sigsworth, "A Study of Victorian Prostitution and
Venereal Disease," in Suffer and be Still

V. WOMEN'S LIVES AS PORTRAYED IN NOVELS

The following are only suggestions, you may pick a novel of your
choice after consulting with the instructor.

Emile Zola, L'Assommoir or Germinal or Nana
George Gissing, The Odd Women
Gabriele Reuter, Aus Guter Familie: Leidensgeschichte eines
Madchens
Benjamin Disraeli, Sybil
Jane Austen, Emily or Charlotte Bronté, or George Eliot
Alexandre Kuprin, Yama
Sholem Asch, The God of Vengeance
or choose an author whose work you would like to read...

VI. FEMINISM

Edith Hurwitz, "The International Sisterhood, in BV

Sheila Rowbotham, Hidden from History, chaps. 8-10, 15

Amy Hackett, "Feminism and Liberalism in Wilhelmine
Germany," in Liberating Women's History

European Women, part V

(Supplementary Reading)
Richard Evans, The Feminist Movement in Germany: 1894-
1933
C. Pankhurst, Unshackled. The Story of how We Won the
Vote

VII. WOMEN AND SOCIALISM

Marilyn Boxer and Jean Quataert, Socialist Women, chaps.
1,2,4,5,6 (Italy, Germany, France)

European Women, part VI

(Supplementary Reading)
Jean Quataert, Reluctant Feminists in German Social
Democracy, 1885-1917

Boxer and Quataert, Socialist Women, chaps. 3,7 (Russia)

Barbara Engel, "Women as Revolutionaries: The Case of the
Russian Populists," in BV

Bernice Rosenthal, "Love on the Tractor: Women in the Russian
Revolution and After, in BV

(Supplementary Reading)
Richard Stites, The Women's Liberation Movement in Russia

VIII. WOMEN AND WAR

G. Braybon, Women Workers in the First World War: The British
Experience

(Supplementary Reading)
Vera Brittain, Testament of Youth

Jean Quataert, Reluctant Feminists (part D "Wartime Divisions")

IX. WOMEN UNDER DEPRESSION AND FASCISM

Renate Bridenthal, "Something Old, Something New: Women
between the Two World Wars," in BV

Claudia Koonz, "Mothers in the Fatherland: Women in Nazi
Germany," in BV

Tim Mason, "Women in Germany, 1925-1940: Family, Welfare and
Work," History Workshop (1976)

(Supplementary Reading)
Margery Spring-Rice, Working-Class Wives (England, 1930's)

Leila Rupp, <u>Mobilizing Women for War:German</u> <u>and American</u>
  <u>Propaganda, 1939-1945</u>
Jill Stephenson, <u>Women in Nazi Society</u>

(films)"Mädchen in Uniform"
      "Rosie the Riveter"

*   *   *   *   *   *   *   *

It is recommended that the following boods be purchased:

1.<u>Becoming Visible, Women in European History</u>, Renate Bridenthal
  and Claudia Koonz (Houghton Mifflin, NY, 1977)

2.<u>European Women, A Documentary History</u>, by Eleanor Riemer
   and John Fout (eds), (Schocken,NY, 1980)

3.<u>Socialist Women</u>, by Marilyn Boxer and Jean Quataert

4.One of the following:

    <u>A Vindication of the Rights of Women</u>, Mary Wollstonecraft
                  or
    <u>On the Subjection of Women</u>, Mill and Taylor

Reprints, novels and edited books will be placed on reserve
at the library. The books are also available at Womanbooks,
92nd and Amsterdam Ave.

New York University   History G57. 1253
                        M. Nolan
                        Spring 1981

Women in European Society and Politics

This course will explore the economic, social and political
position of women in Britain. France and Germany from the eighteenth
century to the 1930s. It will focus on women's work, women in the
family and women's political activity.

The course meets Tuesday, 4:20-6:00. You are expected to
do the reading and participate actively in discussions. You are
expected to write two ten-page papers.

Books marked with an asterisk have been ordered at the bookstore. All other materials will be on reserve at Bobst or in the
history department office (19 University Place, room 400) or in
both places.

I.   Introduction: Problems of Conceptualization
     February 3

II. Women in preindustrial society
     February 10

     Vann, R. "Toward a New Lifestyle: Women in preindustrial
          capitalism," in Bridenthal, R. and Koonz, C., Becoming
          Visible, pp. 192-216.
     Kleinbaum, A "Women in the Age of Light," in Bridenthal
          and Koonz, pp. 217-35.

     Hufton. Olwen "Women and the Family Economy in Eighteenth
          Century France," French Historical Studies. IX, Nr. 1,
          Spring 1975.
     Eisenstein, Zillah, Capitalist Patriarchy and the Case for
          Socialist Feminism, first essay by Eisenstein. pp. 4-35,
          and essay by Hartman, H. pp. 206-47.

III. Women in industrializing Societies
     February 17

     *Scott, J. and Tilly. L. Women, Work and Family, entire.
          If you have read Scott and Tilly, please read
     Pinchbeck, Ivy, Women Workers and the Industrial Revolution

IV. Women and Protest in preindustrial Societies
     February 24

     Hufton, Olwen. "Women in Revolution, 1789-96," Past and
          Present, 53, 1971.
                              104

Rowbotham, Sheila, Women, Resistance and Revolution,
   Chapters 1 and 2
*Wollstonecraft, Mary. A Vindication of the Rights of
   Woman, Chapters I-IV, IX, XIII

V. Women and Protest in the Nineteenth Century
    March 3

Taylor, Barbara, "The Men are as Bad as Their Masters,"
   Feminist Studies, V, Nr. 1, Spring 1979. pp. 7-40.
Thompson, Dorothy. "Women and Nineteenth-Century Radical Politics:
   A Lost Dimension," in Mitchell, Juliet and Oakley, Ann,
   The Rights and Wrongs of Women.
Thomas, Edith The Women Incendaries, Chapters 1,2,4, 5, 7,
   8, 10-12 and pp. 223 - 30.

VI Theories about Women
    March 10

*Engels Friedrich The Origins of the Family, Private Property
   and the State. entire.
Mill, JS. The Subjection of Women, pages to be assigned.

VII Family and Sexuality: The Middle Classes
     March 17

*Banks, J A. and Banks, Olive. Feminism and Family Planning in
   Victorian England, entire.
Hartman, Mary. Victorian Murderesses , Introduction, Chapters 1,
   3, 4, conclusion.

VIII. Family and Sexuality: The Working Class
       March 31

Davidoff, Leonore, "Mastered for Life: Servant and Wife in
   Victorian and Edwardian England," Journal of Social
   History, 7, Nr 4, Summer 1974.
Davin, Anna. "Imperialism and Motherhood " History Workshop
   Journal, Issue 5, Spring 1978, pp. 9-88
Oren Laura, "Welfare of Women in Laboring Families: England
   1860-1950," Feminist Studies I, Nr. 3-4, 1973, pp. 107-25.
Rapp R , Rosen, E and Bridenthal, R. "Family History Examined "
   Faminist Studies V, Nr. 1, Spring 1979 pp. 174-200.
*Maternity, Letters from Working Women ed. by Margaret Davies
   , read 50-60 pages of your choice

IX Prostitution
     April 7

     Walkowitz. Judith, <u>Prostitution and Victorian Society</u>, entire.

 X. The Women's Movement in Britain
     April 14

     Pankhurst. Emmeline, <u>My Own Story</u>, entire,
     Strachey, Ray. <u>The Cause</u>. Chapters XV-XVII,

XI. The Women's Movement in Britain
     April 21

     Liddington, Jill and Norris, Jill, <u>One Hand Tied Behind Us</u> entire.

XII. The Women's Movement in Germany
     April 28

     *Evans, Richard. <u>The Feminist Movement in Germany, 1894-
          1933</u>, entire.

XIII. Women and Working-class Movements
      May 5

      Thönnessen, Werner. <u>The Emanicpation of Women</u>, entire.
      *<u>Life As We Have Known It</u>. ed. by Margaret Davies. Read 60-
           70 pages of your choice,

XIV.. Women and Fascism
      May 12

      Bridenthal, Renata, "Beyond Kinder, Küche, Kirche: Weimar
           Women at Work," <u>Central European History</u> VI. 1973, pp. 148-6(
      Koonz Claudia, "Nazi Women Before 1933." <u>Social Science
           Quarterly</u>, March 1976.
      Mason, Tim, "Women in Nazi Germany," <u>History Workshop Journal</u>,
           Issue 1, Spring 1976, pp. 74-133 and Issue 2. Autumn,
           1976, pp 5-32

History 27.8J (SCG)
Women in Modern Europe
Spring 1981
Renate Bridenthal
Brooklyn College. CUNY

Course description

The history of women in Europe from the Industrial and French Revolutions to
the present. Changes in and interaction of women's activities in work, the
family, politics (including feminism), and the relationship of these changes
to those in women's sexuality, relationships, and in contemporary concepts of
women's nature. Stress is on women as a group, rather than on individual
heroines.

Course requirements

Two exams: mid-term and final, each 1/3 of grade.
Two book reviews: Davies and Zola (see below): 20% of grade.
Class participation: being there in body and mind: remainder of grade.

Required books

R. Bridenthal and C. Koonz, eds., Becoming Visible: Women in European
    History (Houghton Mifflin, 1977).

E. Riemer and J. Fout, eds., European Women: A Documentary History, 1980-1945.
    (Schocken Bks., 1980).

Alice Rossi, ed., Essays on Sex Equality, by J.S. and H.T. Mill, (University
    of Chicago Press, 1977).

Marge L. Davies, ed., Life as We Have Known It, by Co-operative Working Women,
    (W.W. Norton reprint, 1975).

Emile Zola, Germinal.

SYLLABUS, Part I		Readings
Feb. 3-5	Introduction	Introd. to BV and R&F.
Feb. 12	Pre-industrial family economy.	BV, ch. 8.
Feb. 17-19	Pre-industrial ideology and politics.	BV, ch. 9. BV, ch. 10: R&F, #16.
Feb. 24-26	Capitalist industrialization.	BV, ch. 11 & 12. R&F, #1,4,28,30.
Mar. 3-5	Politics of class and gender.	BV, ch. 13. R&F, #5-12, 17,29.
Mar. 10-12	Liberal Feminism.	BV, ch. 14. R&F, #19-22.
Mar. 17-19	Liberal Feminism.	Rossi, essays by Mill and Mill. Entire.
Mar. 24	Mid-term.	
Mar. 26	Socialist feminism.	Lecture.

SYLLABUS, Part II

	Required	Recommended
Apr. 2		
Women Revolutionaries	BV, ch. 15 R&F, #23, 24	WE, ch. 24, Pt. III & ch. 25, Pt. VI - (sections, Russia)
Apr. 7-9		
Women as producers and reproducers in the 20th century.	BV, ch. 18 R&F. #15, 31-40.	WE: ch. 26, Pt. II on "Home Front" & ch. 27, Pt. III.
Apr. 14-16		
Woman and Her Body.	R&F. Pt. IV Entire (#42-53)	WE: ch. 25, Pts. I & II. ch. 27, Pt. II
Apr. 28-30		
Contemporary Alternatives: the USSR	BV, ch. 16. R&F, #25, 41	WE: ch. 26, Pt. III; ch. 27, Pt. I; ch. 28, Pt. II sections on Russia.
May 5-7		
Contemp. Alternatives: Anarchist Spain, Nazi Germany	BV, ch. 17 BV, ch. 19 R&F, #26, 27	WE: ch. 25, Pt. IV on Spain; ch. 28, Pt. I, Pt. II on Nazi Germany.
May 12-14		
Modern European Women, East and West	lectures	
May 19		
Gender alternatives	slide show	

BV - Becoming Visible
R&F - Reimer & Fout documentary, # refers to document number (not page)
WE - The Western Experience, vol. III.

Recommended supplemenatry readings in The Western Experience, vol. III by
Chambers, Grew, Herlihy, Rabb and Woloch.

Pre-industrial society: Ch. 20, Parts I-IV.

French Revolution: Ch. 20, Parts V-VI, and ch. 21.

Industrialization: Ch. 23, Parts I-II.

Liberal feminism: Ch. 22, Parts II-III and ch. 23, Part III.

Socialist feminism: ch. 25, Parts III-V.

Guidelines for book reviews of <u>Life as We Have Known It</u>, ed. by M.L. Davies and <u>Germinal</u> by Emile Zola.

In approximately 1000 to 1500 words (4 to 6 double spaced typed pages) write a comparative review, noting the similarities and differences in the lives of women in France and England as described in these two books, with respect to the following themes:

1. What kind of paid employment was usual for working class women?

2. What was motherhood like for them?

3. What were their relationships with men of their class like?

4. What were their relationships with other women of their class like?

5. What were their relationships with people of other classes?

6. What was their leisure like? What kind of activities did it include?

7. What kind of political awareness did they have, if any, and what kind of actions were available to them?

8. Do you get a different sense of the experience as told by the women themselves than by a male novelist? If so, what is the difference?

9. Free space: any thoughts, comments, questions, that came to your mind as you read the books or wrote this review.

Western European Jewry
from the French Revolution to the Twentieth Century

I. The Struggle for Emancipation

Jan. 24   (1) Introduction

Jan. 31   (2) The French Revolution

Salo Baron, "Ghetto and Emancipation," Menorah
Journal (1928), pp. 515-526.

_____, "Newer approaches to Jewish Emancipation,"
Diogenes (Spring 1960), pp. 56-81.

*Jacob Katz, Out of the Ghetto, pp. 1-56.

*Arthur Hertzberg, The French Enlightenment and the
Jews, pp. 314-368.

Recommended: La Revolution francaise et l'emancipation
des juifs (8 vols.)

Feb. 7   (3) Napoleon and the Jews

Diogene Tama, Transactions of the Parisian Sanhedrin.

Simeon Maslin, Selected Documents of Napoleonic Jewry,
pp. 35-39, 56-60, 74-78.

Recommended: Robert Anchel, Napoleon et les juifs
Frances Malino, The Sephardic Jews of Bordeaux.

Feb. 14   (4) The German Experience

H.D. Schmidt, "The Terms of Emancipation, 1781-1812,"
Leo Baeck Institute Yearbook, I (1956), pp. 28-47.

Herbert Strauss, "Pre-emancipation Prussian Policies
towards the Jews, 1815-1847," LBIYB, XI (1966),
pp. 107-136.

Reinhard Rurup, "Jewish Emancipation and Bourgeois
Society," LBIYB, XIV (1969), pp. 67-91.

Recommended: Jacob Toury, Der Eintritt der Juden ins
Deutsche Burgertum.

II. Jewish Responses to Emancipation

Feb. 21   (5) The Ideology of Assimilation

*Solomon Maimon, Autobiography.

*Michael Meyer, The Origins of the Modern Jew,
pp. 57-114.

Michael Marrus, The Politics of Assimilation, pp.
86-121.

Feb. 28   (6) Social and Demographic Changes

*Jacob Katz, Out of the Ghetto, pp. 104-123, 176-190.

Monika Richarz, "Jewish Social Mobility in Germany
during the Time of Emancipation (1790-1871), LBIYB,
XX (1975), pp. 69-78.

Fritz Stern, Gold and Iron, pp. 461-493.

Recommended: Phyllis Albert, The Modernization of
French Jewry.

Mar. 7   (7) Religious Accommodation: Reform Judaism

David Philipson, The Reform Movement in Judaism,
pp. 1-89, 107-269, 284-328.

W. Gunther Plaut, The Rise of Reform Judaism,
pp. 27-42, 50-70, 133-145, 185-199.

Mar. 21   (8) Neo-Orthodoxy and Positive-Historical Judaism

Plaut, pp. 80-90.

*Louis Ginzberg, Students, Scholars, and Saints,
pp. 195-216.

Sampson Raphael Hirsch, The Nineteen Letters of
Ben-Uziel.

*Katz, pp. 142-160.

Recommended: Noah Rosenbloom, Tradition in an Age
of Reform.

Mar. 28   (9) Wissenschaft des Judentums

*Meyer, pp. 144-182

Max Wiener, Abraham Geiger and Liberal Judaism,
pp. 3-80, 138-146, 149-215.

*Heinrich Graetz, The Structure of Jewish History, ed.
Ismar Schorsch, pp. 1-124.

III. Anti-Semitism and Its Impact

Apr. 4   (10) The New Antisemitism

Paul Massing, Rehearsal for Destruction, pp. 1-109, 277-310.

Uriel Tal, Christians and Jews in Germany, pp. 31-80, 160-222, 290-305.

Fritz Stern, Gold and Iron, pp. 494-531.

Recommended: Shulamith Angel-Volkov, The Rise of Popular Anti-Modernism in Germany.

Apr. 11   (11) Anti-Semitism and Jewish Politics

Ismar Schorsch, Jewish Reactions to German Anti-Semitism, pp. 1-177.

Marrus, pp. 122-162, 196-242.

Recommended: Jehuda Reinharz, Fatherland or Promised Land.

Apr. 25   (12) Herzl and the Rise of Western Zionism

Amos Elon, Herzl, pp. 1-247.

Theodor Herzl, The Jewish State.

May 2   (13) The Zionist Challenge

Schorsch, pp. 179-209.

Marrus, pp. 243-285.

*Martin Buber, On Judaism, pp. 11-55.

*Available in paperback

Requirements of the course

Undergraduates: a mid-term, 8-10 page paper, and a final exam.
Graduate students: a major research paper.

History W4513x   **Columbia University**   Professor Hyman
Fall 1979   502 Fayerweather Hall
                                                                            Ext.: 5253

European Jewry in the Twentieth Century

I.   Introduction

      Sept. 6:   The Post-Emancipation Era

II.   The Impact of Immigration

      Sept. 11:   The Arrival of the Immigrants. Lloyd Gartner,
                                The Jewish Immigrant in England,
                                pp. 1 - 99, 142 - 186.

      Sept. 13:   The Jewish Labor Movement in Comparative
                                Perspective. Lloyd Gartner, pp. 100 - 141
                                Recommended: Paula Hyman, From Dreyfus to
                                Vichy, pp. 89 - 114.

      Sept. 18:   Natives and Immigrants: Communal Politics.
                                Szajkowski, Zosa: "The European Attitude to
                                Eastern European Jewish Immigration, 1881 - 1893",
                                Publication of the American Jewish Historical
                                Society, XLI (1951 - 52), pp. 126 - 162;
                                Gartner, pp. 187 - 240; P. Hyman, "From
                                Paternalism to Cooptation: The French Jewish
                                Consistory and the Immigrants, 1906 - 1939,"
                                YIVO Annual of Jewish Social Science, XVII (1978),
                                pp. 217 - 237.

      Sept. 20:   East Meets West: Buber, Rosenzweig,and Kafka
                                Max Mayer, "A German Jew Goes East," Leo Baeck
                                Institute Yearbook, III (1958), pp. 344 - 357;
                                Alexander Carlebach, "A German Rabbi Goes East,"
                                LBIYB, VI (1961), pp. 60 - 68; Martin Buber,
                                Hasidism and Modern Man, pp. 21 - 69.

III.   World War I

      Sept. 25:   The Jews in the War

      Sept. 27:   Zionism and the Balfour Declaration. Isaiah Fried-
                                man, The Question of Palestine, pp. 25 - 64,
                                227 - 332; Recommended: I. Friedman, Germany,
                                Turkey, Zionism, 1897 - 1918.

      Oct.   2:   National Minority Rights; *Simon Dubnow,
                                Nationalism and History, pp. 131 - 142; Oscar
                                Janowsky, The Jews and Minority Rights,
                                pp. 264 - 369.

IV. The Jewish Renaissance

Oct. 4: Hermann Cohen and Leo Baeck, Hermann Cohen, <u>Religion of Reason</u>, pp. 1 - 34; *Leo Baeck, <u>The Essence of Judaism</u>, pp. 9 - 80, 257 - 275.

Oct. 9: Social Context. *Edmond Fleg, "Why I am a Jew", in: <u>The Zionist Idea</u> (ed. A. Hertzberg), pp. 479 - 485.

Oct. 11: Buber and Rosenzweig. *Martin Buber, <u>On Judaism</u>. pp. 3 - 174; *Nahum Glatzer, <u>Franz Rosenzweig: His Life and Thought</u>, pp. 9 - 250; Recommended: Franz Rosenzweig, <u>On Jewish Learning</u>

V. Jews in European Culture and Society

Oct. 16: Making it - Mobility and Assimilation. Lamar Cecil, "Jew and Junker in Imperial Berlin," in: <u>LBIYB</u>, XX (1975), pp. 47 - 58; Recommended: Jakob Wasserman, <u>My Life as German and Jew</u>

Oct. 18: The Jew as Radical Intellectual - The Radical Intellectual as Jew (1); *Peter Gay, <u>Freud, Jews, and Other Germans</u>, pp. 93 - 188.

Oct. 23: The Jew as Radical Intellectual (2) - The Case of Freud. *Gay, pp. 29 - 92; *John Murray Cuddihy, <u>The Ordeal of Civility</u>, pp. 17 - 103.

VI. East European Jewry between the Wars

Oct. 25: Entering the 20th Century. *Lucy Dawidowicz, <u>The Golden Tradition</u>, pp. 27 - 89; Recommended: Vago and Mosse, eds. <u>Jews and Non-Jews in Eastern Europe</u>

Oct. 30: The Political Situation of Polish Jewry. Celia Heller, <u>On the Edge of Destruction</u>, pp. 1 - 139.

Nov. 1: The Culture and Politics of Polish Jewry. Heller, pp. 143 - 298.

Nov. 8: The Jews in the Soviet Union. Solomon M. Schwarz, <u>The Jews in the Soviet Union</u>, pp. 90 - 218, 292 - 308; Recommended: (1) Lionel Kochan, <u>The Jews in Soviet Russia since 1917</u>; (2) Zvi Gitelman, <u>Jewish Nationality and Soviet Politics</u>

VII. Zionism and the New Generation

Nov. 13: The Impact of Zionism. Stephen Poppel, <u>Zionism in Germany</u>, pp. 21 - 135; Chanoch Rinott, "Major Trends in Jewish Youth Movements in Germany," in:

LBIYB, XX (1974), pp. 77 - 95; Paula Hyman, "Challenge
to Assimilation: French Jewish Youth Movements Between
the Wars," in Jewish Journal of Sociology, XVIII, 2
(Dec. 1976), pp. 105 - 114.

VIII. The Holocaust

Nov. 15:   Nazism and German Jewry. Karl Schleunes, The Twisted
           Road to Auschwitz, pp. 62 - 262.

Nov. 20:   Jewish Responses to Nazism in Germany. *Lucy Dawidowicz,
           A Holocaust Reader, pp. 35 - 53, 143 - 170;
           Leo Baeck Institute Yearbook, I (1956), pp. 57 - 104;
           Recommended: John K. Dickinson, German and Jew

Nov. 27:   World Jewry Confronts Nazism. Nahum Goldmann, The
           Autobiography of Nahum Goldmann, pp. 119 - 173;
           Moshe Gottlieb, "The First of April Boycott and the
           Reaction of the American Jewish Community," American
           Jewish Historical Quarterly, LVII (1968), pp. 516 - 556;
           Recommended: David Weinberg, A Community on Trial,
           pp. 72 - 221.

Nov. 29:   The Refugee Problem

           Henry Feingold, The Politics of Rescue, pp. 3 - 68,
           126 - 166, 295 - 307. Recommended: Arieh Tartakower
           and Kurt Grossmann, The Jewish Refugee

Dec. 4:   Dimensions of the Holocaust. *Lucy Dawidowicz, The
           War against the Jews, pp. 143- 200.

Dec. 6:   Jewish Responses to Nazi Persecution. *Dawidowicz,
           War, pp. 265 - 479; *Dawidowicz, Reader, pp. 334 - 380.

IX. Conclusion

Dec. 11:   The Reconstruction of European Jewry

COURSE REQUIREMENTS:

Undergraduates: Midterm, final exam, and 8 - 10 page paper

Graduate students: Final exam and major research paper

* Available in paperback

University of Toronto
Department of History

History 398Y

THE HOLOCAUST   M.R. Marrus

1980-81

Lecture: Tuesday, 1:00

This course surveys the destruction of two-thirds of European Jewry by the Nazis
during the Second World War. The first term explores Nazi policy towards the
Jews in the context of anti-Jewish ideology, bureaucratic structures, and the
varying conditions of occupation and domination in Europe under the Third Reich.
The second term continues the latter theme, but emphasizes the world outside --
reactions of Jews, European populations and governments, the Allies, churches and
political movements.

Students will attend weekly tutorial groups to discuss issues raised in lectures
and assigned readings. These tutorials are an integral part of the course and
satisfactory attendance at them is essential in order to obtain standing. There
will be a test at the end of the first term, a paper due at the end of the second,
and a final examination. The final grade in the course will be computed as follows:
a tentative grade will be established by averaging the results of the test, essay,
and final examination. Each student's tutorial participation will then be assessed,
and the tentative grade previously calculated may then be adjusted upwards or down-
wards by as much as ten percentage points.

Weekly readings address specific themes, but are not intended to provide compre-
hensive coverage. Students are encouraged to read as widely as possible in the
supplementary and alternative readings to investigate diverse interpretations,
and to use a variety of source material. Assignments will be less heavy in the
second term, when students will report to tutorial groups on their term papers.
The Sigmund Samuel Library should have copies of the syllabus material, including
photocopied articles, on short-term loan. In addition, students should purchase
copies of the following, which are available in the Textbook Store:

    Lucy Davidowicz, The War Against the Jews (1975)
    Terence Des Pres, The Survivor (1976)
    Alexander Donat, The Holocaust Kingdom (1965)
    Alfred Rosenberg, Race and Race History (1970)

Students need not purchase the following book, but as the best general study of
the destruction process it will be very useful for reference purposes:

    Raul Hilberg, The Destruction of the European Jews (1967)

The following surveys or documentary collections should also be helpful for most
themes raised in the course:

    Uwe Dietrich Adam, Judenpolitik im Dritten Reich (1972)
    *Lucy Davidowicz, ed., A Holocaust Reader (1976)
    *Raul Hilberg, ed., Documents of Destruction (1971)
    *Nora Levin, The Holocaust (1973)
    *Leon Poliakov, Harvest of Hate

116   ...2

FIRST TERM: THE PROCESS OF DESTRUCTION

Week   Lecture topic and Tutorial Readings

September 9   INTRODUCTION: THE HOLOCAUST AS HISTORY

September 16   ANTECEDENTS I: THE JEWS AND MODERN EUROPEANS

                    *Hannah Arendt, The Origins of Totalitarianism (1958) Part I
                    *Norman Cohn, Warrant for Genocide (1969)
                     Helen Fein, Accounting for Genocide (1979) pp. 3-18
                    *George L. Mosse, Toward the Final Solution (1978)
                    *Leon Poliakov, The Aryan Myth (1976)

September 23   ANTECEDENTS II: THE JEWS AND THE GERMANS

                    *Lucy Dawidowicz, The War Against the Jews (1975), Ch. 2

                Supplementary:

                     Sydney M. Bolkosky, The Distorted Image: German-Jewish
                         Perceptions of Germans and Germany (1975)
                    *George L. Mosse, Germans and Jews (1970)
                    _____, The Crisis of German Ideology (1964)
                     Werner E. Mosse, ed., Entscheidungsjahr 1932 (1966)
                     Uriel Tal, Christians and Jews in Germany (1975)

September 30   THE JEWS AND THE NAZIS

                    *Lucy Dawidowicz, The War Against the Jews (1975), Ch. 1
                    *Alfred Rosenberg, Race and Race History (1970), omitting
                         Ch. 3.

                Supplementary:

                     Eberhard Jäckel, Hitler's Weltanschauung (1972)
                     Peter H. Merkl, Political Violence under the Swastika (1975)
                    *George L. Mosse, Toward the Final Solution (1978),
                         Chs. 11-12

                                                          ...3

October 7   PERSECUTION OF THE JEWS IN GERMANY, 1933-41

                    *Lucy Dawidowicz, The War Against the Jews (1975),
                        Chs. 3, 5, 9.

                Supplementary:

                    Hannah Arendt, Eichmann in Jerusalem (1963) Ch. 5
                    Helmut Genschel, Die Verdrängung der Juden aus der
                        Wirtschaft im Dritten Reich (1966)
                    *Raul Hilberg, The Destruction of the European Jews
                        (1961), Chs. V, VI part 1
                    *Helmut Krausnick and Martin Broszat, Anatomy of the
                        SS State (1968), pp. 39-76
                    Karl A. Schleunes, The Twisted Road to Auschwitz, 1933-
                        1939 (1970

October 14   EVOLUTION OF THE FINAL SOLUTION

                    *Lucy Dawidowicz, The War Against the Jews (1975),
                        Chs. 6, 7, 8
                Supplementary:

                    *Hannah Arendt, Eichmann in Jerusalem (1963), Chs. 6, 7
                    Martin Broszat, "Hitler und die Genesis der 'Endlosung':
                        aus Anlass der Thesen von David Irving," Vierteljahrsheft
                        für Zeitgeschichte, 25 (1977), 739-75.
                    Christopher R. Browning, The Final Solution and the German
                        Foreign Office (1978), Ch. 5
                    Norman Rich, Hitler's War Aims, Vol. II, The Establishment
                        of the New Order (1974), Ch. 1

October 21   THE MACHINERY OF DESTRUCTION: PARTY, SS, BUREAUCRACY

                    *Lucy Dawidowicz, The War Against the Jews (1975), Ch. 4

                Supplementary:

                    *Hannah Arendt, Eichmann in Jerusalem (1963), Chs. 3,8.
                    Christopher Browning, The Final Solution and the German
                        Foreign Office (1978), Chs. 2, 3, 9.
                    *Raul Hilberg, The Destruction of the European Jews (1961)
                        Chs. 3, 7.
                    Edward N. Peterson, The Limits of Hitler's Power (1969)

                            118

...4

October 21   *Norman Rich, Hitler's War Aims, Vol. I, Ideology,
(cont'd.)   the Nazi State, and the Course of Expansion
                    (1973), Part I.

October 28   GHETTOIZATION IN THE EAST: I: CONCENTRATION

                    *Alexander Donat, The Holocaust Kingdom (1963), Chs. 1, 2.

                 Supplementary:

                    *Abraham I. Katsh, ed., The Warsaw Diary of Chaim
                        A. Kaplan (1973)
                    Yitzhak Katznelson, Vitel Diary (1972)
                    Emanuel Ringelblum, Polish-Jewish Relations (1976)
                    *_____, Notes from the Warsaw Ghetto (1974)
                    Isaiah Trunk Judenrat (1972)
                    Leonard Tushnet, The Pavement of Hell (1972)

November 4   GHETTOIZATION IN THE EAST II: DEPORTATION

                    *Lucy Dawidowicz, The War Against the Jews (1975),
                        Chs. 10, 11, 14, 16

                 Supplementary:

                    same as previous week

November 11   THE DEATH CAMPS I: STRUCTURE

                    *Lucy Dawidowicz, The War Against the Jews (1975), Ch. 7
                    *Alexander Donat, The Holocaust Kingdom (1965), pp. 241-71

                 Supplementary:

                    *Martin Broszat and Helmut Krausnik, Anatomy of the SS
                        State (1968)
                    *Alexander Donat, ed., The Death Camp Treblinka (1979)
                    *Raul Hilberg, The Destruction of the European Jews
                        (1961), Ch. IX

November 11   Eugen Kogon, <u>The Theory and Practice of Hell</u>
(cont'd.)   *Primo Levi, <u>Survival in Auschwitz</u> (1962)
                 Anna Pawelczynska, <u>Values and Violence in Auschwitz</u> (1979)
                 *Gita Sereny, <u>Into that Darkness</u> (1976)
                 Jean-Francois Steiner, <u>Treblinka</u> (1967)

November 18   THE DEATH CAMPS II: PATHOLOGY

                 *Terrence Des Pres, <u>The Survivor</u> (1976)

                 Supplementary (in addition to works of previous week):

                 *Bruno Bettelheim, <u>The Informed Heart</u> (1960)

November 25   JEWISH RESISTANCE IN EASTERN EUROPE

                 *Alexander Donat, <u>The Holocaust Kingdom</u> (1965), Ch. 3
                 *Lucy Dawidowicz, <u>The War Against the Jews</u> (1975),
                     Chs. 12, 13, 15.

                 Supplementary:

                 *Reuben Ainsztein, <u>The Warsaw Ghetto Revolt</u> (1979)
                 _____, <u>Jewish Resistance in Nazi-Occupied</u>
                     <u>Eastern Europe</u> (1974)
                 *Yehuda Bauer, <u>They Chose Life</u> (1973)
                 _____, <u>The Jewish Emergence from Powerlessness</u>
                     (1979), pp. 26-40.
                 Michel Borowicz, <u>L'Insurrection du ghetto de Varsovie</u>
                     (1966)
                 *Yuri Suhn, <u>They Fought Back</u> (1975)
                 Isaiah Trunk, <u>Judenrat</u> (1972), Chs. 16, 17
                 Yad Vashem Institute, <u>Jewish Resistance During the Holocaust</u>
                     (1971)

December 2   COUNTING THE VICTIMS: A BALANCE SHEET

...6

120

SECOND TERM: THE WORLD OUTSIDE

January 6   WHO KNEW WHAT? WHEN? HOW?

Walter Laqueur,"Jewish Denial and the Holocaust,"
Commentary, December 1979, 44-55
_____, "Hitler's Holocaust: Who Knew What,
When & How?" Encounter, July 1980, 6-25

Supplementary:

John S. Conway, "Frühe Augenzeugenberichte aus Auschwitz:
Glaubwürdigkeit und Wirkungsgeschichte,"
Vierteljahrshefte für Zeitgeschichte, 27 (1979),
260-84

Alex Grobman, "What Did They Know? The American Jewish
Press and the Holocaust, " American Jewish History,
LXVIII (1979), 353-66.

January 13   ITALY: THE HALF-HEARTED ALLY

Gene Bernardini, "The Origins and Development of Racial
Antisemitism in Fascist Italy," Journal of Modern
History, 49 (1977), 431-53
Renzo De Felice, Storia degli ebrei italiani sotto il
fascismo (1961)
Michael Ledeen, "The Evolution of Italian Fascist Anti-
semitism," Jewish Social Studies, XXXVII (1975), 3-17
Meir Michaelis, Mussolini and the Jews (1978)
Leon Poliakov and Jacques Sabille, Jews Under Italian
Occupation (1954)

January 20   SATELLITES I: HUNGARY AND RUMANIA

Randolph L. Braham, The Hungarian Labor Service System (1977)
_____, The Destruction of Hugarian Jewry,
2 vols. (1963)
_____, "The Jewish Question in German-Hungarian
Relations during the Kallay Era," Jewish Social
Studies, XXXIX (1977), 183-208.
Christopher Browning, The Final Solution and the German
Foreign Office (1978)
Raul Hilberg, The Destruction of the European Jews (1961)
Nicholas Nagy-Talavera, The Green Shirts and the Others
(1970)
Bela Vago and George L. Mosse, eds., Jews and Non-Jews in
Eastern Europe (1974)

January 27   SATELLITES II: VICHY FRANCE

        Joseph Billig, Le Commissariat general aux questions
            Juives, 3 vols. (1955-60)
        Claude Levy and Paul Tillard, Betrayal at the Vel d'Hiv
            (1967)
        *Raul Hilberg, The Destruction of the European Jews
            (1961), pp. 389-21
        *Robert O. Paxton, Vichy France (1972)
        Zosa Szajkowski, Analytical Franco-Jewish Gazetteer (1966)

February 3   OCCUPIED STATES: HOLLAND, DENMARK

        Helen Fein, Accounting for Genocide (1979), pp.
            144-52, Ch. 10
        *Raul Hilberg, The Destruction of the European Jews(1961)
        Jacob Presser, The Destruction of the Dutch Jews (1969)
        Leni Yahil, The Rescue of Danish Jewry (1969)

February 10   THE ALLIES: BRITAIN, AMERICA AND THE REFUGEES

        Henry Feingold, The Politics of Rescue (1970)
        Saul S. Friedman, No Haven for the Oppressed (1973)
        *Arthur D. Morse, While Six Million Died (1968)
        A.J. Sherman, Island Refuge (1973)
        Bernard Wasserstein, Britain and the Jews of Europe (1979)
        David S. Wyman, Paper Walls: America and the Refugee
            Crisis (1968)

February 17   READING WEEK

February 24   THE CHURCHES AND THE HOLOCAUST

        Owen Chadwick, "Weizsäcker, the Vatican, and the
            Jews of Rome," Journal of Ecclesiastical History,
            28 (1977), 179-99
        Helen Fein, Accounting for Genocide (1979), Ch. 4
        *Gunther Lewy, The Catholic Church and Nazi Germany
            (1964), Ch. 10
        John F. Morley, Vatican Diplomacy and the Jews during
            the Holocaust (1980)

...8

March 3   THE POLITICS OF RESCUE I: BARGAINING WITH THE NAZIS

> *Yehuda Bauer, The Jewish Emergence from Powerlessness
> (1979), 7-25
> _____, The Holocaust in Historical Perspective
> (1978), Ch. 4
> *Andre Biss, A Million Jews to Save (1973)
> Yisrael Gutman and Efraim Zuroff eds., Rescue Attempts
> during the Holocaust (1977)
> *Raul Hilberg, The Destruction of the Europen Jews
> (1961), pp. 715-29

March 10   THE POLITICS OF RESCUE II: MILITARY PROPOSALS

> Dino A. Brugioni and Robert G. Poirer, "The Holocaust
> Revisited," (U.S. Central Intelligence Agency
> Report, 1979)
> Bernard Wasserstein, Britain and the Jews of Europe
> (1979), Ch. 7
> David S. Wyman, "Why Auschwitz was never Bombed,"
> Commentary, 65 (May 1978), 37-46

March 17   1945-48: DEALING WITH THE SURVIVORS

> *Alexander Donat, The Holocaust Kingdom (1965),
> pp. 271-96
> Yehuda Bauer, Flight and Rescue: Brichah (1970)
> *Raul Hilberg, The Destruction of the European Jews pp.729-38
> Malcolm J. Proudfoot, European Refugees (1956), Chs. 10, 11
> Marcus Smith, The Harrowing of Hell (1972)

March 24   WAR CRIMES: JUDGEMENT AT NUREMBERG

> Joseph Borkin, The Crime and Punishment of I.G. Farben
> (1979)
> *Raul Hilberg, The Destruction of the European Jews
> (1961), pp. 684-704
> Werner Maser, Nuremberg: A Nation on Trial (1979)
> Léon Poliakov, Le Procès de Nuremberg (1971)
> Bradley Smith, Reaching Judgement at Nuremberg (1977)

PROGRAM IN SCIENCE IN HUMAN AFFAIRS

SHA 294: Disease and Doctors in the Modern West

Fall 1981   Professor Geison

Organization: Papers, Examinations, Grades

This course follows the standard format of two lectures and one precept each
week. There will be a final examination, but no midterm. In lieu of a mid-
term, each student will write an essay on a topic that falls within the pur-
view of the course. This essay, 15-25 double-spaced typed pages in length,
is due Friday, December 11th. Further instructions on the essay will be
distributed later. There will be no class meetings or additional assignments
during the reading period.

The final grade will be determined roughly as follows: final exam (40%),
essay (40%), precept (20%).

Readings

All readings below are required and, for the sake of precept discussion,
should be done in advance of the associated precept meetings. I will be
glad to suggest additional sources in connection with the required essay
and for those who may have special interest in particular topics.

The following works, which form part of the weekly reading assignments, are
required for purchase:

1.   Source Book of Medical History, compiled with notes by Logan Clendenning
     (Dover paperback, 1942).

2.   William H. McNeill, Plagues and Peoples (Doubleday paperback, 1976).

3.   Richard H. Shryock, The Development of Modern Medicine (Wisconsin
     paperback, 1979).

4.   Thomas McKeown, The Role of Medicine: Dream, Mirage, or Nemesis?
     (Princeton paperback, 1979).

LECTURE TOPICS AND READINGS BY WEEK

I.   Health, Doctors, and the History of Medicine

     Owsei Temkin, "The Meaning of Medicine in Historical Perspective,"
        in The Double Face of Janus and Other Essays in the History of
        Medicine (Baltimore, 1977), pp. 41-49.   R131.T4

     Owsei Temkin, "Health and Disease," in The Double Face of Janus,
        pp. 419-440.   R131.T4

     McNeill, Plagues and Peoples, Chapters 1 and 2 (pp. 15-76).

II. **The Medical World of Antiquity and the Middle Ages**

McNeill, Plagues and Peoples, Chapter 3 (pp. 77-148).

Henry Sigerist, The Great Doctors, Chapters 2, 8-9. 8954.857.4

Clendenning, Source Book of Medical History, pp. 1-94 (skim).

III. **The Renaissance Upheaval in Medical Thought and Practice**

McNeill, Plagues and Peoples, Chapters 4 and 5 (pp. 149-234).

Sigerist, Great Doctors, Chapters 12-15.

Clendenning, Source Book of Medical History, pp. 95-141.

IV. **Medicine and the Scientific Revolution of the 17th Century**

E.H. Ackerknecht, A Short History of Medicine, pp. 113-129. R131.A18.1968

Clendenning, Source Book of Medical History, pp. 142-169, 221-237.

Keith Thomas, Religion and the Decline of Magic (Charles Scribners'
paperback, 1971), pp. 3-21, 177-211. 5511.902

Alfred White Franklin, "Clinical Medicine," in Medicine in Seventeenth Century England, ed. A.G. Debus (UCLA, 1974), pp. 113-145.
R486.M43

V. **The Transition to Modernity: Health, Medicine, and Mortality in
the 18th Century**

Shryock, Development of Modern Medicine, pp. 57-108.

Clendenning, Source Book of Medical History, pp. 194-208, 204-253,
291-305, 441-468.

VI. **Life and Death in the 19th Century: Disease Patterns, Public Health,
and Vital Statistics, 1800-1880**

McNeill, Plagues and Peoples, Chapter 6 (pp. 235-291).

Shryock, Development of Modern Medicine, Chapter 12 (pp. 211-247).

Edwin Chadwick, Report on the Sanitary Condition of the Labouring
Population of Great Britain (1842), ed. M.W. Flinn, pp. 18-26,
58-66, 75-79, 421-425. 89417.406.17.2

Robert Tomes, "Why We Get Sick (1856)," in Medical America in the
Nineteenth Century: Readings from the Literature, ed. G.H. Brieger
(Baltimore, 1972), pp. 256-262. R151.B75

VII. From Urine Flasks to Stethoscopes: Hospitals, Instruments, and the
Social Role of Healers, 1800-1880

Shryock, Development of Modern Medicine, Chapter 9 (pp. 151-169).

Stanley Reiser, Medicine and the Reign of Technology, (London, 1978),
pp. 23-44.   R145.R44

Clendenning, Source Book of Medical History, pp. 306-330, 502-509,
530-539, 572-587.

VIII. Quackery, Sects and Science, or Varieties of Response to Therapeutic
Uncertainty: Medical Thought and Practice, 1800-1880

Shryock, Development of Modern Medicine, Chapter 13 (pp. 248-272).

Elisha Bartlett, "An Inquiry into the Degree of Certainty in Medicine;
and into the Nature and Extent of Its Power Over Disease (1848),"
in Medical America in the Nineteenth Century, ed. G.H. Brieger,
pp. 98-106.   R151.B75

Edwin L. Godkin, "Orthopathy and Heteropathy (1867)," in ibid., pp.
75-83.   R151.B75

Rudolf Virchow, "Scientific Medicine and Therapeutic Standpoints
(1849)," in Disease, Life and Man, pp. 40-66.   8957.938

Claude Bernard, Introduction to the Study of Experimental Medicine
(1865), pp. 190-226.   8957.171

IX. From Infectious to Chronic Diseases: Disease Patterns and Vital
Statistics since 1880

McKeown, The Role of Medicine, Chapters 3-6 (pp. 29-78) and 8 (pp.
91-116).

Judith W. Leavitt and Ronald L. Numbers, "Sickness and Health in
America: An Overview," in Sickness and Health in America: Readings
in the History of Medicine and Public Health (Wisconsin, 1978), pp.
3-10.

Shryock, Development of Modern Medicine, Chapter 15 (pp. 304-335).

X. Specialization, Professionalization and Medical Education in the
Brave New Medical World: The Organization and Social Role of
Healers since 1880

Shryock, Development of Modern Medicine, Chapters 16 (pp. 336-355)
and 18-19 (pp. 381-430).

Clendenning, Source Book of Medical History, pp. 634-675.

Robert Hudson, "Abraham Flexner in Perspective: American Medical

Education, 1865-1910," Bulletin of the History of Medicine, 46
(1972), 545-561.

Abraham Flexner, Medical Education in the United States and Canada
(1910), pp. 3-51, 156-166, 178-181.   8957.351.3

XI. The Bacteriological Revolution and the Drama of Specific Cures:
Medical Thought and Practice since 1880

Shryock, Development of Modern Medicine, pp. 273-303.

Clendenning, Source Book of Medical History, pp. 378-406, 603-621.

Hubert A. Lechevalier and Morris Solotorovsky, Three Centuries of
Microbiology (Dover paperback, 1974), pp. 210-259, 437-492.   8954.998

Leo Zimmerman and Ilza Veith, Great Ideas in the History of Surgery
(Dover paperback, 1967), pp. 461-518.   QR21. L4.1974

XII. The Current Debate: Shifting Attitudes toward Health, Disease and
Medicine

Shryock, The Development of Modern Medicine, pp. 432-457.

McKeown, The Role of Medicine, skim previously unassigned chapters.

Reiser, Medicine and the Reign of Technology, pp. 158-195.   R145.R44

Walsh McDermott et al., "Health Care Experiment at Many Farms,"
Science 175 (1972), 23-31.   8001.863

Nick Eberstadt, "The Health Crisis in the USSR," New York Review of
Books, February 19, 1981, pp. 23-31.

Highly recommended -- and not only because of its wonderfully apt
title -- is Doing Better and Feeling Worse: Health in the United
States, ed. John Knowles, Winter 1977 issue of Daedalus.

Also highly recommended is Susan Sontag, Illness as Metaphor.

History 284   Winter,   1980-1981

SICKNESS AND HEALTH IN SOCIETY: 1492 TO THE PRESENT

Martin S. Pernick

Scope of the Course: Doctors, Disease, and Society

Medical history includes more than the history of doctors and their discoveries. In addition, it includes the history of sickness and health. From devastating epidemics of cholera and yellow fever to the quiet suffering of malnutrition, diseases have deeply marked the evolution of society. In turn, social changes haved dramatically altered the patterns of illness and health.

This course will study four different historical periods, exploring such issues as: the effect of medical discoveries, personal lifestyles, and environmental conditions on human health; the health problems of specific social groups including Indians, women, blacks, children, immigrants, industrial workers, and the poor; the roles of ethics, economics, and politics in medical decisionmaking; the changing meanings of terms like "health," "disease," "cause," and "cure,"; the dissemination and impact of medical innovations; and the changing structure of the medical professions.

The specific examples in the readings will be drawn from US and British history primarily. Each lecture will include comparisons between the English speaking world and other Western nations or Third World countries, as appropriate. This course is open to all undergraduates and assumes no previous knowledge of history or medicine. Lectures are Mondays and Wednesdays, 7-8:30 pm.

128

TOPIC I   DISEASE, TRADE, AND CONQUEST: THE OLD WORLD AND THE NEW

Read for 1/14

        "Childhood" Diseases and the European Conquest of the Americas

Alfred W. Crosby, The Columbian Exchange: Biological and Cultural Consequences
     of 1492 (1972) 35-62.

James P. Ronda, "'We Are Well as We Are': An Indian Critique of 17th-Century
     Christian Missions," William and Mary Quarterly (January 1977) 66-82.

Read for 1/19

                  Part I -- Syphilis: An American Disease in Europe?

Alfred W. Crosby, The Columbian Exchange 122-60.

              Part II -- After 1492: The Continuing Destruction

Sherburne F. Cook, "The Significance of Disease in the Extinction of the New
     England Indians," Human Biology (1973) 485-508.

Virginia R. Allen, "The White Man's Road: Physical and Psychological Impact of
     Relocation on the Southern Plains Indians," Journal of the History of Medicine
     and Allied Sciences (April 1975) 148-163.

              Part III -- The "Lessons" of Medical History: The Fallacy
                          of Biodeterminism

P.M. Ashburn, The Ranks of Death (1937) epilogue.

Read for 1/21

                  Part I -- Death in the Colonies:
              "Our" Perceptions Versus "Their" Perceptions

Anne Bradstreet, Works, ed. by J. Hensley, (orig. 1660s), 235- 42.

Maris Vinovskis, "Angels' Heads and Weeping Willows: Death in Early America," in
     The American Family in Social-Historical Perspective, ed. by Michael Gordon
     (2nd ed, 1978) 546-63.

                  Part II -- Smallpox Inoculation:
              Medicine, Religion, and Communal Responsibility

John B. Blake, "The Inoculation Controversy in Boston 1721-1722," (1952) in Leavitt
     and Numbers, Sickness and Health in America 231-39.

Perry Miller, "The Judgment of the Smallpox," in The New England Mind From Colony
     to Province (1953) 345-66.

TOPIC II   HEALTH AND SOCIETY 1790-1880

Read for 1/26

                The Political Meaning of Health in the Enlightenment

George Rosen, "Political Order and Human Health in Jeffersonian Thought,"
    Bulletin of the History of Medicine (1952) 32-44.

Richard H. Shryock, Medicine and Society in America (1960) chap III.

Martin S. Pernick, "Politics, Parties, and Pestilence: Epidemic Yellow Fever in
    Philadelphia and the Rise of the First Party System," in Leavitt and Numbers,
    Sickness and Health in America 241-56.

    1/28   QUIZ #1

Read for 1/28, 2/2, and 2/4

                    Cholera and Social Medicine

Charles Rosenberg, The Cholera Years (1962) chaps 1-6, 8-11.

Martin S. Pernick, "Cholera, Public Health, and the Reform Movements of Pre-Civil
    War America," typescript.

Read for 2/2 (continued)

            Preventing Disease: A Personal or a Public Responsibility?
            Conflicting 19th Century Views on the Cause of Sickness

Lemuel Shattuck, Report of the Sanitary Commission of Massachusetts (1850)
    pp. 200-212, 266-72.

J. B. F. Walker, M.D., "Is It Wicked to be Sick?" The Water-Cure Journal
    (September, 1861).

Read for 2/4 (continued)

            Curing Disease: From Heroic to Environmental Therapies

Leon S. Bryan, Jr. "Blood-Letting in American Medicine, 1830-1892," Bulletin
    of the History of Medicine (1964) 516-29.

Charles Rosenberg, "The Therapeutic Revolution," in Vogel and Rosenberg,
    The Therapeutic Revolution (1980)

Charles Rosenberg, "Florence Nightingale on Contagion: The Hospital as Moral
    Universe" in Healing and History (1979) 116-36.

TOPIC II (continued)

<u>Read for 2/9</u>

Part I -- Environmental Therapy and Insanity

Gerald Grob, <u>Mental Institutions in America</u> (1973) 4-12, 174-256.

Christopher Lasch, "Origins of the Asylum," in <u>The World of Nations</u> (1974) 3-17.

Part II -- What is a Disease?

H. Tristram Engelhardt, "The Disease of Masturbation: Values and the Concept of Disease," in Leavitt and Numbers, <u>Sickness and Health</u> 15-24.

Barbara Sicherman, "The Uses of a Diagnosis: Doctors, Patients, and Neurasthenia," in Leavitt and Numbers, <u>Sickness and Health</u>, 25-38.

<u>Read for 2/11</u>

Women as Patients/Women as Doctors

Charles Rosenberg and Carroll Smith Rosenberg, "The Female Animal: Medical and Biological Views of Women," in <u>No Other Gods</u> (1973) 54-70.

"Female Physicians," <u>Philadelphia Bulletin</u> (1859) typescript copy.

Regina Markell-Morantz, "The Connecting Link: The Case for the Woman Doctor in 19th-Century America," in Leavitt and Numbers, <u>Sickness and Health</u> 117-27.

Martin S. Pernick, "Sex and Pain in 19th Century Medicine," typescript selections from <u>A Calculus of Suffering: Pain, Professionalism, and Anesthesia in 19th Century American Medicine</u>, forthcoming (1982).

<u>Read for 2/16</u>

Race, Economics, and Yellow Fever in the South:
Part I -- Antebellum

Jo Ann Carrigan, "Privilege, Prejudice, and the 'Stranger's Disease' in 19th Century New Orleans," <u>Journal of Southern History</u> (1970) 568-78.

Part II -- The "New South"

Gerald M. Capers, "Yellow Fever in Memphis in the 1870s," <u>Mississippi Valley Historical Review</u> (1938).

2/18 MIDTERM EXAM

TOPIC III   HEALTH AND SOCIETY IN THE GOLDEN AGE OF BACTERIOLOGY 1880-1920

Read for 3/2 and 3/4

From Big Truths to Littler Truths:
Germs and the Specific Cause of Infection

Paul de Kruif, Microbe Hunters (1926) chaps 3-6.

Charles V. Chapin, "Dirt, Disease, and the Health Officer," (1902)

James H. Cassedy, "The Flamboyant Colonel Waring: An Anticontagionist in the
Age of Pasteur and Koch," in Leavitt and Numbers, Sickness and Health 305-12.

Charles Rosenberg, "Florence Nightingale on Contagion," review from Topic II (2/4)

Read for 3/9

Specific Etiology, Laboratory Science, and the New
Medical Education

Abraham Flexner, Report on Medical Education (1910) 43-59, 143-55, 178-81.

Robert Hudson, "Abraham Flexner in Perspective," in Leavitt and Numbers,
Sickness and Health, 105-116.

Gerald Markowitz and David Rosner, "Doctors in Crisis: Medical Education and
Medical Reform During the Progressive Era 1895-1915," in Reverby and Rosner,
Health Care in America, 185-205.

Richard Shryock, "Nursing Emerges as a Profession," in Leavitt and Numbers,
Sickness and Health 203-16.

Read for 3/11

The "New Immigration" and the "New Public Health"

"Americanization by Bath," The Literary Digest (August 1913) 280-81.

"The White Man's Burden," and "What Mississippi Has Done," Journal of the Outdoor
Life (1910) 274-75; (1914) 28.

"European Immigration by Country, Selected Years," typescript

Judith Walzer Leavitt, "Politics and Public Health: Smallpox in Milwaukee 1894-95,"
in Leavitt and Numbers, Sickness and Health 403-14.

TOPIC III (continued)

Read for 3/16

Health in the Factory / Factory Methods in Health

Livingston Farrand, "Health and Productive Power," National Conference on Charities and Corrections (1913).

"Consumptives Cost the Rest of Us $500,000,000 a Year," American City (1912) 26-27.

"Standardization of Health Conservation," Journal of the Outdoor Life (1910) 119.

"Child Health and the Laboratory," Charities (1903) 3.

John R. Shillady, "Cooperation of Tuberculosis Agencies with Labor Unions and Factories," Journal of the Outdoor Life (1913) 228-31.

Read for 3/18

Part I -- Health Education and Persuasion

"The Awakening of Ivan Meyervitz," Fresh Air Magazine (1910) 12-13.

William White, "The Secret of Proper Tuberculosis Education," Journal of the Outdoor Life (1910) 41.

Martin S. Pernick, "The Ethics of Preventive Medicine--Thomas Edison's Tuberculosis Films: Mass Media and Health Propaganda," Hastings Center Report (June 1978) 21-27.

Richard Shryock, "The Historical Significance of the Tuberculosis Movement," in Medicine in America (1966) 31-48.

Part II -- Health Legislation and Force

Daniel Fox, "Social Policy and City Politics: Tuberculosis Reporting in New York, 1889-1900," in Leavitt and Numbers, Sickness and Health 415-32.

Jacobson v. Massachusetts 197 US 11, (1905).

Read for 3/23

Part I -- Medicine and Sex: VD, Psychology

John C. Burnham, "The Progressive Era Revolution in American Attitudes Towards Sex," Journal of American History (1973) 885-908.

F. Cauthorn, "Some Thoughts Suggested by the Campaign Against Venereal Diseases," Medical Record (NY) (1921) 23-24.

Carl Scheffel, "Venereal Diseases: Educational Vs. Sanitary and Legal Methods to Suppress," Modern Medicine (Chicago) (1921) 248-49.

Required Viewing: The End of the Road (1919). videocassette on reserve

TOPIC III (Continued)

Read for 3/23 (continued)

Part II -- Professionalism and Motherhood

Frances Kobrin, "The American Midwife Controversy," in Leavitt and Numbers, Sickness and Health 217-25.

Sarah Comstock, "Mothercraft: A New Profession for Women," Good Housekeeping (1914) typescript selections.

Read for 3/25

The Specificity of Medical Science and the Rise of Life Expectancy: Is There a Connection?

Paul de Kruif, Microbe Hunters (1926) chap 12

Rene Dubos, Mirage of Health (1959) 101-10, 151-65.

"Sickness and Health in America: An Overview," in Leavitt and Numbers, Sickness and Health, 3-10.

Daphne Roe, "The Sharecroppers' Plague," Natural History (1974).

   3/30 QUIZ # 2

Read for 3/30

The End of the Golden Age: Flu, Fear, and Force

Stuart Galishoff, "Newark and the Great Influenza Pandemic of 1918" Bulletin of the History of Medicine (1969) 246-58.

The New York Times, selections from October, 1918, typescript.

Alfred W. Crosby, Epidemic and Peace 1918 (1976), 22-24, 203-207 and passim.

Read for 4/2

Health in Hard Times: Polio and Priorities
Part I -- Priority Decisions Among Social Problems

Walter C. Clarke, "Health Protection in Hard Times," radio script broadcast
    July 22, 1933 WEVD-New York.

"Infantile Paralysis is Dangerous," Metropolitan Life Insurance Company (1920)

National Foundation-March of Dimes Fundraising Letter, January, 1945.

"The Need is for More" New York World-Telegram (1946) typescript.

"Panic or Reason in Polio?" American Journal of Public Health (1946)

"Who Gets Your Charity Dollars?" Saturday Evening Post (1954)

Leonard Kriegel, The Long Walk Home, pp 55-59.

Part II -- Priority Decisions Among Individual Patients

John R. Paul, History of Poliomyelitis, 324-34, 338-45, 308-12.

Leonard C. Hawkins, The Man in the Iron Lung, 13-15, 103-114.

Leonard Kriegel, The Long Walk Home, 19-27.

Read for 4/8

From Genetics to Genocide?? Medicine and the Holocaust

Mark Haller, Eugenics (1963) 3-7, 95-110

Philip Reilly, Genetics, Law and Social Policy (1977) 62-86, 121-48.

Lucy Dawidowicz, The War Against the Jews (1975) chap 7.

L. Alexander, "Medical Science Under Dictatorship," New England Journal of Medicine
    241 (July 14, 1949) 39-47.

Alfredo Jadresic, "Doctors and Torture, An Experience as a Prisoner," Journal
    of Medical Ethics. 6(1980) 124-27.

Symposium on the Uses of the Holocaust Analogy, Hasting Center Report
    (August, 1976), supplement, 19pp.

TOPIC IV (continued)

Read for 4/13

How Much Health is "Enough?"
Disease Eradication Versus Disease Control in Third World Health Priorities

Fred L. Soper, "Rehabilitation of the Eradication Concept in Prevention of
Communicable Disease," Public Health Reports (1965).

L. J. Bruce-Chwatt, "Malaria Eradication," Bulletin of the New York Academy
of Medicine (1969) 999-1015.

Required Viewing: The Mosquito (Walt Disney, 1945) videocassette on reserve.

Read for 4/15

Who Should Decide?:
The Federal Government Role in US Medical Decisionmaking

Stephen Strickland, Politics, Science, and Dread Disease (1972) ix-xi, 233-59.

Ronald L. Numbers, "The Third Party: Health Insurance In America," in Leavitt
and Numbers, Sickness and Health 139-53.

Read for 4/20

Who is Responsible for Health and Disease?:
The Unresolved Issues

John Knowles, "The Responsibility of the Individual," in Doing Better and Feeling
Worse, (1977).

Samuel Epstein and Joel Swartz, "Fallacies of the Lifestyle Cancer Theories,"
Nature (January 15, 1981) 127-30.

Richard F. Spark, "Legislating Against Cancer," The New Republic (June 3, 1978)
16-19

Required Viewing: Choose to Live (American Cancer Society, 1940)
Let My People Live (Urban League and National TB Association, 1944)
videocassettes on reserve.

4/27 FINAL EXAMINATION

History 123
Fall, 1983

M. A. Miller
207 E. Duke **University**
x 3575

MADNESS AND SOCIETY IN HISTORICAL PERSPECTIVE

Required Readings (available at the university book store and at the Book
    Exchange)

    Foucault, M. Madness and Civilization
    Freud, S. On the History of the Psychoanalytic Movement
    Peterson, D. (ed.) A Mad People's History of Madness
    Rosen, G. Madness in Society
    Rothman, D. Discovery of the Asylum
    Szasz, T. The Myth of Mental Illness
    Zilboorg, G. A History of Medical Psychology

Related General Works:

    Alexander, F. The History of Psychiatry
    Ellenberger, H. The Discovery of the Unconscious
    Fine, R. A History of Psychoanalysis

Documentary Collections on Psychiatric History:

    Bateson, G. (ed.) Perceval's Narrative
    Burton, R. The Anatomy of Melancholy
    Conolly, J. The Treatment of the Insane Without Mechanical Restraints
        (1856)
    Galt, J. The Treatment of Insanity (1846)
    Grob, G. (ed.) Origins of the State Mental Hospital in America
    Hunter, R. and I. Macalpine (eds.) Three Hundred Years of Psychiatry
    Jarvis, E. Insanity and Idiocy in Massachusetts (1855)
    Skultans, V. (ed.) Madness and Morals
    Szasz, T. (ed.) The Age of Madness

SYLLABUS

1. Introduction: An Overview of the History of Mental Illness

    Peter Conrad and Joseph Schneider, Deviance and Medicalization, chapter 3,
        pp. 38-72: "The Emergence of Mental Illness" (Medical Model of Madness)

    G. Mora, "Historical and Theoretical Trends in Psychiatry," Comprehensive
        Textbook of Psychiatry, 2nd edition, II, volume 1, pp. 1-75.

    E. H. Ackerknecht, A Short History of Psychiatry

2. Madness Among the Ancients

    G. Zilboorg, History of Medical Psychology, pp. 36-58: Greece, from

Hippocrates to Aristotle; pp. 58-92: Rome, through Galen

Bennett Simon, Mind and Madness in Ancient Greece

E. R. Dodd, The Greeks and the Irrational

George Rosen, Madness in Society, pp. 71-136 ("Greece and Rome")

3. Medieval and Renaissance Madness

    G. Zilboorg, pp. 93-143 (Dark Ages and Demonology); pp. 144-174 (Witch-craft)

    G. Rosen, Madness in Society, 1-18 ("Psychopathology in the Social Process"). 139-150 ("Western & Central Europe during the Late Middle Ages and the Renaissance"), 195-225 ("Psychic Epidemics")

    William Bouwsma, "Anxiety & the Formation of Early Modern Culture," B. C. Malament (ed.), After the Reformation, 215-46.

    Guido Ruggiero, "Excusable Murder: Insanity and Reason in Early Renaissance Venice," Journal of Social History (Fall 1982):109-119.

    Stanley W. Jackson, "Unusual Mental States in Medieval Europe: Medical Syndromes of Mental Disorder, 400-1100 A.D.," Journal of the History of Medicine 27 (1972):262-97.

4. Early Modern Europe: Spiritual and Secular Madness

    Zilboorg, pp. 175-244, "The First Psychiatric Revolution" (on Vives, Paracelsus, Agrippa and Weyer)

    Rosen, Madness in Society, pp. 151-94: "Irrationality and Madness in 17th and 18th Century Europe"; "Some Origins of Social Psychiatry: Social Stress and Mental Disease from the 18th Century"

    R. Neugebauer, "Medieval and Early Modern Theories of Mental Illness," Archives of General Psychiatry, 36 (April, 1979):477-83

    M. Foucault, Madness and Civilization, chapters 1-5

    D. Peterson, A Mad People's History of Madness, pp. 3-63

    Michael MacDonald, Mystical Bedlam: Madness, Anxiety and Healing in 17th Century England

    D. P. Walker, Unclean Spirits: Possession and Exorcism in France and England in the Late 16th and Early 17th Centuries

    Max Byrd, Visits to Bedlam: Madness and Literature in the 18th Century

    Richard Hunter and Ida Macalpine (eds.) Three Hundred Years of Psychiatry (documents from the 16th through the 18th centuries, pp. 1-564)

5. The Formation of Modern Psychiatry and Psychiatric Institutions

    A. General
           Zilboorg, pp. 311-341 ("Age of Reconstruction" on Pinel); pp.342-
           378 ("The Discovery of Neurosis," on Mesmer and Charcot); pp. 379-
           478 ("The Era of Systems," from Esquirol & Tuke to Kraepelin)
           Peterson, pp. 64-135
           Szasz, Age of Madness, pp. 18-126

    B. France (on Janet, Charcot and Pinel)
           Henri Ellenberger, The Discovery of the Unconscious, chapters 1-6
           Dora Weiner, "Health and Mental Health in the Thought of Philippe
           Pinel," Charles Rosenberg (ed,), Healing and History: Essays
           for George Rosen, pp. 59-85
           Jan Goldstein, "The Hysteria Diagnosis and the Politics of Anti-
           Clericalism in Late 19th Century France," Journal of Modern
           History, June 1982, pp. 209-39
           Theodore Zeldin, "Worry, Boredom and Hysteria," France, 1848-1945,
           II, 823-75

    C. England (Tuke, Maudsley et al.)
           Vida Skultans, Madness and Morals, pp. 1-28
           Ida Macalpine and Richard Hunter, George III and the Mad-Business
           (espec. Part IV, "Georgian Psychiatry," pp. 267-363)
           G. Bateson (ed.), Perceval's Narrative. A Patient's Account of his
           Psychosis, 1830-32
           R. Hunter and I. Macalpine (eds.), Three Hundred Years of Psychiatry,
           pp. 567-1084 (documents on the 19th century)

    D.. On the U.S.
           Ruth Caplan, Psychiatry & The Community in 19th Century America
           Norman Dain, Concepts of Insanity in the U.S. 1789-1865
           _____, Disordered Minds. The First Century of Eastern State
           Hospital in Williamsburg, Virginia
           Albert Deutsch, The Mentally Ill in America
           Gerald Grob, The State of the Mentally Ill: A History of Worcester
           State Hospital, 1830-1920
           _____, Mental Institutions in America: Social Policy to 1875
           _____, Edward Jarvis & the Medical World of 19th Century America
           Tod Savitt, Medicine and Slavery, ch. 8, "Insanity," pp. 247-249
           S. P. Fullinwider, Technicians of the Finite: The Rise and Decline of
           the Schizophrenic in American Thought, 1840-1960

    E. On the Soviet Union
           Joseph Wortis, Soviet Psychiatry
           A. Galachyan, "Soviet Union," A. Kiev (ed.) Psychiatry in the Com-
           munist World
           Mark Field, "Soviet Psychiatry," American Journal of Psychotherapy,
           21, 2 (April 1967):230-43
           Nancy Rollins, Child Psychiatry in the Soviet Union

6. "The Great Confinement": Revisionist Theory in Psychiatric Historiography

A. France
   M. Foucault, Madness and Civilization, chapters 6-9
   _____, Mental Illness and Psychology (espec. pp. 64-75: "The
   Historical Constitution of Mental Illness")
   G. Bleandonu and G. de Gaufey, "The Creation of the Insane Asylums
   of Auxerre and Paris," R. Forster and O. Ranum (eds.), Deviants
   & The Abandoned in French Society, 180-212
   H. C. Erick Midelfort, "Madness and Civilization in Early Modern
   Europe: A Reappraisal of Michel Foucault," B. C. Malament (ed.),
   After the Reformation, pp. 247-65

B. England
   A. Scull, Decarceration
   _____, Museums of Madness
   _____, "Madness and Segregative Control: The Rise of the Asylum,"
   Social Problems 24 (1977):337-51
   William Parry-Jones, The Trade in Lunacy: A Study of Private Madhouses
   in England in the 18th and 19th Centuries
   Vieda Skultans, English Madness. Ideas on Insanity, 1580-1890
   H. Miller, "The Abuse of Psychiatry," Encounter, May 1970, pp. 24-31

C. Ireland
   Mark Finnane, Insanity and the Insane in Post-Famine Ireland
   Nancy Scheper-Hughes, Saints, Scholars and Schizophrenics. Mental
   Illness in Rural Ireland

D. United States
   David Rothman Discovery of the Asylum; Conscience and Convenience
   Richard Fox, So Far Disordered in Mind: Insanity in California, 1870
   1930
   Ervin Goffman, Asylums
   Thomas Szasz, The Myth of Mental Illness
   _____, The Manufacture of Madness
   Gerald Grob, "Rediscovering Asylums," Morris Vogel and Charles
   Rosenberg (eds.), The Therapeutic Revolution, pp. 135-157.
   A. Scull (ed.), Madhouses Mad-Doctors and Madmen: A Social History
   of Psychiatry in the Victorian Era

7. Psychoanalysis

H. Ellenberger, Chapters 7-11

G. Zilboorg, pp. 479-525

Reuben Fine, A History of Psychoanalysis

S. Freud, Introductory Lectures in Psychoanalysis

_____, The Wolf Man. Edited by M. Gardiner

_____, On the History of the Psychoanalytic Movement

Nathan Hale, Freud and the Americans, Vol. I: The Beginnings of Psychoanalysis in the U.S., 1876-1917

_____, James Jackson Putnam and Psychoanalysis (Correspondence with
Freud)

"Historical Review of the Contribution of Psychoanalysis to Psychiatry,
pp. 10-31 in Ida Macalpine and Richard Hunter, Schizophrenia 1677
(Published in 1956 in a limited edition of only 750 copies
this book contains the translated diary of a 17th-century painter,
Christoph Haizmann, who recorded his psychotic experience of
demoniacal possession. Nine of his paintings depicting his fantasies
are also included. The book, in addition, contains Freud's analysis
of the original diary and other related psychoanalytic material.)

Some recent studies on psychoanalysis of special historical interest
include:

Bruno Bettelheim, Freud and Man's Soul (a reinterpretation of psychoanalysis
based on the argument that Freud has been inaccurately translated and
thus misunderstood in English).

A. Carotenuto. A Secret Symmetry. Sabina Spielrein between Freud and
Jung. (The story of a brilliant Russian student in analytic training
with Jung whose affair with her mentor was brought to Freud's attention. Includes Speilrein's recently discovered correspondence with
Jung and Freud.)

Russell Jacoby. Social Amnesia. (A critical examination of post-Freudian
psychoanalytic theory from Adler to Laing in which Freud is praised
for his revolutionary work.)

David Stannard. Shrinking History. On Freud and the Failure of Psychohistory. (A devastating critique of historians' efforts to apply psychoanalytic theory to historical study.)

Shelly Turkle. Psychoanalytic Politics. Freud's French Revolution. (An
analysis of the conjuncture between the 1968 upheaval in France and the
popularity of Lacan's interpretation of Freud. Includes a discussion of
the resistance to psychoanalysis in France prior to 1968.

In addition, there are recent biographies of significant psychoanalytic
theorists and practitioners, including the following:

Helen Swick Perry, Psychiatrist of America. The Life of Harry Stack
Sullivan

Celia Bertin, Marie Bonaparte (a founder of psychoanalysis in France)

Myron Sharaf, Fury on Earth. A Biography of Wilhelm Reich

8. Twentieth Century Developments

   A. The Critique from Within
       Thomas Szasz, The Myth of Mental Illness
       David Ingleby (ed.), Critical Psychiatry: The Politics of Mental
          Health
       David Cooper, Psychiatry and Anti-Psychiatry
       R. D. Laing, The Divided Self
       Peterson, pp. 136-354
       Szasz, Age of Madness, pp. 127-362

   B. Psychiatric Epidemiology
       G. Grob (ed.), Insanity and Idiocy in Massachusetts. Report of
          the Commission on Luncacy, 1855 by Edward Jarvis, 1-73
       B. Malzberg and E. S. Lee, Migration and Mental Disease (Introduc-
          tion by D. S. Thomas, 1-42)
       H. Goldhamer and A. Marshall, Psychosis and Civilization
       S. C. Plog, "Social Complexity," Plog and Edgerton, Changing
          Perspectives in Mental Illness, 285-312
       R. W. Fox, So Far Disordered in Mind: A History of Insanity in
          California, 104-134
       B. P. Dohrenwend, "Social and Cultural Influences on Psycho-
          pathology," Annual Review of Psychology 25 (1974):417-452
          _____, "Sociocultural and Social-Psychological Factors in the
          Genesis of Mental Disorders," Journal of Health and Social
          Behavior 16 (Dec. 1975):365-392
          _____, Mental Illness in America

9. Related Topics (with Selected Examples of the Literature)

   A. The History of Mental Disorders
       Ilse Veith, Hysteria. History of a Disease
       Helmut Thomas, Anorexia Nervosa
       A. Lewis, "Melancholia: A Historical Review," The State of Psy-
          chiatry, pp. 71-110
       O. Temkin, The Falling Sickness: A History of Epilepsy from the
          Greeks to the Beginnings of Modern Neurology

   B. Psychiatric Biographies
       Jean Stouse, Alice James
       Stephen Trombley, All That Summer She Was Mad. Virginia Woolf,
          Female Victim of Male medicine
       Bernard Straus, The Maladies of Marcel Proust

10. Recent Evaluations of Psychiatric Treatment and Theory

    Walter Reich, "Psychiatry's Second Coming," Psychiatry 45 (Aug. 1982):
       189-196

    Richard Restak, "Psychiatry in America," The Wilson Quarterly 7, 4
       (Autumn, 1983):95-125

STUDIES ON THE EUROPEAN RIGHT

Thursday, 4-6   M.R. Marrus

Some works on fascism and the extreme right:

*Gilbert Allardyce, ed., The Place of Fascism in European History (1971)
_____, "What Fascism Is Not: Thoughts on the Definition of
a Concept", American Historical Review, 48 (1979), 367-88, and
comments by Stanley Payne, Ernst Nolte, and Allardyce, 389-98
Hans Buchheim, Totalitarian Rule (1968)
*F.L. Carsten, The Rise of Fascism (1967)
*Alan Cassels, Fascism (1975)
*Renzo De Felice, Interpretations of Fascism (1977)
*_____, Fascism: An Informal Introduction to its Theory and
Practice (1977)
*Charles Delzell, ed., Mediterranean Fascism (1970)
*Nathanael Greene, ed., Fascism: An Anthology (1978)
*A. James Gregor, Interpretations of Fascism (1974)
Alastair Hamilton, The Appeal of Fascism (1971)
H.R. Kedward, Fascism in Western Europe (1971)
*Martin Kitchen, Fascism (1976)
*Walter Laqueur, ed., Fascism: A Reader's Guide (1976)
*Walter Laqueur and George L. Mosse, eds., International Fascism (1966)
Stein Ugelvik Larsen et al, eds., Who Were the Fascists? (1980)
*Arno Mayer, Dynamics of Counterrevolution in Europe (1971)
*George L. Mosse, ed., International Fascism (1979)
*Ernst Nolte, The Three Faces of Fascism (1966)
Stanley Payne, Fascism: Comparison and Definition (1980)
Amos Perlmutter, Modern Authoritarianism (1981)
*Nicos Poulantzas, Fascism and Dictatorship (1974)
*Hans Rogger and Eugen Weber, eds., The European Right (1965)
W. Schieder, ed., Faschismus als soziale Bewegung (1976)
*Anthony D. Smith, Nationalism in the Twentieth Century (1979)
H.-U. Thamer and Wolfgang Wipperman, Faschismus und neofaschistiche
Bewegung (1977)
*Eugen Weber, Varieties of Fascism (1964)
*John Weiss, The Fascist Tradition (1967)
Wolfgang Wippermann, Faschismustheorien (1975)
*S.J. Woolf, ed., European Fascism (1969)

*Denotes works available in paperback.

.....2

143

September 16   Introduction

September 23   The Nationalist Revival in France: Prefascism?

                    William C. Buthman, The Rise of Integral Nationalism
                         in France
                    Michael Curtis, Three Against the Third Republic (1959)
                    Paul Mazgaj, The Action Française and Revolutionary
                         Syndicalism (1979)
                    Rene Remond, The Right in France (1971)
                    David Shapiro, The Right In France (1890-1919)
                    Robert Soucy, Fascism in France: the Case of Maurice
                         Barres (1972)
                    Zeev Sternhell, La droite révolutionnaire, 1885-1914
                         (1978)
                    Eugen Weber, Action francaise (1962)
                    _____, The Nationalist Revival in France (1959)

September 30   The Rise of Fascism in Italy

                    Tobias Abse, "Syndicalism and the Origins of Italian
                         Fascism", Historical Journal, 25 (1982), 247-58
                    Paul Corner, Fascism in Ferrara (1975)
                    Renzo De Felice, Mussolini il rivoluzionario (1965)
                    _____, Mussolini il fascista (1966)
                    A. James Gregor, Young Mussolini and the Intellectual
                         Origins of Fascism (1979)
                    P. Milza and S. Bernstein, Le fascisme italien (1980)
                    *A. William Salomone, ed., Italy from the Risorgimento
                         to Fascism (1970), chs. III, IV, V
                    Domenico Settembrini, "Mussolini and the Legacy of Revo-
                         lutionary Socialism", Journal of Contemporary
                         History, 11 (March 1976), 239-68
                    Frank M. Snowden, "From Sharecropper to Proletarian: the
                         Background to Fascism in Rural Tuscany, 1880-1920",
                         in John A. Davis, ed., Gramsci and Italy's Passive
                         Revolution (1979)
                    Paolo Spriano, The Occupation of the Factories: Italy,
                         1920 (1975)
                    Edward R. Tannenbaum, The Fascist Experience (1972),
                         chs. 1, 2
                    Roberto Vivarelli, "Revolution and Reaction in Italy,
                         1918-1922", Journal of Italian History, I
                         (Autumn 1978), 235-63
                    S.J. Woolf, "Mussolini as Revolutionary", in Walter Laqueur
                         and George L. Mosse, eds., Left-Wing Intellectuals
                         Between the Wars (1966), 187-96

                                144

                                                        3

October   7   Mussolini's Fascist Regime, 1922-40

Alberto Aquarone, "Italy: the Crisis and Corporative
        Economy", Journal of Contemporary History,
        4 (1969), 37-58
Paul Corner, "Fascist Agrarian Policy and the Italian
        Economy in the Inter-War Years", in Davis, ed.,
        Gramsci and Italy's Passive Revolution
Renzo De Felice, Mussolini il fascista, Vol. II,
        L'organizzazione dello stato fascista (1968)
A. James Gregor, Italian Fascism and Developmental
        Dictatorship (1979)
Adrian Lyttelton, "Italian Fascism", in *Walter
        Laqueur, ed., Fascism: A Reader's Guide (1979)
        _____, "Fascism in Italy: the Second Wave",
        in *Walter Laqueur and George L. Mosse, eds.,
        International Fascism (1966), 75-100, and
        Roland Sarti, ed., The Ax Within (1974), 59-86,
        and George L. Mosse, ed., International Fascism
        (1979)
Piero Melograni, "The Cult of the Duce in Mussolini's
        Italy", Journal of Contemporary History, 11
        (March 1976), 221-37
P. Milza and S. Bernstein, Le fascisme italien (1980)
David Roberts, The Syndicalist Tradition and Italian
        Fascism (1979)
Giovanni Sabbatucci, "Fascist Institutions: Recent
        Problems and Interpretations", Journal of
        Italian History, 2 (Spring 1979), 75-92
Gaetano Salvemini, Under the Axe of Fascism (1971)
Roland Sarti, ed., The Ax Within (1974), passim.
        _____, "Fascist Modernization in Italy: Tradi-
        tional or Revolutionary?" American Historical
        Review, LXXV (April 1970), 1029-45
Denis Mack Smith, Mussolini (1982)
Edward R. Tannebaum, The Fascist Experience (1972),
        chs. 3, 4, 5, and passim.

October 14   The Origins of National Socialism in Germany

*William S. Allen, The Nazi Seizure of Power (1965)
Eberhard Jäckel, Hitler's Weltanschauung (1972)
Max H. Kele, Nazis and Workers: National Socialist
        Appeals to German Labor, 1919-1933 (1972)
Peter Loewenberg, "The Psychohistorical Origins of the
        Nazi Youth Cohort", American Historical Review,
        76 (1971), 1457-1502
Peter H. Merkl, Political Violence Under the Swastika
        (1975), esp. 668-716
*George L. Mosse, The Crisis of German Ideology (1964)

145

October 14   The Origins of National Socialism in Germany - cont'd

     Detief Mühlberger, "The Sociology of the NSDAP: the
       Question of Working-Class Membership", Journal
       of Contemporary History, 15 (July 1980), 493-511
     Jeremy Noakes, The Nazi Party in Lower Saxony (1971)
     Dietrich Orlow, The History of the Nazi Party, 1919-1933
       (1969)
     *Geoffrey Pridham, Hitler's Rise to Power (1973)
     Ronald Rogowski, "The Gauleiter and the Social Origins of
       Fascism", Comparative Studies in Society and
       History, 19 (1977), 399-430
     *Peter Stachura, Nazi Youth in the Weimar Republic (1975)

October 21   The Hitlerian Revolution

     Thomas Childers, "The Social Basis of the National Social-
       ist Vote," Journal of Contemporary History, 11
       (1976), 17-42
     *Gordon Craig, Germany, 1866-1945 (1978), Chs. XV, XVI
     *Theodor Eschenberg et alia, The Path to Dictatorship,
       1918-1933 (1966)
     Peter Hayes, "A Question Mark with Epaulettes? Kurt von
       Schlieicher and Weimar Politics", Journal of
       Modern History, 52 (March 1980), 35-65
     Detief Mühlberger, "The Sociology of the NSDAP: the Ques-
       tion of Working-Class Membership, Journal of
       Contemporary History, 15 (July 1980), 493-511
     *A.J. Nicholls, Weimar and the Rise of Hitler (1968)
     Dietrich Orlow, The History of the Nazi Party (1969),
       esp. ch. 7
     Nico Passchier, "The Electoral Geography of the Nazi Land-
       slide: the Need for Community Studies", in S.U.
       Larsen et alia, eds., Who Were the Fascists? (1980)
     Peter D. Stachura, "'Der Fall Strasser': Gregor Strasser,
       Hitler, and National Socialism, 1930-1932," in Peter
       D. Stachura, ed., The Shaping of the Nazi State (1978)
     Heinrich August Winkler, "German Society, Hitler, and the
       Illusion of Restoration, 1930-33," Journal of Contem-
       porary history, 11 (1976), 1-16; and also in *George
       L. Mosse, ed., International Fascism (1979), 143-60

October 28   Nazism as Regime, 1933-39

     *Karl Dietrich Bracher, The German Dictatorship (1970), ch. V
     Martin Broszat, The Hitler State (1981)
     Gordon Craig, Germany, 1866-1945 (1978), ch. XVII
     Sebastian Haffner, The Meaning of Hitler (1979)

.....5

October 28   <u>Nazism as Regime, 1933-39</u> - cont'd

         William Jannen, Jr., "National Socialists and Social Mobil-
            ity," <u>Journal of Social History</u>, 9 (1976), 339-66
         Ian Kershaw, "The Führer Image and Political Integration:
            The Popular Conception of Hitler in Bavaria during
            the Third Reich", in Gerhard Hirschfeld and Lothar
            Kettenacker, eds., <u>Der "Führerstaat": Mythos and</u>
            <u>Realität. Studien zur Struktur und Politik des</u>
            <u>Dritten Reiches</u> (Stuttgart, 1981)
            _____, <u>Der Hitler-Mythos, 1920-1945. Volksmeinung</u>
            <u>und Propaganda im Dritten Reich</u> (Stuttgart, 1981)
         Robert Koehl, "Feudal Aspects of National Socialism", in
            *Henry Ashby Turner, Ed., <u>Nazism and the Third</u>
            <u>Reich</u> (1972), 151-74
         T.W. Mason, "The Primacy of Politics -- Politics and Econo-
            mics in National Socialist Germany", in *Henry Ashby
            Turner, ed., <u>Nazism and the Third Reich</u> (1972),
            175-200
            _____, <u>Sozialpolitik im Dritten Reich</u> (1977)
         *George L. Mosse, <u>Nazism</u> (1978)
         Edward Peterson, <u>The Limits of Hitler's Power</u> (1969)
         Wolfgang Sauer, "National Socialism: Totalitarianism or
            Fascism?" <u>American Historical Review</u>, LXXIII (1967),
            404-24, also in *Henry A. Turner, ed., <u>Reappraisals</u>
            <u>of Fascism</u> (1975), 93-116
         *David Schoenbaum, <u>Hitler's Social Revolution</u> (1967)
         Fred Weinstein, <u>The Dynamics of Nazism</u> (1980)

November 4   <u>The Extreme Right in France in the 1930s</u>

         Gilbert Allardyce, "The Political Transition of Jacques
            Doriot", in *Walter Laqueur and George L. Mosse,
            eds., <u>International Fascism</u> (1966), 56-74
         Serge Bernstein, <u>Le 6 février 1934</u> (1975)
         Henri Dubief, <u>le decline de la IIIe Republique</u> (1976), Part 3
         William D. Irvine, <u>French Conservatism in Crisis</u> (1979)
         _____, "French Conservatives and the 'New Right'
            during the 1930s," <u>French Historical Studies,</u> VIII
            (Fall 1974), 534-62
         Klaus-Jürgen Müller, "French Fascism and Modernization",
            <u>Journal of Contemporary History</u>, 11 (1976), 75-107
         Antoine Prost, <u>Les Anciens Combattants</u> (1977)
         René Rémond, <u>The Right in France</u> (1971)
         Robert Soucy, "The Nature of Fascism in France", in *Walter
            Laqueur and George L. Mosse, eds., <u>International</u>
            <u>Fascism</u> (1966), 27-55, and in *Nathanael Greene, ed.,
            <u>Faxcism: An Anthology</u> (1968), 275-300

November 4   The Extreme Right in France in the 1930s - cont'd

                Robert Soucy, "French Fascist Intellectuals in the 1930s:
                      An Old New Left?" French Historical Studies, VIII
                      (Spring 1974), 445-58
                Eugen Weber, "France", in Hans Rogger and Eugen Weber,
                      eds., The European Right (1965), 71-127

November 11   The Authoritarian Right in Spain

                Shlomo Ben Ami, "The Dictatorship of Primo de Rivera: A
                      Political Assessment", Journal of Contemporary
                      History, 12 (1977), 65-84
                Raymond Carr, Spain, 1808-1939 (1966)
                            , The Spanish Tragedy (1977)
             *Gabriel Jackson, The Spanish Republic and Civil War (1965)
                Stanley Payne, Falange: A History of Spanish Fascism (1966)
                            , "Spanish Fascism in Comparative Perspec-
                      tive," in *Henry A. Turner Jr., ed., Reappraisals
                      of Fascism (1966), 174-69
                Hugh Thomas, "The Hero in the Empty Room: Jose Antonio and
                      Spanish Fascism" in *George L. Mosse, ed., Inter-
                      national Fascism (1979), 345-54, and in *Walter
                      Laqueur and George L. Mosse, eds., International
                      Fascism (1966), 174-82
                            , "Spain", in S.J. Woolf, ed., European Fascism
                      (1969), 280-301

November 18   Vichy: The Authoritarian Right in France

                Robert Aron, The Vichy Regime (1958)
                Roger Bourderon, "Was Vichy Fascist? A Tentative Approach
                      to the Question", in *John C. Cairns, ed., France:
                      Illusion, Conflict, and Regeneration (1978),
                      200-227
                Stanley Hoffman, "Collaborationism in France during the
                      Second World War", Journal of Modern History, 40
                      (1968), 375-95
                Fred Kupferman, Pierre Laval (1976)
                Michael R. Marrus and Robert O. Paxton, Vichy France and
                      the Jews (1981)
             *Robert O. Paxton, Vichy France: Old Guard and New Order
                      (1972)
                Geoffrey Warner, Pierre Laval and the Eclipse of France
                      (1969)

November 25   Hungary and Rumania: Fascism on the Periphery

> George Barany, "The Dragon's Teeth: The Roots of
>   Hungarian Fascism", in *Peter F. Sugar, ed.,
>   Native Fascism in the Successor States (1971),
>   73-81
> Randolph Braham, The Politics of Genocide: The Holocaust
>   in Hungary, 2 vols. (1981)
> Istvan Deak, "Hungary", in Hans Rogger and Eugen Weber,
>   eds., The European Right (1965), 364-407
> Miklos Lacko, "Ostmitteleuropäischer Faschismus", Viertel-
>   jahrshefte für Zeitgeschichte, 21 (1973) 39-51
>   _____, Arrow-Cross Men, National Socialists (1969)
> NicholA M. Nagy-Talavera, The Green Shirts and the Others:
>   A History of Fascism in Hungary and Rumania (1970)
> György Ranki, "The Problem of Fascism in Hungary", in *Sugar,
>   ed., Native Fascism (1971), 65-72
>   _____, "The Fascist Vote in Budapest in 1939", in
>   S.U. Larsen et alia, Who Were the Fascists? (1980)
> Henry L. Roberts, Rumania (1951)
> *Joseph Rothschild, East Central Europe Between the Wars
>   (1974)
> *Peter F. Sugar, ed., Native Fascism in the Successor States
>   (1971)
> Eugen Weber, "Rumania", in Rogger and Weber, eds., The
>   European Right, 501-76
>   _____, "The Men of the Archangel", in *George L. Mosse,
>   ed., International Fascism (1979) 317-44, and in
>   *Walter Laqueur and George L. Mosse, eds., Interna-
>   tional Fascism (1966), 101-26

December 2   Hungary and Rumania: Fascism on the Periphery - cont'd

Fall 1979   **Columbia University**   Robert O. Paxton

HISTORY G8378x: COLLOQUIUM ON FASCISM

Tuesdays, 2:10-4 p.m.

I. BACKGROUND

Sept. 11: Introduction to the course.
C. S. MAIER, "Some Recent Studies of Fascism,"
          Journ.Mod.Hist. 48:3 (Sept.1976), 506-521
F.L.CARSTEN, The Rise of Fascism (as possible)

Sept. 18: Who Joined? Patterns of Recruitment and Growth
Eugen Weber, "The Men of the Archangel," in Walter Laqueur
   & Geo.Mosse, eds., INTERNATIONAL FASCISM, pp. 101-126.
Paul CORNER, Fascism in Ferrara, Chap. 7, "The Rank and File
   of Fascism," pp. 137-169
Thomas Childers, "The Social Bases of the National Socialist
   Vote," in Walter Z. LAQUEUR, Theories of Fascism, pp. 17-42
   (also Journ. Contemp. History XI:4 (Oct.1976), 17-42)
Daniel Lerner, "The Nazi Elite," in Harold D. LASSWELL, Revo-
   lutionary Elites: Studies in Coercive Ideological Movements,
   esp. pp. 194-8, 279-300.
Rudolf HEBERLE, From Democracy to Nazism, Chap. 3, pp. 32-89.
Tim Mason, "National Socialism and the Working Class," in
   NEW GERMAN CRITIQUE, No. 11 (Spring 1977), pp. 49-93.

Sept. 25: Seizure of Power - I: At the Grass Roots
William Sheridan ALLEN, The Nazi Seizure of Power
Paul R. CORNER, Fascism in Ferrara

Oct. 2: Seizure of Power - II: At the Top
Karl Dietrich BRACHER, The German Dictatorship, pp. 168-227.
Alan BULLOCK, Hitler: A Study in Tyranny, revised ed., pp.
   145-311 (earlier pp. as possible)
Adrian LYTTELTON, The Seizure of Power: Fascism in Italy,
   1919-29, Chaps. 1-6, 10 (pp. 1-148, 237-268).

II. POLICIES AFTER POWER

Oct. 9: Relations with Traditional Elites
Party and State: K. D. BRACHER, German Dictatorship, pp. 228-247
                 Franz NEUMANN, Behemoth, pp. 37-129, 365-399
                 A. LYTTELTON, Seizure of Power, Chaps. 7-8,11,
                    (pp. 149-201, 269-307)
Officer Corps: Gordon R. CRAIG, The Politics of the Prussian
                    Army, pp. 427-503
               Giorgio Rochat, "The Fascist Militia and the Army,"
                    in Roland SARTI, ed., The Ax Within, pp. 43-56
Churches: K.D.BRACHER, German Dictatorship, pp. 379-390
          A. LYTTELTON, Seizure of Power, pp. 416-421
Industry: A. LYTTELTON, Seizure of Power, Chap. 9, pp. 202-236.
          H. A. Turner, "Big Business and the Rise of Hitler,"
             in H. A. TURNER, ed., Nazism & the Third Reich, 89-108
             (also in AHR LXXV:1 (Oct. 1969), pp. 56-70)

Oct. 16: Fascism and the Social Order
David SCHOENBAUM, Hitler's Social Revolution. Class and Status
  in Nazi Germany, Chaps. 1-2, 5-9 (pp. 1-72, 152-294)
T.W.MASON, "Labour in the Third Reich"
  in Past & Present No. 33, 1966
Cesare Vannutelli, "The Living Standard of Italian Workers, 1929-
  39," in Roland SARTI, ed., The Ax Within, pp. 139-160.

Oct. 23: Fascism and the Economy
D. S. LANDES, The Unbound Prometheus, pp. 359-419, 459-480.
John A. GARRATY, "The New Deal, National Socialism, and the
  Great Depression"
          in AHR LXXVIII:4 (Oct. 1973), pp. 907-944
T. W. Mason, "The Primacy of Politics," in Stuart Woolf, ed.,
  NATURE OF FASCISM, pp. 165-195. Also in H. A. TURNER, ed.,
  Nazism and the Third Reich, pp. 175-200.
A. AQUARONE, "Italy: The Crisis and the Corporative Economy
          in Journ.Contemp.Hist.IV:4(Oct.1969),37-58
A. LYTTELTON, Seizure of Power, Chaps. 12-13 (pp. 308-363)
Franz NEUMANN, Behemoth, pp. 221-361

Oct. 30: Fascism and War
Alan MILWARD, The German Economy at War, Chap. 1 - 2, pp. 1-53.
T. W. MASON, "Some Causes of the Second World War"
  in Past & Present No. 29, 1964
Alexander DALLIN, German Rule in Russia, Chaps. 15, 18, 30 (pp.
  305-319, 376-408, 660-678).
Klaus HILDEBRAND, The Foreign Policy of the Third Reich (background)
Denis MACK SMITH, Mussolini's Roman Empire

III. SOME INTERPRETATIONS

Nov. 6: Fascism as Response to Cultural Crisis
Fritz STERN, The Politics of Cultural Despair
Ernst NOLTE, Three Faces of Fascism, Parts I & V (pp. 3-21, 429-462)
Klaus Epstein, "A New Study of Fascism," in H. A. Turner, ed.,
  REAPPRAISALS OF FASCISM, pp. 2-23
George MOSSE, The Nationalization of the Masses (selectively)

Nov. 13: Fascism and Modernization
A. F. K. Organski, "Fascism and Modernization," in S. J. Woolf,
  ed., NATURE OF FASCISM, pp. 19-41
H. A. Turner, "Fascism and Modernization," in H.A.Turner ed.,
  REAPPRAISALS OF FASCISM, pp. 117-139
Ralf DAHRENDORF, Society and Democracy in Germany, Chap. 25, pp.402-18
Alexander GERSCHENKRON, Economic Backwardness in Historical Per-
  spective, pp. 5-30
Antonio GRAMSCI, Prison Notebooks, "Americanism & Fordism," 277-318.
Roland SARTI, "Fascism and Modernization in Italy"
  in AHR LXXV: 4 (Apr. 1970), pp. 1029-1045
Renzo DE FELICE, Fascism: An Informal Introduction to its
  Theory and Practice
Heinrich A. WINKLER, "From Social Protectionism to National
  Socialism: the German Small Business Movement in Comparative
  Perspective"   Journ. Mod. Hist. Mar.'76

Nov. 20: Fascism as Capitalist Defense
  Anton G. RABINBACH, "Towards a Marxist Theory of Fascism and
    National Socialism"   New German Critique,
    No. 3 (Fall 1974), pp. 127-153.
  Palmiro TOGLIATTI, Lectures on Fascism (selectively)   271-284, 299-335
  Nicos POULANTZAS, Fascism and Dictatorship, 11-24, 57-88, 139-167, 237-258
  Jane Caplan, "Theories of Fascism: Nicos Poulantzas as Historian"
    History Workshop No. 3 (1977)

IV. SOME COMPARISONS

Nov. 27: Fascism in Industrial and Agrarian Settings
  Barrington MOORE, Jr., Social Origins of D'ship & D'cracy, 413-483
  Henry L. ROBERTS, Rumania: Political Problems of an Agrarian
    State, pp. 3-93, 130-169, 223-241.
  Eugen Weber, "Romania," in Hans ROGGER & E. Weber, eds., The
    European Right, pp. 501-574.
  Istvan Deak, "Hungary," in Ibid., pp. 364-407.
  Arno MAYER, Politics and Diplomacy of Peacemaking, Chaps. 16,
    17, 21, 24, pp. 520-603, 716-749, 827-852.
  A.H.Oliveira-Marques, "Revolution and Counterrevolution in
    Portugal," in Manfred KOSSOK, ed., Studien über die Revolution,
    pp. 403-418.
  H. Martins, "Portugal," in S. J. WOOLF, ed., European Fascism, 302-336.

Dec. 4: Fascism and Authoritarianism
  Juan Linz, "An Authoritarian Regime: Spain," in Erik ALLARDT,
    ed., Cleavages, Ideologies, and Party Systems, pp. 291-341.
  Stanley Payne, "Spanish Fascism in Comparative Perspective,"
    in H.A.Turner, ed., REAPPRAISALS OF FASCISM, pp. 142-169.
  Andrew Whiteside, "Austria," in Hans ROGGER & E. Weber, eds.,
    The European Right, pp. 308-363.
  Ludwig Jedlicka, "The Austrian Heimwehr," in Walter Laqueur,
    ed., INTERNATIONAL FASCISM, pp. 127-144.
  Robert J. Soucy, "The Nature of Fascism in France," Ibid., pp.
    27-55.
  R.O.PAXTON, Vichy France, pp. 136-233, 330-357.

Dec. 11: An Overview
  Juan Linz, "Some Notes Toward a Comparative Study of Fascism
    in Sociological Historical Perspective," in Walter LAQUEUR,
    ed., Fascism: A Reader's Guide, pp. 3-121
  Eugen Weber, "Revolution? Counterrevolution? What Revolution?"
    in Ibid., pp. 435-467.

ASSIGNMENTS:

1. Oral presentation (10-15 minutes): each member of the colloquium will
   act as rapporteur to launch one discussion. On the basis of wider
   reading and thought, the rapporteur will set the assigned reading
   in historiographical and logical context, and identify major issues
   for discussion.

2. Paper (15 pp.). Not a research paper but a review essay embodying
   critical evaluation of the work of some student of fascism, or of
   works concerning a single issue or hypothesis. DUE Fri. Dec. 14.
   Please discuss topic with me in advance.

REVOLUTION AND FASCISM IN SPAIN, ITALY AND PORTUGAL

History 340   Mr. Payne

Description: This course examines the dramatic political and social conflict
of Spain, Italy and Portugal in modern times. No other countries present such
a broad and full gamut of radical ideologies, movements and institutional
changes since the nineteenth century. Main emphases will be on the break-
through of modern liberalism, the rise of the revolutionary left, the onset of
fascism, the Spanish Civil War, the Portuguese revolution and the contemporary
challenge of terrorism. The course will conclude with a brief analysis of the
contemporary democratic systems in all three countries and the serious conflicts that face them. Study will be to some extent topical and comparative,
analyzing all three countries in terms of similar conflicts, movements and
phases of development.

Lectures: There will be three lectures each week, about 40-45 minutes in
length, punctuated and/or followed by questions or discussion. In addition,
there will be a fourth hour of discussion section.

Exams and Assignments: There will be six- and twelve-week exams (each one
hour) and a two-hour final exam. In addition, all students must submit a
three-page essay by December 2 analyzing a major aspect of their reading.

Students registered for <u>four credits</u> must also prepare a brief research
paper or a longer essay on reading, defined by individual consultation with
the instructor no later than September 25. This will be due on December 2.

<u>Graduate students</u> should consult with the instructor about their own
requirements.

Grading: For <u>3-credit students</u>, each of the first two exams will make up 25%
of the final grade. The final will amount to 40 to 50%, and the 3-page essay
5 to 10%.

For 4-credit students, the first two exams will each make up nearly 20%
of the grade, the paper 20 to 25%, and the final nearly 40%.

Required Reading (paperbacks):

S. G. Payne, <u>A History of Spain and Portugal</u> (UW) Vol. 2
Salvatore Saladino, <u>Italy from Unification to 1919</u> (AHM)
A. J. Gregor, <u>Italian Fascism & Developmental Dictatorship</u>
Burnett Bolloten, <u>The Spanish Revolution</u> (North Carolina)
R. Carr & J. P. Fusi, <u>Spain: Dictatorship to Democracy</u> (Allen & Unwin).

Schedule of Topics:

August	Readings
31 Background	Payne, 351–414

September

2 The Liberal Revolution in Spain & Portugal	Payne, 415–52, 513–25
4 The Carlist Counterrevolution	---
9 Democratic Revolution & Two-Pary Liberalism	Payne, 453–505, 525–47
11 The Risorgimento & Unification of Italy	Saladino, 1–23
14 Oligarchic Liberalism & Trasformismo	Saladino, 24–51
16 Stagnation of Liberalism & the Colonial Problem: 1) Spain & Portugal	Payne, 508–12, 547–50
18 2) Italy	Saladino, 52–93
21 Open	
23 Origins of the Revolutionary Left in Spain and Italy	Payne, 601–03; Gregor, 3–31
25 Giolittismo & Liberal Democracy, 1902–1914	Saladino, 94–133
28 Maura's "Revolution from Above" and Liberal Reformism in Spain	Payne, 578–601
30 The Portuguese Republic, 1910–1918	Payne, 550–68

October

2 Open	
5 Six-Weeks Exam	
7 Italian Nationalism & the Great War	Saladino, 134–63; Gregor, 32–95
9 The Postwar Crises: 1) Socialist Maximalism & the Rise of Fascism in Italy	Gregor, 96–126
12 The Postwar Crises: 2) Spain, 1917–1923	Payne, 607–18
14 The Postwar Crises: 3) Portugal, 1918–1926	Payne, 568–77
16 Mussolini's Triumph	----
19 Institutionalization of the Mussolini Regime	Gregor, 127–213
21 Democratic Breakthrough & Political Breakdown: A Comparative Perspective	Payne, 618–29
23 Salazar's "New State"	Payne, 663–83
26 Fascist Italy at Mid-Passage	Gregor, 214–99
28 Open	
30 The Second Spanish Republic: Opening to the Left, 1930–33	Payne, 630–36

November

2 The Regionalist Problem in Spain	Payne, 505–08, 605–07
4 The Effort to Stabilize the Republic, 1933–36	Payne, 636–41
6 From Popular Front to Civil War	Payne, 614–46; Bolloten, 1–51
9 The Spanish Revolution	Payne, 646–57; Bolloten, 52–236
11 Franco's Victory	Payne, 657–62; Bolloten, 237–477
13 Open	

November
16 TWELVE WEEKS EXAM
18 Mussolini and Hitler   Gregor, 300-34
20 Italy and Spain in World War II   Payne, 684-87
23 The Franco Regime   Payne, 687-97; Carr-Fusi, 1-48
25 The Real Spanish Revolution   Carr-Fusi, 49-167
30 Italian Democracy and Terrorism   ----

December
2 The Portuguese Revolution, 1974-75   ----
4 Portugal from Revolution to Democracy   ----
7 The Democratization of Spain   Carr-Fusi, 168-258
9 Current Problems   ----
11 Open

Reserve Reading:

SPAIN

Carr, Raymond	Spain, 1808-1939
----	The Spanish Tragedy
----	Modern Spain
---- & J. P. Fusi	Spain: Dictatorship to Democracy
Hennessy, C. A. M.	The Federal Republic in Spain
Ullman, Joan C.	The Tragic Week
Boyd, Carolyn	Pretorianism in Liberal Spain
Meaker, Gerald	The Revolutionary Left in Spain, 1914-1923
Malefakis, Edward	Agrarian Reform and Peasant Revolution in Spain
Jackson, Gabriel	The Republic and Civil War in Spain
Thomas, Hugh	The Spanish Civil War
Bolloten, Burnett	The Spanish Revolution
Robinson, R. A. H.	The Origins of Franco's Spain
Trythall, J. W. D.	El Caudillo
Coverdale, John F.	The Political Transformation of Spain after Franco
Payne, S. G.	Falange: A History of Spanish Fascism
----	Politics and the Military in Modern Spain
----	The Spanish Revolution
----	Franco's Spain
----	Basque Nationalism
Clark, Robert	The Basques: The Franco Years and Beyond
Harrison, Joseph	An Economic History of Modern Spain

ITALY

Hostetter, R.	The Italian Socialist Movement
Clough, S. B.	Economic History of Modern Italy
Neufeld, Maurice	Italy: School for Awakening Countries
Salomone, A. W.	Italian Democracy in the Making
Thayer, John	Italy and the Great War
Seton-Watson, C.	Italy from Liberalism to Fascism
Lyttleton, Adrian	The Seizure of Power

Roberts, David	The Syndicalist Tradition and Italian Fascism
Tannenbaum, Edward	The Fascist Experience
Gregor, A. J.	The Ideology of Fascism
----	Interpretations of Fascism
----	The Fascist Persuasion in Radical Politics
----	Italian Fascism and Developmental Dictatorship
Cassels, Alan	Fascism
Payne, S. G.	Fascism: Comparison and Definition
Allum, P. A.	Italy--Republic without Government?
Blackmer, Donald and	
Sidney Tarrow	Communism in Italy and France

PORTUGAL

Marques, A. H. de Oliveira	History of Portugal, v. II
Kay, Hugh	Salazar and Modern Portugal
Wiarda, H. J.	Corporatism and Development
Robinson, Richard	Contemporary Portugal
Wheeler, Douglas	Republican Portugal
L. Graham and	
H. Makler	Contemporary Portugal
Porch, Douglas	The Portuguese Armed Forces and the Revolution
Harvey, Robert	Portugal: Birth of a Democracy
Morrison, R. J.	Portugal: Revolutionary Change in an Open Economy

PRINCETON UNIVERSITY
Department of Politics

Politics 335 - Radical Thought: Marxism

Spring 1979-80   Professor Cohen

    This is a course about Marxism as radical thought and as the
ideology of political movements. The course will examine the development of Marxist ideas and movements in various historical
and social settings.

    Note that the readings sometimes involve a choice on your
part. The literature designated as "recommended" is in no way required; it is cited for students who wish to do some additional or
secondary reading. (Titles marked with an asterisk are on reserve
for this course in Firestone Library.) For students who would like
a general, introductory book on the history of Marxism, I recommend
George Lichtheim's Marxism: An Historical and Critical Study.
Finally, the following required and alternative titles, as well as
a few copies of some recommended titles, are available for purchase
at the University Store:

        *R. Tucker (ed.), Marx-Engels Reader
        *R. Tucker (ed.), Lenin Anthology
        *G. Sorel, Reflections on Violence
        *L. Trotsky, The Revolution Betrayed
        *G. Orwell, Homage to Catalona
        *A. Koestler, Darkness at Noon
        *R. Debray, Revolution in the Revolution?
        *F. Fanon, Wretched of the Earth
        *S. Stojanovic, Between Ideals and Reality
        *L. Kolakowski, Toward a Marxist Humanism
        *H. Marcuse, One-Dimensional Man
        *E. Genovese, Political Economy of Slavery
        *E. Thompson, Making of the English Working Class
        *E. Hobsbawm, Age of Revolution
        *G. Lichtheim, Marxism
        *S. Avineri, Social and Political Thought of Karl Marx
        *C. Sigal, Going Away
        *M. Markovic, From Affluence to Praxis
        *L. Trotsky, My Life
        *S. Cohen, Bukharin and the Bolshevik Revolution
        *P. Nettl, Rosa Luxemburg
        *V. Gornick, Romance of American Communism
        *E. Bernstein, Evolutionary Socialism
        *R. Medvedev, On Socialist Democracy
        *P. Miliband, The State in Capitalist Society
        *N. Poulantzas, Political Power and Social Class

                              157

SCHEDULE OF TOPICS AND READINGS

Week I-III
Feb. 5-21

The Radicalism of Marx and Engels
Reading: *R. Tucker (ed.), The Marx-Engels Reader
(I recommend that students read the whole volume.
For those who cannot, the following minimum readings
are recommended: pp. 3-6, 12-15, 66-125, 143-200,
203-217, 294-438, 469-500, 525-548, 556-573, 577-652,
665-675, 681-717, 730-759.)

Other Recommended Writings by Marx and Engels:
The Poverty of Philosophy
The Holy Family
The Grundrisse (ed. by D. McLellan)
*Capital, Vol. I
The Class Struggles in France
Anti-Duhring
Origin of the Family, Private Property, and the State

Recommended Secondary Literature:
  *R. Tucker, Philosophy and Myth in Karl Marx
  *R. Tucker, The Marxian Revolutionary Idea
  *S. Avineri, The Social and Political Thought of
    Karl Marx
  S. Hook, From Hegel to Marx
  B. Ollman, Alienation: Marx's Conception of Man in
    Capitalist Society
  *D. McLellan, Karl Marx: His Life and Thought
  Z. Jordan, The Evolution of Dialectical Materialism
  *G. Lichtheim, Marxism
  G. Lichtheim, Origins of Socialism
  M. Buber, Paths in Utopia
  H. Lefebvre, The Sociology of Marx
  H. Marcuse, Reason and Revolution
  G. Lukacs, History and Class Consciousness
  P. Sweezy, The Theory of Capitalist Development
  E. Mandel, Marxist Economic Theory
  K. Korsch, Karl Marx

Week IV
Feb. 26-28

Social Democratic Marxism and the Rise of the Mass
Movement
Reading: *Eduard Bernstein, Evolutionary Socialism

Recommended Secondary and Related Literature:
  *P. Gay, The Dilemma of Democratic Socialism
  K. Kautsky, The Class Struggle
  C. Gneuss, "Bernstein," in Revisionism (ed. L.Labedz
  R. Michels, Political Parties

J. Joll, The Second International
*R. Tucker, Marxian Revolutionary Idea, chap. 6
R. Kindersley, The First Russian Revisionists
O. Bauer, The Austrian Revolution
C. Schorske, German Social Democracy, 1905-1917
*G. Lichtheim, Marxism, Part 5, chaps. 5-6
T. Bottomore & P. Goode (eds.), Austro-Marxism

**Week V
Mar. 4-6** Sorel's Reradicalization of Marxism
Reading: *Georges Sorel, Reflections on Violence

Recommended Secondary Literature:
I. Horowitz, Radicalism and the Revolt Against Reason
H. S. Hughes, Consciousness and Society, chaps. 4-5

**Week VI
Mar. 11-13** The Rise of Communism: Bolshevism and the Reradicalization of Marxism
Reading: Lenin, "What Is To Be Done?"; "Imperialism"; "State and Revolution"; "Two Resolutions on Party Unity"; "The Proletarian Revolution and the Renegade Kautsky"; "'Left-Wing' Communism--An Infantile Disorder"; and last writings of 1922-23--all in Tucker (ed.), The Lenin Anthology, pp. 12-114, 204-274, 311-398, 461-476, 496-502, 550-618, 703-748.

Recommended Secondary and Related Literature:

N. Bukharin, Imperialism and World Economy
*S. Cohen, Bukharin and the Bolshevik Revolution, chaps. 1-2
R. Luxemburg, The Mass Strike and the Junius Pamphlet
R. Luxemburg, The Accumulation of Capital
P. Nettl, Rosa Luxemburg
F. Venturi, Roots of Revolution
R. Luxemburg, The Russian Revolution and Leninism or Marxism
L. Haimson, Russian Marxists and the Origins of Bolshevism
I. Deutscher, Prophet Armed: Trotsky, 1879-1921
A. Meyer, Leninism
A. Ulam, The Unfinished Revolution
B. Wolfe, Three Who Made a Revolution
*R. Tucker, The Marxian Revolutionary Idea, chaps. 4-6
S. Baron, Plekhanov: The Father of Russian Marxism
L. Trotsky, Permanent Revolution
L. Trotsky, "The Lessons of October," in The Essential Trotsky

Week VII
Mar. 18-20

Bolshevik Utopianism and the Golden Era of Soviet
Marxism

No Required Reading

Optional Reading (any of the following):
  N. Bukharin and E. Preobrazhensky, The ABC of Communism
  N. Bukharin, Historical Materialism
  L. Trotsky, Terrorism and Communism
  L. Trotsky, Problems of Everyday Life and Other
    Writings
  L. Trotsky, Literature and Revolution
  N. Bukharin, Economics of the Transformation Period
  E. Preobrazhensky, The New Economics
  M. Pokrovsky, Russia in World History: Selected
    Essays
  R. Daniels (ed.), Documentary History of Communism,
    I, pp. 217-321

Recommended Secondary Literature:
  D. Joravsky, Soviet Marxism and Natural Science
  L. Graham, The Soviet Academy of Sciences and the CP
  R. Maguire, Red Virgin Soil: Soviet Literature in
    the 1920's
 *S. Cohen, Bukharin and the Bolshevik Revolution,
    chaps. 3-9
  I. Deutscher, Prophet Unarmed: Trotsky, 1921-1929
  A. Erlich, The Soviet Industrialization Debate
  B. Moore, Soviet Politics: The Dilemma of Power
  R. Daniels, Conscience of the Revolution
  M. Lewin, Lenin's Last Struggle
  S. Fitzpatrick, The Commissariat of Enlightenment
  G. Wetter, Dialectical Materialism
  R. Tucker, Stalin as Revolutionary
  F. Borkenau, World Communism

Week VIII
April 1-3

Stalinism, Fascism, and the Crisis of Marxist Analysis
Reading: *Leon Trotsky, The Revolution Betrayed

Recommended Secondary and Related Literature:
R. Tucker, Soviet Political Mind, chap. 2
I. Deutscher, Prophet Outcast: Trotsky, 1929-1940
*S. Cohen, Bukharin and the Bolshevik Revolution,
    chap. 10
M. Djilas, The New Class
J. Burnham, The Managerial Revolution
N. Krasso (ed.), Trotsky: The Great Debate Renewed
C. Rakovsky, "Bureaucracy and the Soviet State," in
    Essential Works of Socialism (ed. by I. Howe)
R. Hilferding, "State Capitalism or Totalitarian
    State Economy?" ibid.
M. Shachtman, The Bureaucratic Revolution
H. Arendt, The Origins of Totalitarianism
J. Steinberg (ed.), Verdict of Three Decades
V. Serge, Russia Twenty Years After
R. Dahrendorf, Class and Class Conflict in Industrial
    Society, Part I
J. Stalin, Mastering Bolshevism and Works, Vols.12-13
R. Daniels, Documentary History of Communism, Vol. 2
H. Marcuse, Soviet Marxism
R. Medvedev, Let History Judge: The Origins and Con-
    sequences of Stalinism
History of the Communist Party of the Soviet Union
    (Short Course)
C. Friedrich (ed.), Totalitarianism
F. Borkenau, World Communism

Week IX
Apr. 8-10

The Literature of Disillusionment and Exodus
Reading (one of the following):
*R. Crossman (ed.), The God That Failed (on reserve)
*G. Orwell, Homage to Catalona
*A. Koestler, Darkness at Noon
*C. Charney, A Long Journey (on reserve)
*W. Leonhard, Child of the Revolution (on reserve)
*C. Sigal, Going Away
*M. Kempton, Part of Our Time (on reserve)
*E. P. Thompson, "Open Letter to Leszek Kolakowski,"
    and L. Kolakowski,"My Correct Views on Everything"
    --in The Socialist Register for 1973 (pp. 1-100)
    and 1974 (pp. 1-20) (on reserve)
*V. Gornick, The Romance of American Communism
*J. Mitford, A Fine Old Conflict

Recommended Related Literature:
I. Deutscher, "The Ex-Communist's Conscience," in Russia in Transition
M. Merleau-Ponty, Humanism and Terror
D. Cante, The Great Fear
J. Cogley, Report on Blacklisting
J. Steinberg (ed.), Verdict of Three Decades
A. Gide, Return From the USSR
A. Koestler, The Yogi and the Commissar
H. Fast, The Naked God
E. Bentley (ed.), Thirty Years of Treason: Hearings Before the House Committee on Un-American Activities, 1938-68
M. Djilas, The Imperfect Society
R. Garaudy, The Crisis in Communism
G. Hicks, Where We Came Out
J. Freeman, An American Testament
A. Solzhenitsyn, Letter to the Soviet Leaders

Week X
Apr. 15-17

Marxism and Peasant War
Reading:
*Lin Piao, Long Live the Victory of the People's War! (on reserve);
and
*R. Debrary, Revolution in the Revolution?
(or)
*F. Fanon, Wretched of the Earth

Recommended Secondary and Related Literature:
L. Bianco, Origins of the Chinese Revolution
E. Wolf, Peasant Wars of the Twentieth Century
C. Gueverra, Guerrilla Warfare
B. Schwartz, Chinese Communism and the Rise of Mao
C. Johnson, Peasant Nationalism and Communist Power
S. Schram (ed.), Political Thought of Mao
B. Moore, Social Origins of Dictatorship and Democracy
F. Engels, The Peasant Question in France and Germany
F. Engels, The Peasant War in Germany
Mao Tse Tung, Selected Works
S. Avineri (ed.), Karl Marx on Colonialism and Modernization
A. Ulam, The Unfinished Revolution

162

Week XI
Apr. 22-24

The Revival of Critical Marxism
Reading (one of the following):
*S. Stojanovic, Between Ideals and Reality
*L. Kolakowski, Toward a Marxist Humanism
*E. Fromm (ed.), Socialist Humanism
*H. Marcuse, One-Dimensional Man
*M. Markovic, From Affluence to Praxis
*Roy Medvedev, On Socialist Democracy

Recommended Secondary and Related Literature:
P. Baran and P. Sweezy, Monopoly Capitalism
A. DeGeorge, The New Marxism
Praxis (a Yugoslav journal also published in English)
Marxism Today (January 1967 issue of Survey)
L. Labedz (ed.), Revisionism, Part III
H. Parson, Humanist Philosophy in Contemporary
  Poland and Yugoslavia
A. Schaff, Marxism and the Human Individual
H. Marcuse, Eros and Civilization
S. Firestone, The Dialectic of Sex
J. Mitchell, Woman's Estate
A. MacIntyre, Herbert Marcuse
G. Petrovic, Marx in the Mid-20th Century
H. Marcuse, Negations
H. Marcuse, An Essay on Liberation
H. Magdoff, The Age of Imperialism
W. Leonhard, Three Faces of Marxism
G. Sher, Praxis

Week XII
Apr. 29-May 1

Academic Marxism
Reading (one of the following or any other serious
  work of Marxist scholarship):
*E. Genovese, Political Economy of Slavery
*E. Thompson, Making of the English Working Class
*R. Miliband, The State in Capitalist Society
*N. Poulantzas, Political Power and Social Class
*E. Hobsbawm, Age of Revolution (or another of his
  works)
*C. Hill, Century of Revolution (Or another of his
  works)

Or one of these secondary and related works:
*A. Gouldner, The Coming Crisis in Western Sociology
L. Althusser, For Marx
D. Howard and K. Klare (eds.), The Unknown Dimension:
  European Marxism Since Lenin
*M. Jay, The Dialectical Imagination: A History of
  the Frankfurt School and the Institute of Social
  Research 1923-1950

163

L. Graham, <u>Science and Philosophy in the Soviet Union</u>

A. Mayer, <u>Politics and Diplomacy of Peacemaking: Containment and Counterrevolution at Versailles, 1918-1919</u>

*R. Blackburn (ed.), <u>Ideology in the Social Sciences</u>

D. Horowitz (ed.), <u>Marx and Modern Economics</u>

P. Berger (ed.), <u>Marxism and Sociology: Views from Eastern Europe</u>

<u>Marx and Contemporary Scientific Thought: Essays</u>

Reading Period Assignment: Read an account--biographical, auto-
May 5-18   biographical, or fictional--of the life of a Marxist
                  thinker. For example:

*D. McLellan, <u>Karl Marx: His Life and Thought</u>

*I. Deutscher, <u>Prophet Outcast: Trotsky, 1929-1940</u>

*L. Trotsky, <u>My Life</u>

*S. Cohen, <u>Bukharin and the Bolshevik Revolution</u>

*P. Nettl, <u>Rosa Luxemburg</u> (one-vol. ed.)

*L. Fischer, <u>Life of Lenin</u>

*P. Gay, <u>Dilemma of Democratic Socialism: Eduard Bernstein's Challenge to Marx</u>

I. Getzler, <u>Martov</u>

J. Cammet, <u>Gramsci</u>

S. Baron, <u>Plekhanov</u>

*I. Howe, <u>Trotsky</u>

G. Steenson, <u>Karl Kautsky</u>

M. Salvadori, <u>Kautsky and the Socialist Revolution</u>

Professor Santore   Fall 1979
Barnard College

Syllabus

History 29

European Communism in the Era of the Comintern, 1919-1943

I. Introductory Session

September 6:

Discussion of syllabus and course requirements.

II. Historical Background: European Socialism before the Communist International, 1780-1917.

September 13:

1. Lecture #1: The Industrial Revolution and the development of the Socialist vision: early critics of capitalism from Owen to Marx.

2. Readings: Carl Landauer, European Socialism: A History of Ideas and Movements from the Industrial Revolution to Hitler's Seizure of Power, pp. 3-71.

   Sidney Hook, Marx and the Marxists, pp. 11-48, 133-163.

September 20:

1. Lecture #2: The Second Phase: the spread of Socialist ideas after 1848 - Marx, Lassalle, Bakunin, and the First International, 1848-1876.

2. Readings: Edmund Wilson, To the Finland Station, pp. 178-346.

   Hook, pp. 49-64.

September 27: The Second International.

James Joll, The Second International, 1889-1914.

Hook, pp. 65-75, 177-182.

III. V.I. Lenin.

October 4: Life (to 1917)

Adam Ulam, The Bolsheviks: The Intellectual and Political History of the Triumph of Communism in Russia, pp. 1-313.

October 11: Life (1917-1924)

Ulam, pp. 313-579.

Hook, pp. 182-198.

October 18: Doctrine.

        (On Party Organization)

        V.I. Lenin, What is to be Done?, in Helmut Gruber (ed.),
             International Communism in the Era of
             Lenin, pp. 9-29.

        Rosa Luxemburg, The Russian Revolution and Marxism
             or Leninism?, pp. 1-24, 81-108.

        Bertram D. Wolfe, "A Party of a New Type: The
             Foundation Stone of the Communist
             International", in Milorad M. Drachko-
             vitch and Branco Lazitch (eds.), The
             Comintern: Historical Highlights, pp.
             20-44.

        (On War and Nationalism)

        V.I. Lenin, "The Tasks of Revolutionary Social
             Democracy in the European War", and
             "Draft Manifesto Introduced by the
             Left-Wing Delegates at the International
             Conference at Zimmerwald", in Gruber,
             pp. 44-60.

        (On the Thirs International)

        V.I. Lenin, The Third International and its Place
             in History, pp. 5-13.

        Stefan T. Possony, "The Comintern's Claim to Marxist
             Legitimacy", in Drachkovitch and Lazitch,
             pp. 3-19.

IV. The Founding of the Third International, 1919.

   October 25:

        James W. Hulse, The Founding of the Communist
             International.

        Gruber, International Communism in the Era of Lenin,
             pp. 73-123 ("The Creation of the Third
             International", "Spartacus in Berlin",
             "Bela Kun's 133 Days").

V. The Lbb of the Revolutionary Tide in Europe: The Long Period of
   Communist Defeat, 1920-1927.

   November 1:

        Franz Borkenau, World Communism, pp. 161-295.

        Gruber, International Communism, pp. 231-46, 365-42
             ("The Twenty-One Conditions", "A Second
             Red October").

        Issac Deutscher, The Prophet Unarmed: Trotsky, 1921-
             1929, pp. 140-151.

        Fernando Claudin, The Communist Movement: From Comintern
             to Cominform, v. I, pp. 103-25.

VI. The Triumph of Stalin in the USSR.

November 8:Life

> Issac Deutscher, <u>Stalin: A Political Biography</u>, chaps. 1-9.

November 15: Stalin and "Stalinism", an analysis.

> Deutcher, <u>Stalin</u>, chaps. 10-11.
>
> Leon Trotsky, "Why Stalin Triumphed", in <u>The Revolution Betrayed</u>, pp. 86-94.
>
> - - - - - - , "Stalinism and Bolshevism", in Irving Howe (ed.), <u>The Basic Writings of Leon Trotsky</u>, pp. 356-70.
>
> Stephen Cohen, "Bolshevism and Stalinism", in Robert C. Tucker (ed.), <u>Stalinism: Essays in Historical Interpretation</u>, pp. 3-30.
>
> Robert H. McNeal, "Trotskyist Interpretations of Stalinism", in Tucker, pp. 30-52.
>
> Leszek Kolakowski, "Marxist Roots of Stalinism", in Tucker, pp. 283-98.
>
> Robert C. Tucker, "Stalinism as Revolution From Above", in Tucker, **77-108.**
>
> Mihailo Markovic, "Stalinism and Marxism", in Tucker, 299-319.

VII. The Sixth Comintern Congress and the Destruction of German Communist Party, 1928-1934.

November 29:

> Borkenau, <u>World Communism</u>, pp. 332-385.
>
> Claudin, <u>The Communist Movement</u>, I, 126-166.
>
> Rosa Levine-Meyer, <u>Inside German Communism: Memoires of Party Life in the Weimar Republic</u>, pp. 125-188.
>
> Issac Deutscher, <u>The Prophet Outcast: Trotsky, 1929-1940</u>, pp. 33-45, 128-144, 198-202.

VIII. The Popular Front, 1934-1939.

December 6: France.

> Claudin, <u>The Communist Movement</u>, I, 210-242.
>
> Daniel Brower, <u>The New Jacobins: The French Communist Party and the Popular Front</u>.
>
> John Santore, "The Comintern's United Front Initiative of May 1934: French or Soviet Inspiration.", in <u>The Canadian Journal of History/ Annales Canadiennes d'Histoire</u>, XVI, 3, 405-21.

December 13: Spain.

  Claudin, _The Communist Movement_, I, 210-242.

  George Orwell, _Homage to Catalonia_.

  Branco Lazitch, "Stalin's Massacre of Foreign
    Communist Leaders", in Drachkovitch
    and Lazitch, pp. 138-175.

  Boris Souvarine, "Comments on the Massacre", in
    ibid., pp. 175-183.

IX. The Second World War and the Third International: the Comintern's
  last four years, 1939-1943.

  December 20:

    (The War and the act of dissolution)

    Hugh Seton-Watson, _From Lenin to Khrushchev: The
      History of World Communism_, pp. 200-228.

    Franz Borkenau, _European Communism_, pp. 296-336.

    Claudin, _The Communist Movement_, I, 294-304, 15-45.

    (The Comintern: summary and overall assessment, 1919-
    1943)

    Milorad M. Drachkovitch and Branco Lazitch, "The
      Communist International", in Milorad M.
      Drachkovitch (ed.), _The Revolutionary
      Internationals, 1864-1943_, pp. 159-202.

    George Lichtheim, _A Short History of Socialism_,
      pp. 249-66.

    Adam Ulam, _The Unfinished Revolution: As Essay on
      the Sources of Influence of Marxism and
      Communism_, pp. 196-250.

    Geoffrey Barraclough, _An Introduction to Contemporary
      History_, pp. 199-232.

M. A. Miller
207 E. Duke
University

HISTORY OF RUSSIAN ANARCHISM

I. Anarchist Theory and Practice in Historical Perspective
   G. Woodcock, Anarchism
   J. Joll, The Anarchists

II. Pre-revolutionary Russian Anarchism
   A. Lehning (ed.), Michael Bakunin: Selected Writings
   M. Miller (ed.), Peter Kropotkin: Selected Writings on Anarchism and
       Revolution
   M. Miller, Kropotkin
   Marx-Engels-Lenin, Anarchism and Anarcho-Syndicalism

III. Anarchism and the Russian Revolution
   P. Avrich, The Russian Anarchists
   P. Avrich (ed.), Anarchists in the Russian Revolution
   P. Avrich, Kronstadt
   Voline (B. Eichenbaum), The Unknown Revolution
   D. Cohn-Bendit, Obsolete Communism
   L. van Rossum, "Proclamations of the Makhno Movement, 1920," International
       Review for Social History, XIII, 1968, 246-268
   P. Arshinov, History of the Makhnovist Movement
   E. Goldman, My Disillusionment in Russia
   V. Serge, Memoirs of a Revolutionary

IV. Soviet Research on Anarchism and the Revolution in Russia
   S. N. Kanev, "Krakh russkogo anarkhizma," Voprosy istorii, 1968, no. 9
   S. N. Kanev, Oktiabr'skaia revoliutsiia i krakh anarkhizma
   M. Khudiakulov, "Bor'ba kommunisticheskoi partii protiv anarkhizma v
       gody stanofleniia i uprocheniia Sovetskoi vlasti," A. V. Kachurina,
       Bol'sheviki v bor'be protiv melkoburzhuaznykh partii v Rossii
   A. D. Kosichev, Bor'ba Marksizma-Leninzma s ideologiei anarkhizma
   N. S. Prozorova, Bor'ba K. Marksa i F. Engel'sa protiv anarkhizma
   I. B. Zil'berman, Politicheskaia teoriia anarkhizma M. A. Bakunina

Harvard University   **Prof. Donald H. Bell**

<u>CSPS 174b/CSCC 174b</u>: <u>POLITICAL TERRORISM IN HISTORICAL PERSPECTIVE</u>:
                              <u>THE CASE OF WESTERN EUROPE</u>
(Graduate Level)

Description:

    Several recent accounts of contemporary European terrorism
have treated this phenomenon as essentially a throwback to
earlier forms of political violence. Is this a valid interpretation,
or must the recent outbreak of terrorist activity in such nations
as Italy, Germany, Spain and in Northern Ireland be seen as
largely a product of the specific strains and issues of late-
twentieth century society? This seminar will explore the
problem of terrorism in present-day Western Europe and will
attempt by comparative historical analysis to understand both
the political role of terrorist activities and the degree to
which political violence is informed by previous tradition
and example.

Requirements:

    1). Since this course will focus on reading and discussion,
it is therefore required that you keep up with the assignments
and come to class prepared to discuss them.

    2). Your major written requirement will be an 18-20 page
term paper which you will write on a subject of your
choosing after consultation with the instructor.

D.H.Bell
CSPS 174b/CSCC 174b
Spring, 1980

POLITICAL TERRORISM IN HISTORICAL PERSPECTIVE:
THE CASE OF WESTERN EUROPE

I. The Phenomenon of Terror:

Reading:

1). Accounts of Recent Terrorist Activity in Italy, Germany,
Spain, Northern Ireland (R)*

2). Walter Laqueur, Terrorism (P)*, Ch. 1,3, (Ch. 5, optional)

3). Walter Laqueur, The Terrorism Reader,(P), pp. 251-285

4). Michael Walzer, Just and Unjust Wars,(R), pp. 44-47,
127-151, 197-206.

Optional Reading:

1). Franz Fanon, The Wretched of the Earth (R), Ch.1.
("Concerning Violence")

2). Jan Schreiber, The Ultimate Weapon:Terrorists and the
World Order,(R), Ch. 1,2.

II. Historical Case Studies:

A. Nineteenth-Century Russia: The Historical Context:

Reading:

1). Cyril Black, "The Nature of Imperial Russian Society",
in Bruce Mazlish, et al, Revolution: A Reader (R) and (X).

2). Martin Malia, "What is the Intellegentsia?" in
Mazlish, Revolution: A Reader (R) and (X).

3). Walter Laqueur, Terrorism, Ch.2.

4). Isaiah Berlin, "Russian Populism", in Isaiah Berlin,
Russian Thinkers (Aileen Kelly, ed)., or "Introduction," to
Franco Venturi, The Roots of Revolution (both R)

5). Paul Avrich, The Russian Anarchists,(R), Ch. 1,2.

P=Student Purchase
R=Library Reserve
X= Xerox   171

Optional Reading:

1).Franco Venturi, The Roots of Revolution (R), Ch. 1,2,13-18, 20-22

B. Nineteenth-Century Russia: The Intellectual Context:

    1). Ivan Turgenev, Fathers and Sons, Ch. 10, 11.(R)

    2). Walter Laqueur, The Terrorism Reader, (P),pp. 47-90,198-223

    3). Sergei Nechaev, "Catechism of a Revolutionist" (X).

    4). Michael Bakunin, selections (X)

    5). Isaiah Berlin, "Herzen and Bakunin on Individual Liberty," "Fathers and Children", in Isaiah Berlin, Russian Thinkers (R).

    6). V.I. Lenin, "What is to be Done", in Mazlish, Revolution: A Reader (R).

    7). Boris Savinkov, Memiors of a Terrorist,selections (X)

C. Pre-World War I Western Europe:

    1). Barbara Tuchman, The Proud Tower, (R), Ch. 2.,"The Idea and the Deed".

    2). James Joll, The Anarchists, Ch. V-VII.

    3). Walter Laqueur, The Terrorism Reader,pp. 90-112, 193-198.

    4). James Joll, Anarchism, (R), Ch. 10.

    5). Georges Sorel, "Class War and the Ethics of Violence" (X)

    6). Alexander Berkman,"Propaganda by the Deed" (X)

    7). Prince Kropotkin, "The Conquest of Bread" (X). (optional)

D. Spain:

    1). George Woodcock, Anarchism (R), Ch. 12,

    2). Gerald Brenan, The Spanish Labyrinth, Ch. 7-8.

    3). Murray Bookchin, The Spanish Anarchists, (R), Introduction, Ch. 6-8.

    4). Hugh Thomas, "Anarchist Labor Federations in the Civil War" (X)

III. Contemporary Western Europe: The 1960s and 1970s

A. The Background :

Reading:

1). Stanley Hoffmann, "Fragments Floating in the Here and Now"(X)

2). Suzanne Berger, "Politics and Antipolitics in Western Europe in the Seventies"(X)

3). Walter Laqueur, Terrorism, Chapter 5

4). Walter Laqueur, The Terrorism Reader, pp. 159-172

5). Francois Bourricaud, "Individualistic Mobilization and the Crisis of Professional Authority" (X).

B. Case Studies:

1). Italy:

1). John Earle, Italy in the 1970s (R) , Ch. 1-3,7-8,11-12.
                          or,
2). Denis Mack Smith, Italy: A Modern History, (3rd ed.)(R),Ch.

3). J. Bowyer Bell, A Time of Terror, Ch. 11.

4). Alberto Ronchey, "Terror in Italy:Red and Black" (X)

5). Thomas Sheehan, "Italy: Behind the Ski Mask" (New York Review of Books, 8/16/1979) (X)

6). George Woodcock, Anarchism, Ch. 11.

7). Corriere della Sera, 12/27/1979

8). Sabino S. Aquiviva, Guerrilla Warfare and Revolutionary War in Italy (R?)

9). Sabino S. Aquiviva, The Religious Seeds of Revolt (R?)

10).Antonio Negri, Il dominio e il sabataggio: Sul metodo marxista della trasformazione sociale (R?).

11). Elizabeth Wiskemann, Italy Since 1945, Ch. 6-9.

2). Germany:

    1). Jillian Beck, Hitler's Children,(R), slections to be assigned.

    2). Michael Balfour, West Germany, (R), Part II, esp. Ch. 12.

    3). Bommi Baumann, How it All Began (P)

    4). Ovid Demaris, Brothers in Blood (R), Book 3, pp.215-265.

    5). Jan Schreiber, The Ultimate Weapon, Chapter 7.(R).

    6). Walter Laqueur, The Terrorism Reader, pp.176-179,246-251.

    7) Gorgon Craig, Germany, 1866-1945 (R) (optional background).

3). Northern Ireland:

    1). J. Bowyer Bell, A Time of Terror,(R), Ch. 10.

    2). Ovid Demaris, Brothers in Blood (R), Book 4

    3). Roger H. Hull, The Irish Triangle, Ch. I,II. (R).

    4). J. Bowyer Bell, The Secret Army: The Ira, 1960-1970, (R),
    Ch. XVIiI, Epilogue.

    5). Walter Laqueur, Terrorism Reader, pp.112-116, 130-137.

4). Spain:

    1). Raymond Carr and Juan Pablo Fusi, Spain: Dictatorship
to Democracy (selections to be assigned)

    2). Gerald Brenan, "Out of the Labyrinth," (New York Review
of Books, 9/27/1979) (X)

    3). Kenneth N. Medhurst, Government in Spain, Parts 2,3,4,

IV: A "Terrorist International?" : Conclusions :

    1). Walter Laqueur, Terrorism, Conclusion

    2).Walter Laqueur, The Terrorism Reader, pp. 267-

    3). J. Bowyer Bell, A Time of Terror (R),Ch. 12

    4). Christopher Dobson and Ronald Payne, The Carlos Complex, (R),
    Introduction, Ch. 14.

    5). Bernard Avishai, "In Cold Blood", New York Review of Books,
    March 8, 1979. (R or X).

University of Chicago
Department of History

Quantitative Methods for Historians   Mr. John Coatsworth
History 436   Mr. Edward Cook

Introduction

The purpose of this graduate course is to introduce students to quantitative methods of historical research. Since the use of quantitative methods requires both statistical and conceptual skills, attention will be devoted both to the technical aspects of data processing and manipulation as well as problems of research design, modeling, hypothesis testing, and the like.

No prior training in statistics, data processing, mathematics or computer science is required. Arrangements have been made to offer students enrolled in the course an opportunity to take a three week course (six sessions) at the University Computation Center on the use of the Statistical Package for the Social Sciences, the computer program most widely used by historians. The SPSS course costs $25.00, and will meet Tuesday and Thursday at 4 p.m. from October 16 to November 1. Students interested in taking this optional course should register immediately at the Computation Center Business Office at 5737 South University Avenue.

Optional tours of the University Computation Center and the Social Sciences Division terminal facilities in Pick Hall have also been arranged.

A limited budget for computer time is available to all students in the course. Extra time is allocated for those who enroll in the SPSS course. In addition students are entitled to register with the Computation Center for a "get acquainted" account of $25 per quarter.

Requirements

Each student taking the seminar (including auditors) will be required to submit a two to five page essay on his/her current research interests and possibilities for use of quantitative methods by Thursday, October 11. The purpose of this essay is to assist the instructors in selecting relevant materials for lectures and additional readings.

All students (including auditors) will be required to complete the statistical exercises distributed in class during the quarter.

Quantitative Methods for Historians   History 436

Students who wish to receive a letter grade in the course are
required to submit a paper, not less than ten pages in length, demonstrating
the application of quantitative methods in historical research. Students
should select a topic that corresponds to a current research project or
interest, and must consult one of the instructors in the course for approval
of the paper topic by the third week of the quarter.

Books for Purchase

The following books have been ordered for purchase at the Seminary
Bookstore. All readings are available in Regenstein Reserve.

1. Hubert Blalock, Social Statistics (McGraw-Hill).
2. Charles Dollar and Richard Jensen, Historians Guide to Statistics:
   Quantitative Analysis and Historical Research (Holt, Rinehart
   and Winston).
3. Primer, Statistical Package for the Social Sciences (McGraw-Hill).
4. Edward Shorter, The Historian and the Computer: A Practical Guide
   (Prentice-Hall).
5. Roderick Floud, An Introduction to Quantitative Methods for
   Historians.

Course Outline

Week I. Introduction to Computer Technology and Research Design

1. Dollar and Jensen, pp. 139-72, 1-26.
2. Floud
3. Blalock, Chapters 1, 2.
4. Robert A. Berkhofer, A Behavioral Approach to Historical
   Analysis, esp. ch. 1, 12, 13.
5. David Potter, "Explicit Data and Implicit Assumptions in
   Historical Studies," in Louis Gottschalk, ed., Generaliza-
   tion in the Writing of History, pp. 178-94.
6. Edward Shorter, The Historian and the Computer: A Practical
   Guide (entire)

Week II. Text Manipulation by Computer (Michael Dalby)

No new readings.

Quantitative Methods for Historians   History 436

Week III.   Descriptive Statistics and Frequency Distributions

  1. Blalock, Chapters 3-6
  2. Dollar and Jensen, pp. 27-55
  3. Floud, Chapters 1-5
  4. Richard McCormick, "New Perspectives on Jacksonian Politics,"
       Rowney and Graham, pp. 372-84
  5. Maris Vinovskis and Richard Bernard, "Women in Education in
       Ante-Bellum America," paper on reserve
  6. Burton Singer, "Exploratory Strategies and Graphical Displays,"
       Journal of Interdisciplinary History, 7 (1976), pp. 57-70

Week IV.   Introduction to Times Series

  1. Floud, pp. 85-124
  2. D. T. Campbell and H. L. Ross, "The Connecticut Crackdown on
       Speeding: Time Series Analysis in Quasi-Experimental
       Analysis," in Edward Tufte, ed., The Quantitative Analysis
       of Social Problems, pp. 110-25.
  3. Charles Tilly and Edward Shorter, "The Shape of Strikes in
       France, 1830-1900," Comparative Studies in Society and
       History, V. 13 (1971)
  4. Dorothy S. Thomas, "The Impact of the Harvest On Population
       Change," in Paul F. Lazarsfeld and Morris Rosenberg, eds.,
       The Language of Social Research (Glencoe, 1962), pp. 206-13

Week V.   Probability and Sampling; and Cross Tabulation

  1. Blalock, Chapters 7, 15, 21 (Chapters 8-13 recommended)
  2. Floud, pp. 125-33, 155-83
  3. Melvyn A. Hammarberg, "Designing a Sample from Incomplete
       Historical Lists," American Quarterly, 23 (1971), pp. 542-61
  4. R. S. Shofield, "Sampling in Historical Research," in E. A.
       Wrigley, Nineteenth Century Society, pp. 146-90
  5. Richard S. Alcorn & Peter R. Knight, "Most Uncommon Bostonians:
       A Critique of Stephan Thernstrom's The Other Bostonians,"
       Historical Methods Newsletter, 8 (June 1975), pp. 98-120
  6. Patrick L. R. Higonnet & Trevor B. Higonnet, "Class, Corruption,
       and Politics in the French Chamber of Deputies, 1846-1848,"
       Rowney and Graham, pp. 129-47
  7. Daniel Smith and Michael Hindus, "Premarital Pregnancy in
       America, 1640-1771: An Overview and Interpretation,"
       Journal of Interdisciplinary History V (1975), pp. 537-70

Week VI.   Scalograms and Clusters

      1. Dollar and Jensen, pp. 106-26
      2. Barbara Sinclair, "From Party Voting to Regional Fragmenta-
         tion: The House of Representatives, 1933-1956," _American_
         Politics Quarterly, v. 6 (1978), pp. 125-46
      3. Allan G. Bogue, "Some Dimensions of Power in the Thirty-
         Seventh Senate," in William O. Aydelotte, Allan G. Bogue
         and Robert W. Fogel, eds., _The Dimensions of Quantitative_
         Research in History (Princeton, 1972), pp. 285-318

Week VII. Nonparametric Measures of Association

      1. Blalock, Chapters 14, 15
      2. Dollar and Jensen, pp. 56-87, 106-26
      3. Richard Jensen, "Quantitative Collective Biography: An
         Application to Metropolitan Elites," Swierenga, pp. 398-405
      4. Allan Kulikoff, "The Progress of Inequality in Revolutionary
         Boston," _William and Mary Quarterly_, 3rd ser. 28 (July
         1971), pp. 375-412
      5. John Modell, Frank F. Furstenberg Jr., and Theodore Hershberg,
         "Social Change and Transitions to Adulthood in Historical
         Perspective," in Milton Gordon, ed., _The American Family_
         in Social-Historical Perspective (2nd edition), pp. 192-219

Week VIII. Analysis of Variance

      1. Blalock, Chapter 16
      2. Edward M. Cook, Jr., "Local Leadership and the Typology of
         New England Towns, 1700-1785," _Political Science Quarterly_,
         v. 86 (1971), pp. 161-75

Week IX.   Linear Regression and Correlation

      1. Blalock, Chapters 17-20
      2. Floud, pp. 133-51
      3. Dollar and Jensen, pp. 56-87
      4. John L. Shover, "Was 1928 a Critical Election in California?"
         in Rowney and Graham, pp. 385-98

Week X.   Introduction to Multivariate Analysis

1. Blalock, Chapter 19
2. Dollar and Jensen, pp. 87-104
3. S. Hackney, "Southern Violence," in Swierenga, pp. 348-65
4. Paul Burnstein and William Frendenberg, "Changing Public
    Policy: The Impact of Public Opinion, Antiwar Demonstra-
    tions, and War Costs on Senate Voting on Vietnam War
    Motions," American Journal of Sociology, v. 84 (1978),
    pp. 98-122
5. Carl Stone, "Political Determinants of Social Policy
    Allocations in Latin America," Comparative Studies in
    Society and History, v. 17 (1975), pp. 286-308
6. Maris A. Vinovskis, "A Multivariate Regression of Fertility:
    Differentials Among Massachusetts Towns in 1860,"
    (unpublished paper, 1972)

University of California
Los Angeles

History 136G
Tu-Th, 11:00-12:15
Bunche 3170

Mr. Loewenberg
Fall 1983

Psychohistory

The goal of this course is to introduce you to some depth psychological concepts and their uses in historical research. The course structure is designed to present a three-phase approach: 1) a theoretical concept; 2) a clinical demonstration; 3) a historical application. Thus you will see the mental mechanism of projection demonstrated in the Schreber case and applied in pre 1914 European diplomacy; the anal sadistic character demonstrated in the Rat Man Case and applied to Himmler and Nazism; the syndrome "Wrecked by Success" demonstrated on Henrik Ibsen's Rebecca West and applied to John C. Fremont and to the Confederacy.

Class Discussion: Each member of the class will be asked to organize and lead one session's topic.

Paper: You may write an optional paper on "Psychodynamics and Historical Understanding: A Critique and Evaluation" to count for one half of the grade, due on December 1.

Examinations: There will be no midterm. The final examination will be from 11:30 a.m. to 2:30 p.m. on Monday, December 12 in Bunche Hall 3170.

Guest Presenters: We will have three guest presenters, each an accomplished historian, who will discuss their work in psychohistory:

Oct. 25: Professor Judith Hughes, Department of History, U.C. San Diego, on "Emotions and High Politics."

Nov. 10: Professor Mauricio Mazon, Chairman, Department of History, U.S.C., on "Psychohistory and Chicano-American Culture."

Dec. 1: Andrew Rolle, Clelland Professor of History, Occidental College, on "John C. Fremont: A Man Wrecked by Success."

Audio-Visual: We will view the following films to accompany course material:

Oct. 4: "Mother Love," Harlow's Monkey.

Oct. 11: "Sudden Departure," parental deprivation.

Oct. 13: "John," Regression of a boy cut off from his mother during hospitalization.

Oct. 27: "Shyness," Adult to Child Case Studies

Nov. 8: "Four Families," Comparative Child Rearing in India, France, Japan and Canada.

Nov. 15: "The Rat Man," Freud's classic case.

Nov. 22: "Feelings of Depression," Case History.

Office Hours: Mr. Loewenberg's office hours are Tuesday and Thursday just after this class, 12:30 to 1:45 in 8246 Ralph Bunche Hall, telephone: 825-3175.

Outline and Readings

Oct. 4: Introduction
film: "Mother Love" (26 min.)

Oct. 6: Loewenberg, "On Psychohistory: A Statement on Method" in Decoding the Past: The Psychohistorical Approach (N.Y.: Knopf, 1983), pp. 3-8.

Loewenberg, "Psychoanalysis and History: The Scope of the Problem," Ibid., pp. 11-41.

Oct. 11: Loewenberg, "The Education of a Psychohistorian," Ibid., pp. 45-80.

Martin Duberman, "On Becoming an Historian," Evergreen Review, 13:65 (1969) and in his The Uncompleted Past (New York, 1969), pp. 335-356.
In College Library Reserve.

film: "Sudden Departure" (28 min.)

Oct. 13: Loewenberg, "The Psychobiographical Background to Psychohistory: The Langer Family and the Dynamics of Shame and Success," Decoding the Past, pp. 81-95.

film: "John" (45 min.)

Oct. 18: Sigmund Freud, "The Case of Schreber" in Three Case Histories (Collier/Macmillan 07665).

Judith M. Hughes, Emotion and High Politics: Personal Relations at the Summit in Late Nineteenth Century Britain and Germany (Berkeley and Los Angeles: University of California Press, 1983), pp. 1-76.

Oct. 20: Jonathan Steinberg, "The Copenhagen Complex," Journal of Contemporary History; 1:3 (1966), 23-46.
In College Library Reserve.

J. Hughes, Emotion and High Politics, pp. 78-162.

Oct. 25: Guest Presentation by Professor Judith M. Hughes, Department of History, U.C. San Diego.

Oct. 27: Erik H. Erikson, "Identity Crisis in Autobiographic Perspective," in Life History and the Historical Moment (New York: W. W. Norton, 1975), pp. 17-47.

film: "Shyness" (23 min.)

Nov. 1: Points of Technique:

a) Watch the apparently trivial details: S. Freud, "The Moses of Michelangelo" (1914) in Character and Culture (Collier-McMillan, 07620), pp. 80-106.

b) Ambivalence: "Reflections upon War and Death" (1915), Ibid., pp. 107-133.

c) Father Rivalry: "A Disturbance of Memory on the Acropolis" (1937), Ibid., pp. 311-320.

Nov. 3: S. Freud, "Character and Anal Erotism" (1908), Character and Culture, pp. 27-33.

S. Freud, "On the Transformation of Instincts with Special Reference to Anal Erotism" (1917), Ibid., pp. 202-209.

Wilhelm Reich, "The Compulsive Character" in Character Analysis (New York: Noonday, 1949), pp. 193-200. In College Library Reserve.

Nov. 8: film: "Four Families" by Margaret Mead (60 min.)

Nov. 10: Guest Presenter: Professor Mauricio Mazon, Chairman, Department of History, U.S.C. on "Psychohistory and Chicano American History."

Nov. 15: S. Freud, "The Rat Man Case" in Three Case Histories.

film: "Rat Man," (53 min.)

Nov. 17: Discussion of Freud's papers of Nov. 3, Wilhelm Reich, the Rat Man.

Loewenberg, "The Unsuccessful Adolescence of Heinrich Himmler," Decoding the Past, pp. 209-239.

Nov. 22: film: "Feelings of Depression" (30 min.)

Stanley M. Elkins, "Slavery and Personality," in Robert J. Brugger, ed., Ourselves/Our Past: Psychological Approaches to American History (Baltimore: Johns Hopkins University Press, 1981), pp. 141-164.

Nov. 29: Sigmund Freud, "Some Character Types Met With in Psychoanalytic Work" (1916), in Character and Culture, pp. 157-181, especially "Those Wrecked by Success," pp. 162-179.

Kenneth M. Stampp, "The Southern Road to Appomattox," in
The Imperiled Union: Essays on the Background of the Civil War
(New York: Oxford University Press, 1980), pp. 246-269.
In College Library Reserve.

Loewenberg, "Austro-Marxism and Revolution: Otto Bauer, Freud's
'Dora' Case, and the Crises of the First Austrian Republic," in
Decoding the Past, pp. 161-204.

Dec. 1: Guest Presenter: Andrew Rolle, Clelland Professor of History,
Occidental College, on "John C. Fremont: A Man Wrecked By Success."

Dec. 6: Generational Theory and Psychohistory:

Loewenberg, "The Psychohistorical Origins of the Nazi Youth Cohort,"
in Decoding the Past, pp. 240-283.

George Forgie, "Abraham Lincoln and the Melodrama of the House
Divided," in Our Selves, Our Past, pp. 179-204.

Dec. 8: Open for review.

Dec. 12: Final Examination, 11:30 a.m. - 2:30 p.m.

HISTORY 4521v Spring 1983
Historiography

Requirements: midterm and final exam (take-home); one of the
questions of the final exam may be developed into a short,
10 page paper and be substituted for the final exam. Graduate
students who take the course for E-credit write one more, short,
paper. In the reading list the readings marked G, are required
for graduate students on top of what has been designated as
required for the whole class.

Background reading, reference etc.: some of the obvious choices
for textbooks and background reading are out of print. For a
general introduction I shall regularly refer to H. Stuart Hughes,
History as an Art and as a Science (available in bookstore).
The following titles for Philosophy of History, W.H. Walsh, Philosophy
of History, R. Aron, Introduction to the Philosophy of History; for
Historiography: G.P. Gooch, History and Historians in the Nineteenth
Century, Tr.R. Tholfsen, Historical Thinking, G.G. Iggers, New
Direction in European Historiography

Readings:

1) Introduction
    a) Myth and History:

        Required: E. Cassirer, An Essay on Man, Ch. 5, 7, 10 or
                  idem, The Myth of the State, Part I
                  M.J. Finley, "Myth, Memory and History", in
                  History and Theory, 1965
                  M. Mandelbaum, The Anatomy of Historical Knowledge,
                  Part I/II
                  B. Halpern, "Myth and Ideology in Modern Usage",
                  in History and Theory
        Recommended: S. Toulmin, The Discovery of Time; R. Berkhofer,
                  A Behavioral Approach to Historical Analysis,
                  Ch. 10, 11; G.S. Kirk, Myth, its Meaning and
                  Functions in Ancient and other Cultures, p 261-
                  285. (G)

    b) The Claims of Scientific History

                  D.H. Fischer, Historian's Fallacies. (G)
                  H. Meyerhof ed. The Philosophy of History in our Time.
                  (art. by Hempel, White, Nagel)

2) The New History of the 18th Century; a Mythical Structure?

        Required: C. Becker, The Heavenly City of 18th Century Philosopher:
                  F. Stern, ed., The Varieties of History, on Voltaire
                  P. Gay, The Enlightenment, Book III, Ch. 7

3) The Ambiguity of the 18th Century Legacy

    Required: G.A. Wells, " Herder's two Philospphies of History"
                    Jöurnal History of Ideas, 1960.
             R. Nisbet, Social Change and History, Intro., Part I,
               II sect. 4.
             J.B. Bury, The Idea of Progress, Ch. 7 through 19.

    Recommended: I. Berlin, Vico and Herder (G)
               F. Meinecke, Historism,Ch. on Montesquieu, Voltaire,
                 Burke, Herder (G).
               Voltaire, Essav sur les Moeurs, Ch. LXXIV, CXCVII
               Montesquieu, Spirit of the Laws, Book I, II, XVII-XIX
               Vico, New Science, Introduction;I, 4;II, Introd.;
               II sect. 4;III;IV sect 1-12;V; Conclusion.
               J.G. Herder, Reflections on the Philosphy of the
               History of Mankind, Ch. I, II, VII, VII

4) New Theoretical Concepts in the Early 19th Century
    a)Ranke and Possibilist Historicism

    Required: G.G. Iggers, ed., The Theory and Practice of History,
            Intro. and selections p. 51-101
            idem   The German Conception of History,
            Ch. II, III, UV,
            relevant readings in Stern, op. cit.

    Recommended: Meinecke, op. cit., Ch. on Ranke

    b)Determinist Historicism: Comte and Hegel

    Required: Hegel, Philosophy of Right, Part III sect. iii
            (The State)
            idem, Reason in History

    Recommended: W.H. Walsh, op. cit. Ch. VII
               S. Hook, From Hegel to Marx
               J. S Mill, August Comte and Positivism
               A. Comte, Positive Philosophy, Book VI (Social Physics)
                 Ch. 3-12
               H. Th. Buckle, Civilization in England, Introductory
                 Chapter, (in Stern, op. cit.)
               I. Berlin, Historical Inevitability (G)

    c)Determinist Historicism ??? The case of Marx

    Required: K. Marx, German Ideology
            idem, The Grundrisse, ed., D. McClellan, 16-46
            William H. Shaw, Marx's Theory of History
    Recommended: S. Avineri, The Social and Political Thought of
               Karl Marx
               S. Hook, op. cit. (G)
               G. Lichtheim, From Marx to Hegel
               K. Marx, Precapitalist Economic Formations, introductio
               by E.J. Hobsbawm.

5) Ideological (or Mythical ???) structures of 19th Century Historiography
    a)Nationalism

        Read sections in Stern of 19th century historians; also
        introductory chapters in J. Michelet's History of the French
        Revolution; also required: P. Geyl, Debates with Historians
        on Ranke, Michelet, Macaulay.

    b)Conservatism and Progressivism

        Required: Geyl, op. cit.
                 Ranke, (Xerox from Iggers)

    Recommended: R. Hoffstadter, The Progressive Historians

6) Some Positions against Historicism

        Required: F. Nietzsche, "Use and Abuse of History: in
                 Thoughts out of Season.
                 K. Popper, The Poverty of Historicism

    Recommended: Berlin, Inevitability

7) The Crisis of Historicism: Epistemology and the Problem of Object-
ivity

        Required: W. Dilthey, Pattern and Meaning in History
                 C. Becker, "What are Historical Facts: and "Written
                 History as an Act of Faith" in: H. Meyerhof
                 The Philosophy of History in Our Time
                 R.G. Collingwood, The Idea of History, Part IV,
                 and Part V.
                 M. Mandelbaum,The Anatomy of Historical Knowledge,
                 Part III

    Recommended: W. Walsh, op. cit.
                 K. Popper, The Logic of Scientific Discovery
                 Meyerhof, ed. op. cit.: articles Hempel, White,
                 Nagel, Aron.(G)

8) The Crisis of Historicism: the Solution of Max Weber

        Required: M. Weber, "Objectivity in Social Science and
                 Social Policy" in Methodology of the Social
                 Sciences
                 idem, "Science as a Vocation:, in H.H. Gerth and
                 C. Wright Mills, From Max Weber
                 H. Stuart Hughes, Consciousness and Society,
                 chapter on Weber

    Recommended: R. Bendix, Max Weber.

9) The Loss of Unity and Efforts at New Integration
   a) The consequences of specialization

       Required: W.O. Aydelotte, "Quantification in History", in
                 American Hist. Review, 1966
       R.W. Fogel, "The New Economic History:, in Econ. Hist. Review,
                 1966
                 A. Lovejoy, Introduction to the first issue of
                    Journal of the History of Ideas
                 J. Huizinga, "The Task of Cultural History" in Men
                    and Ideas
   Recommended: B. Mazlish, ed., Psycho-Analysis and History
                 T.W. Fogel, Time on the Cross

   b) New integration

       Required: F. Braudel, The Mediterranean etc., Introduction,
                 Conclusion and a close reading of the Table
                 of Contents
                 M. Bloch, The Historian's Craft
                 G.G. Iggers, New Directions, last 2 chapters

   Recommended: R. Berkhofer, A Behavourial Approach to History
                 L. Febvre, Pour une Histoire à part entière
                 A. Danto, Analytical Philosophy of History
                 F. Braudel, Ecrits surl'Histoire (English translation
                 available), 41-84;175-238.

10) Once more: History , Myth or Science?

       Required: K. Popper, op. cit.
                 Meyerhoff, ed., op. cit. the essays by Croce, Hempel
                 White, Nagel
                 M. Foucault, The Order of Things, Chs. I,V,VI,VII,X.
                 Hayden White, Metahistory

   Recommended: A. Danto, op. cit.
                 R. van Zandt, The Metaphysical Foundation of American
                 History

New York University   Bender/Nolan
                                HISTORICGRPHY

Part I: General Issues

Week I   Introduction to the course

Week II   Vocation, Values, and Constructive Imagination

          Max Weber, "Politics as Vocation" and "Science as Vocation,"
             in Hands Gerth and C. Wright Mills, eds. From Max Weber (1958)
             pp. 77-128, 129-56.

          William H. Dray, "Some Causal Accounts of the American Civil
             War," Daedalus, 91 (1962), 578-92.

          Thomas Kuhn, The Structure of Scientific Revolutions (1962 et. seq.)

          Lawrence W. Levine, "The Historian and the Culture Gap," in L.P.
             Curtis, ed. The Historian's Workshop (1970), 307-326.

Week III Classic Social Thinkers and Historical Analysis

          Karl Marx, The German Ideology (1846, 1947), part I (pp. 3-78)

          Max Weber, The Theory of Social and Economic Organizsation
                       (1947ed.), pp. 88-104.

          Emile Durkheim, The Rules of Sociological Method (1895, 1938), Chap.
             I, "What is a Social Fact"

Week IV   History as Structure/History as Event

          James Henretta, "Social History as Lived and Written," AHR
             (December, 1979), 1293-1322.

          Emmanuel LeRoy Ladurie, "The 'Event' and the 'Long Term' in
             Social History: The Case of the Chouan Uprising," in his
             The Territory of the Historian (1979), pp. 111-31.

          Joan Kelley-Gadol, "The Social Relation of the Sexes: Methodological
                     Implications of Women's History,"Signs, 1 (1976), 809-23.

          Lawrence Stone, "The Revival of Narrative," Past and Present (198).

          Fernand Braudel, "History and the Social Sciences: The Long Term,"
             in Fritz Stern, ed. The Varieties of History (1972), 403-29.

                                    188

Week V   The Quest for Meaning and the Problem of Causation

Clifford Geertz, The Interpretation of Cultures (1973), pp. 3-30, 412-53.

Carlo Ginzburg, The Cheese and Worms (1976/1980)

J.G.A. Pocock, "Languages and their Implications: The Transformation of the Study of Political Thought," in his Politics, Language and Time (1973), pp. 3-41.

Part II Case Studies: Witchcraft

Week VI   Witchcraft, Witchhunts, and Social Tension

Paul Boyer and Stephen Nissenbaum, Salem Possessed

Alan McFarlane, Witchcraft in Tudor and Stuart England, chaps. 11-12

H. Trever-Roper, "The European Witch-craze of the Sixteenth and Seventeenth Centuries, " in his The Crisis of the Seventeenth Century, pp. 90-192.

Week VII   Witchcraft and World Views

Keith Thomas, Religion and the Decline of Magic, chaps. 14-18, 21-22.

Clark, "Inversion, Misrule and the Meaning of Witchcraft," Past and Present, 87 (1980), 98-127.

Carlo Ginzburg,The Night Battles, selections

Week VIII Witchcraft Reassessed

John Demos, Entertaining Satan (1982)

Part III Case Studies: The Rise of Capitalism

Week IX   Transition from Feudalism to Capitalism

Karl Marx, Capital, part VIII, "The So-called Primitive Accumulation."

Henri Pirenne, "Stages in the Social History of Capitalism," AHR, (1914), pp494-515.

Robert DuPlessis, "The Transition Debate," Radical History Review (Winter, 1977), 3-38.

Hans Medick, "The Proto-industrial Family Economy," Social History, 3 (October, 1976), 291-315.

David Levine, "Production, Reproduction and the Proletarian Family in England," (unpub. manuscript, copyright, February, 1983), 28pp.

Week X   Ideas, Ideologies, and Economic Change

            Max Weber, The Protestant Ethic and the Spirit of
                 Capitalism,(1905, 1958)

            Albert Hirschman, The Passions and the Interests, (1977)

Week XI   States, Politics, and Paths of Transition

            Barrington Moore, Social Origins of Dictatorship and
                 Democracy, (1966)

Part IV   Case Studies: Society, Culture, Ideas in Renaissance
                          Florence
───
Week XII   Study in the City

            Jacob Burckhardt, The Civilization of the Renaissance in
                 Italy, (1860), vol. I, pp. 21 - 150.

            Samuel Kline Cohn, Jr., The Laboring Classes in Renaissance
                 Florence, (1980)

Week XIII   Society and Culture: Painting and Architecture

            . Richard Coldthwaite, The Building of Renaissance Florence,
                 (1980)

            Michael Baxandall, Painting and Experience in Fifteenth
                 Century Italy, (1972), esp. pp. 1 - 118, 151 - 153.

Week XIV   Social Origin, Meaning, and Implication of Ideas

            Felix Gilbert, Machiavelli and Cuicciardini, (1965),
                 pp. 1 - 200.

            Quentin Skinner, Machiavelli, (1981)

            J.G.A. Pocock, "Civic Humanism and Its Role in Anglo-
                 American Thought," in his: Politics, Language, and
                 Time, (1973), pp. 80 - 103.

            Isaiah Berlin, "The Originality of Machiavelli," in his:
                 Against the Current, (1980), pp. 25 - 79.

                              190

About the Editor

John Santore received his Ph.D. in modern European history from Columbia University in 1976 and has taught at Rutgers University (1976-1977) and Barnard College (1977-1981). In 1981, he served as the Associate Director of the Columbia University Center for Italian Studies and was a lecturer at the New York University School of Continuing Education in 1982-1983. A specialist in twentieth-century Europe, his reviews and articles have appeared in the Canadian Journal of History and History: Review of New Books.

Markus Wiener Publishing announces the publication of innovative, educational materials in history from leading American scholars.

Selected course outlines and reading lists in history as reference books for faculty members, librarians and graduate students.

EUROPEAN HISTORY

Vol. 1 **Ancient History**
edited by Sarah B. Pomeroy
Hunter College of C.U.N.Y.
and Stanley Burstein
California State University of Los Angeles

Vol. 2 **Medieval History**
edited by Penelope Johnson
New York University

Vol. 3 **Early Modern European History**
edited by Jeffrey Merrick
Barnard College, Columbia University

Vol. 4 **Modern European History:**
1789 to the Present
Vol. I: Chronological and National Courses

Vol. 5 **Modern European History:**
1789 to the Present
Vol. II: Topical and Thematic Courses
edited by John Santore
New York University

AMERICAN HISTORY

Vol. 6 **American History I**
Survey and Chronological Courses

Vol. 7 **American History II**
Selected Topics in Cultural, Social and
Economic History

Vol. 8 **American History III**
Selected Topics in Twentieth Century History
edited by Warren Susman and John Chambers
Rutgers University

Vol. 9 **Women's History**
edited by Annette Baxter
Barnard College, Columbia University

For information, write to
Markus Wiener Publishing, Inc.
551 Fifth Avenue, Suite 3210
New York, N.Y. 10176